"Miriam Adeney lifts the veil that has obscured the faces of Muslim women and reveals their variety. With anthropological skill she details the everyday lives those faces express. And with spiritual sensitivity she describes how each looked through another—torn—veil to see the glory of God in the face of Jesus Christ."

J. DUDLEY WOODBERRY, *Dean Emeritus and Professor of Islamic Studies, School of World Mission, Fuller Theological Seminary*

"Miriam Adeney has come up with a great and timely book on ministering to Muslim women. This book is rich with case studies of Muslim women who have come to the Lord Jesus in various regions of the world. And it is rich in missiological insights for those desiring to work with Muslim women in a spectrum of ethnic settings."

DON MCCURRY, *President, Ministries to Muslims*

"At last the book I have been waiting for! Yes, Muslim women are coming to faith in Christ. Miriam Adeney has given us fascinating accounts of their paths to Christ and highlighted the reasons for their faith. I find the ethnographic material and the missiological suggestions to be perceptive and helpful for all who are drawn to love and minister to these women. I highly recommend Daughters of Islam to both students and experienced workers."

DONNA SMITH, *Women's Ministries Consultant, Arab World Ministries*

"Miriam Adeney writes with unusual clarity and persuasiveness to dispel long-held misguided notions about Muslim women. She applies her anthropological and missionary insights and experiences to bring hope and guidance to those who long to see these women come to Jesus. Readers will be inspired and richly rewarded by her passion and practicality."

JIM REAPSOME, *Editor at Large, Evangelical Missions Quarterly*

"Miriam always likes to ask the question no one else is asking! This book does just that— challenging and encouraging those who desire to understand Muslim women. With her rich crosscultural background, as well as her training in both journalism and anthropology, Miriam Adeney is uniquely qualified to bring together insights on these women's world and worldview. This long anticipated study brings her fresh perspective to current discussions."

MEG CROSSMAN, *Director, Perspectives Partnership*

"Miriam Adeney, a gifted storyteller, has woven together riveting tales of Muslim women from around the world. This book is packed full of up-to-date information on the Muslim world and draws the reader into seeing that world through the eyes and from behind the veils of Muslim women. Adeney's training as an anthropologist is evident in her rich ethnographic description of Muslim life, but her commitment as a missiologist pushes her beyond fascinating description to help the reader understand how to engage these women with the liberating and transforming power of the gospel. The missiological world has been waiting for this book for a long time, and now that it is here, one can't help but believe that this is another kairos moment for our sisters in the Muslim world."

DARRELL WHITEMAN, *Professor of Cultural Anthropology and Dean, E. Stanley Jones School of World Mission and Evangelism, Asbury Theological Seminary*

"For too long the world of Muslim women has been shrouded in silence and darkness to most Christians in the West. Miriam Adeney has lifted the veil on their world and the ways in which the light of the gospel touches them with hope. Their stories bring the women into our lives so that they seem to jump up from the pages, insisting that we listen to their hearts and take seriously their spiritual journey."

COMMISSIONER KAY F. RADER, *former World President of Women's Organizations, The Salvation Army*

"In our world of high abstractions, broad generalizations and stereotypes, it is a blessing to see a work, like Scripture, that talks about real people and helps us experience and learn from their lives. Miriam Adeney introduces us to Christian women from Muslim backgrounds, and she masterfully helps us understand the high costs of their conversions and witness. These stories not only inform us, they challenge us in our complacent Christian lives to identify with our sisters—and to recommit ourselves to a radical commitment to our one Lord. This book is a model in helping us develop an awareness of the nature of the worldwide church."

PAUL G. HIEBERT, *Professor of Mission and Anthropology, Trinity Evangelical Divinity School*

"Miriam Adeney's careful study of daughters of Islam exposes the reader to the commonalities and diversities of Muslim women worldwide. She stirs our hearts with the experiences of those who have found in Christ a loving Savior and offers suggestions for our use in ministry and witness."

DELLANNA O'BRIEN, *retired Executive Director, Woman's Missionary Union*

"Absolutely packed with fascination. Often gripping drama. It is the work of one of the most significant missiologists today. Thus it is also weighty with striking insight and sensitivity. Focuses on a large and unknown world in which ordinary American intuition is worth practically nothing. More of a revelation than an education! Men better read this too."

RALPH D. WINTER, *General Director, Frontier Mission Fellowship*

Daughters of Islam

Building Bridges with Muslim Women

Miriam Adeney

InterVarsity Press

Downers Grove, Illinois
Leicester, England

InterVarsity Press, USA
P.O. Box 1400, Downers Grove, IL 60515-1426, USA
World Wide Web: www.ivpress.com
E-mail: mail@ivpress.com

Inter-Varsity Press, England
38 De Montfort Street, Leicester LE1 7GP, England
World Wide Web: www.ivpbooks.com
E-mail: ivp@uccf.org.uk

InterVarsity Press®, U.S.A., is the book-publishing division of InterVarsity Christian Fellowship/USA®, a student movement active on campus at hundreds of universities, colleges and schools of nursing in the United States of America, and a member movement of the International Fellowship of Evangelical Students. For information about local and regional activities, write Public Relations Dept., InterVarsity Christian Fellowship/USA, 6400 Schroeder Rd., P.O. Box 7895, Madison, WI 53707-7895, or visit the IVCF website at <www.ivcf.org>.

Inter-Varsity Press, England, is the book-publishing division of the Universities and Colleges Christian Fellowship (formerly the Inter-Varsity Fellowship), a student movement linking Christian Unions in universities and colleges throughout the United Kingdom and the Republic of Ireland, and a member movement of the International Fellowship of Evangelical Students. For information about local and national activities write to UCCF, 38 De Montfort Street, Leicester LE1 7GP.

Cover photograph: Iran/SuperStock

USA ISBN 0-8308-2345-X
UK ISBN 0-85111-260-9

Printed in the United States of America ∞

Library of Congress Cataloging-in-Publication Data

Adeney, Miriam, 1945-
    Daughters of Islam: building bridges with Muslim women / Miriam Adeney.
        p.cm.
    Includes bibliographical references.
    ISBN 0-8308-2345-X (pbk.: alk. paper)
        1. Missions to Muslims. 2. Muslim women—Religious life. 3. Christianity and other religions—Islam. 4. Islam—Relations—Christianity. I. Title.

BV2625 .A33 2002
266'.088'2971—dc21

                                                                                    2001051945

British Library Cataloguing in Publication Data

A catalogue record for this book is available from the British Library.

| 20 | 19 | 18 | 17 | 16 | 15 | 14 | 13 | 12 | 11 | 10 | 9 | 8 | 7 | 6 | 5 |
| 17 | 16 | 15 | 14 | 13 | 12 | 11 | 10 | 09 | 08 | 07 | 06 | 05 | 04 | 03 |

Contents

Preface

We stand on the edge of a great immensity when we write about ministry among Muslim women. Recognizing the godfearing spirit of many Muslims, the sacrificial service of generations of Christian witnesses and the great grace of God, we approach humbly.

We want to follow the spirit of Raymond Lull, Kenneth Cragg and J. Dudley Woodberry, who have shown large-hearted appreciation for Muslim peoples and for the beauty of their cultures.

We want to follow in the steps of Lilias Trotter, Mildred Cable and Maud Carey, who trekked deep into the heart of the Muslim world—southern Algeria, the Gobi desert, interior Morocco—to share their delight in Christ with women and men.

We want to follow the thinking of Samuel Zwemer, Constance Padwick and Don McCurry, who used their heads as well as their hearts to construct a comprehensive overview of Muslims, priority issues, and systematic strategies that would serve sound stewardship.

Finally, we want to follow on to find the joy of the Lord as our strength. Justin, Daniel and Derek, men from Africa who studied at Regent College, have modeled this for me. Along with their wives, Grace, Anne and Gladys, they showed me that witness to Muslims is a relaxed and joyous business, even in the face of pain and danger, because it is always and altogether God's work before it is ours.

The burden of this book, ministry among Muslim women, is not new.

What is new in our time is vastly increased opportunities and resources. Samuel Zwemer and Constance Padwick, Lilias Trotter and Maud Carey did not begin to have available the resources that lie at our fingertips, nor the comparatively easy access to all parts of the globe.

To whom much has been given, from them much is required.

*   *   *   *   *

Why write a women's book? Many well-researched books on Muslim ministry have rolled off the presses of the world. Much of the wisdom in these books applies to women. I would be a fool to try to duplicate the wealth of history, theology and ecclesiology available already. For balance, the reader must dig into sources listed in the footnotes.

However, secular research on Muslim women also sparkles with gems. Anthropological books, films, articles and curricula about Muslim women abound. Unfortunately, few lay Christians or even mission executives read this material. Drowning in faxes, reeling from international political explosions, hungry for funds, the overworked mission leader may value data about Muslim women in theory yet never get around to pursuing it in fact. Then, sadly, strategy decisions that affect women are made in ignorance.

For teaching and speaking, I regularly tap into ethnological resources on Muslim women. An urge emerged: Why not make this material accessible to Christian witnesses? Why not gather data on Muslim women's multifaceted worlds and present it in a user-friendly package? Why not integrate and apply it?

That is my aim in this book. To educate about important parts of Muslim women's lives. To elucidate some mission strategies. To offer examples. And to encourage.

*   *   *   *   *

Daughters of Islam features five chapters of case studies, each containing roughly three cases. Each is the story of a Muslim-background woman for whom Jesus is Lord. These chapters introduce us to sisters who are Arab, Iranian, Malay, Indonesian and African. In other chapters we meet Muslim-background followers of Jesus who are Indian or Pakistani, Turkish or Uzbek.

Interspersed with the case study chapters are a brief introduction to

Muslim women; a chapter on women's diversity, featuring Arabs; and chapters on themes important for ministry among Muslim women: ethnotheology, family relations, teaching and learning styles and finances.

All of us missiologists come to our subject groping, like the fabled blind men who stumbled on an elephant. One man was encircled by the elephant's trunk. Another felt the leg. Still another grasped the tail. So, too, a missiological New Testament scholar may sense the trunk of our common subject. A missiological historian may palpate the leg. A missiological theologian may clutch the tail. The danger lies in assuming that any one of us has grabbed the whole elephant.

Since I am an anthropologist, my feel for the elephant of missiology is anthropological. Loving the Lord with my mind means studying culture patterns and applying my findings to mission. This book reflects that. Anthropological awareness has given birth to chapters like "Money Matters," "Learning Styles" and "Sex, Singles, Husbands, Children"—Christianity below the neck, where women always have had to apply it.

How thrilling it would be if complementary books on ministries among Muslim women would be penned by Old Testament and New Testament specialists, theologians, ethicists, evangelists, church growth consultants, Christian educators and counselors. Geographical focus would increase the value of the works, particularly if they were composed in the Urdu, Arabic, Swahili, Malay and Uzbek languages.

Still, "of making of many books there is no end, and much study is a weariness of the flesh" (Ecclesiastes 12:12). Making mission strategies never seems to end either. And with all our talk about tentmakers and the Two-Thirds World and nonresident missionaries and multi-individual decision-making units, weariness can set in, as the writer of Ecclesiastes noted. At bottom, what really matters?

Surely in the end what counts is the perennial necessity of mission: human beings witnessing, discipling and serving in the appropriate language. And the perennial disciplines: Bible study, prayer, fellowship, holiness, love, perseverance. Anthropological, theological and strategic insights have their place. We would be poor stewards if we ignored them. But in our zeal to be contemporary, we must be careful not to bypass the basics.

There are many awesome stories that are not told in this book. In various countries today, thousands of former Muslims follow Jesus Christ as Lord. Many are rural or village people. Others are well-educated professionals. In one country they still call themselves Muslims, completed Muslims. Elsewhere there are mobile churches of Muslim-background nomads. We cannot tell all those stories here. This book is just a beginning. It is our hope simply that the cases, data and strategies in this volume will spark dialogue, research, more storytelling and better mission work.

* * * * *

Finally, what is truth in reporting? Biographers agonize over this. While writing this book I traveled to Africa, Asia, France and Russia, and I interviewed former Muslim women in all those places. Other women I interviewed in North America. Some stories came secondhand through church or mission people who had brought Muslim women to faith in Christ and walked beside them.[1] I interviewed in English, occasionally through translation. English was not the first language for any of these women, though many handled it competently.

Most of the women I interviewed are educated. Many are cosmopolitan. A few are rural or village women. One was a nomad. One is a poor urban working woman. Some live in their home countries, others in Europe or North America. The chapter on five kinds of Arab women sensitizes us to these differences.

It also alerts us to women who may be neglected by Christian witnesses. Take political radicals, for example. Given their strong group support and the motivating energy generated by commitment to a cause, such women probably are not particularly open to a new Lord. We assume that. But do we know? Who has reached out to them? A contextualized apologetic tailored for such women never has been developed, as far as I know. Yet strong potential bridges exist. The political radical hungers for justice and righteousness. The fundamentalist thirsts for God's kingdom values expressed in community. As women, they may be sensitive to the vulnerable and experienced in nurturing concrete needs. Where is the bridge builder who can take these girders and suspension wires and cast an evangelistic span across the rivers on whose banks these women live?

As a rule, I have changed the women's names in order to protect confidentiality. Where possible I have used a woman's own words, as is evident from the contrast in style between one woman's remarks and another's. In various spots I have invented dialogue to tell the story shared with me in narrative form. Where I have been able to check my account with others who were present at an interview, or who know the woman, we have found accuracy high.

Do these women remember their stories accurately? Do they unconsciously overemphasize certain elements in such a way that historical reality is distorted? At best, we see through a glass darkly. All our tellings are incomplete. Whether on the woman's or the author's part, misrepresentations occasionally will occur. For these inadvertent errors I apologize in advance.

What I can assert is that no woman was a new convert. Each had been seriously committed to the Lord Jesus Christ for more than a year, in many cases for more than a decade. And each had a good reputation with several other mature Christians. This "cloud of witnesses" testifies to each woman's authenticity.

Since the interviews, spanning seven years, a couple of women have gone through dark nights of the soul, according to word-of-mouth reports. Others have blazed gloriously through dire problems. In other words, these women are as complex and as common as the rest of us: treasures in jars of clay.

1

Why Muslim Women Come to Christ

Hagar. Single mother. Victim of forced sex. Abandoned in the desert with no child support.

Yet an integral part of the story of Abraham, that great leader of faith. Jews, Christians and Muslims all trace their heritage through Abraham.

Originally Hagar was a slave—illiterate chattel at the bottom of the heap. Her owner was Sarah, Abraham's wife.

But Sarah was infertile. For years she struggled to get pregnant. After awhile it was heartbreaking. Finally, still determined to have children in the house, Sarah did what she thought was the next best thing: she pushed Hagar at Abraham. Maybe her marriage contract required her to provide an heir through a servant if she couldn't produce one herself.

Then the plot thickened. As soon as Hagar got pregnant, Sarah regretted her move. Hagar started showing off. Sarah retaliated by abusing her servant. Hagar couldn't take it. She ran off.

Alone in the desert, Hagar had no future. But God came to Hagar and stopped her in her tracks with his presence and his promises.

The angel of the LORD found Hagar near a spring in the desert; it was the spring that is beside the road to Shur. And he said, "Hagar, servant of Sarai, where have you come from, and where are you going?"

"I'm running away from my mistress Sarai," she answered.

Then the angel of the LORD told her, "Go back to your mistress and submit to her." The angel added, "I will so increase your descendants that they will be too numerous to count."

The angel of the LORD also said to her:
"You are now with child
    and you will have a son.
You shall name him Ishmael,
    for the LORD has heard of your misery. . . ."

She gave this name to the LORD who spoke to her: "You are the God who sees me," for she said, "I have now seen the One who sees me." (Genesis 16:7-11, 13)

When God confronted this pregnant, single nobody, how did she respond? She said, "God, you see me." In spite of the desolate wilderness that surrounded her, in spite of the social structure in which she was insignificant, the miracle was that God saw her. God knew her as an individual. She was not alone in the universe. She was a creature of God. That changed the direction of her life. She turned around, went back and was obedient to Sarah.

Still, fourteen years later, Hagar got kicked out again. This time it was permanent.

The reason was simple. Some years after Hagar's baby was born, Sarah surprised everybody, most of all herself. She got pregnant and gave birth to a boy.

One day Hagar's son teased Sarah's.

Sarah exploded. "Get rid of that slave woman and her son!" she said to Abraham. "That slave woman's son will never share in the inheritance with my son Isaac!"

So Abraham turned Hagar and Ishmael out of his camp. He gave them some food and water and sent them away. Hagar hiked with her boy. Maybe she hoped for a passing caravan where they could hitch a ride. But none appeared. The day came when the water was all used up. This time there was no spring.

When the water in the skin was gone, she put the boy under one of the bushes. Then she went off and sat down nearby, about a bowshot away, for she thought, "I cannot watch the boy die." And as she sat there nearby, she began to sob. (Genesis 21: 15-16)

Then God came to Hagar again.

God heard the boy crying, and the angel of God called to Hagar from heaven and said to her, "What is the matter, Hagar?" (v. 17)

What was the *matter?* Hagar must have been ready to spit out a bitter riposte, when the angel continued:

Do not be afraid. God has heard the boy crying as he lies there. Lift the boy up and take him by the hand, for I will make him into a great nation.

Then God opened her eyes and she saw a well of water. (vv. 17-19)

In Muslim tradition, too, God provided water for Hagar and Ishmael, although the details differ from the biblical story. When Abraham sent Hagar and Ishmael away, according to Muslim teaching, he resettled them in Mecca, a desolate place in the wilderness. He commissioned them to be pioneer missionaries, spreading the true faith in this unreached region. Together Abraham and Hagar built the Ka'bah, a small building, and dedicated it to the worship of the one God. Later, when Hagar searched desperately for water, the fountain of Zamzum miraculously sprang up.[1] Twenty-five hundred years later, the Ka'bah and Zamzum would figure in the story of the prophet Muhammad. Today they are central sites visited by those who make the annual pilgrimage to Mecca.

Muslims trace their heritage from Abraham through Ishmael, Abraham's oldest son. Some consider this their genetic ancestry. For others it is metaphorical. Either way, Hagar stands as the mother of the line.

In Jewish-Christian tradition, Hagar, along with Abraham and Sarah, is one of the people of God who has shown us a little more of what it means to interact with God. She is part of our roots.

This book focuses on "daughters of Hagar," women of Muslim ancestry who have experienced the grace of God through the Lord Jesus Christ. As God provided a spring in the desert for a needy woman four thousand years ago, so today he pours out life and freshness for vulnerable women all over the globe.

Who Are Muslim Women?

Almost one-tenth of the world's population are Muslim women.

Who are they? Arabs, first of all. The prophet Muhammad was an Arab, and Islam's most sacred site is in Arabia. To Arabia pilgrims journey by the millions every year. Beyond Arabia, the Arab world extends north through the Fertile Crescent and west across North Africa.

East from Arabia we find Iranian Muslim women, who are different from Arabs ethnically and religiously. Most are Shiite Muslims rather than Sunni. West and North is Turkey. This nation once dominated the Muslim world. It hosted the last great caliphate. Today Muslims speaking Turkic languages number well over one hundred million. Over sixty million live in the region of the former Soviet Union, in the great frontier states of Central Asia. Because of a robust birth rate, this population is growing fast.

The biggest bloc of Muslims in the world is in South Asia—Pakistan, India, Bangladesh, Afghanistan. In Southeast Asia is the single biggest Muslim-majority nation, Indonesia. Here too are Muslim-oriented Malaysia and the Muslim section of the Philippines. Women tend to take active roles in leadership in daily life in these Southeast Asian communities.

Mosques are being constructed up and down the continent of Africa, where many Muslims live. Islam is most pervasive in East Africa, just a dhow's sail away from Arabia. China supports nearly twenty-five million Muslims, who live especially in the northwest but also in little enclaves scattered throughout the country. Europe is building new mosques rapidly, both for the "guest workers" and immigrants from Muslim countries and for local converts. It is estimated that in the United States there are four to six million Muslims.

Who are Muslim women? Clearly they differ according to their national or ethnic identity. A woman's concerns also will be shaped by
☐ her role in the life cycle
☐ her economic situation

☐ her ideological community

☐ her personality

Consider the life cycle. Women dream new dreams and feel fresh needs at different points in their lives, such as

☐ a daughter in her father's house

☐ a single professional woman sharing an apartment with other young women

☐ a married mother

☐ a childless married woman

☐ a divorced mother, head of household

☐ a widowed grandmother living in her son's household

Sometimes knowing a woman's role in the life cycle is more important than knowing her nationality.

Economically, several of the richest countries in the world are Arab. Yet in other Arab communities poverty is cruel. Certainly among the Muslims of South Asia are many malnourished women, side by side with million-aires. Some Muslim women have Ph.D.s and big stock portfolios. Millions of others are illiterate. Some rich women move regularly between homes in Arabia, France, London and the United States. These are not necessarily "liberated" women. Some of the very rich may not be allowed to drive cars or to go out without a male companion or a veil.

As for religion, many Muslim women have been taught little about Islamic doctrines and theology. They resort to folk religion, shrines, sacrifices, amulets, divination and spirit possession as often as they turn to Muslim institutions. Others are well grounded in the teachings of the faith. Some belong to radical fundamentalist sisterhoods. For others, political activism in solidarity with other Muslims or conationals is what counts, rather than religious activism.

Vocationally, too, there is diversity. Even in a simple village, some women may specialize as herbalists, while others are textile weavers, others food dryers, others cheese makers, others perfumists, others Qur'anic reciters, others musicians, others occult women and others land speculators.

Finally, each woman has unique gifts from God, a distinct personality and distinct life experiences and opportunities.

What Draws Muslim Women to Christ

No disrespect for Islam is intended when we write about Muslim women coming to Christ. Spending time with Muslims, I have been blessed by their high concept of the nature of God. Their prayerful life. Their emphasis on community. Their insistence that faith must be expressed in the public sector. Their concern for ethics in society. Again and again, Islam points us to our Creator.

Yet if a faith doesn't lead to God in Christ, it misses something right at the core. In Christ, God visited this planet in human form. In Christ's death, God experienced the depths of human pain. In Christ's resurrection, God generated the power for new beginnings, for transformation of life. Muslims continually refer to God as "the merciful and compassionate." It is in Christ that God most fully demonstrates those qualities. This is why Muslim women come to Christ. Through Christ, the God whom they knew far off and incompletely becomes their personal Father.

There are all sorts of specific paths by which Muslim women come to the Lord Jesus Christ.

☐ Some come when they read the gospel story.

☐ Others come because they see Jesus in visions or dreams.

☐ Others, during a struggle with demons or spirits, find that the name of Jesus brings liberation and help.

☐ Some have been abused in dysfunctional relationships and find Jesus offering them healing and dignity.

☐ Others have been schooled in the ideals of righteousness and long for justice in their society. They find the power for this in the Lord Jesus.

☐ Some come because of Christ's affirmation of women.

☐ Some who have lived promiscuously cry out for a moral foundation for their own lives.

☐ Others fear death and long for assurance of paradise.

☐ Two women whom I interviewed hungered for God almost single-mindedly from their earliest childhood.

☐ Many come because their family has decided jointly to follow the Lord Jesus Christ.

Muslim women are human beings, and their motives are complex.

However, several milestones recur on these journeys again and again:
- [ ] Scripture
- [ ] spiritual power encounters
- [ ] the love of Christians
- [ ] sex and beauty issues
- [ ] social justice issues

Myths About Ministry with Muslim Women

In the popular mind and in anthropological studies, missionaries often have been labeled paternalistic, judgmental, condescending and colonialist. In his book *Orientalism*, for example, Edward Said argues that missionaries and other expatriates during the Age of Empire viewed Muslim history, culture and ethics through Western lenses. Therefore their reports were faulty.[2]

There is some truth to this. An article in the magazine of the premier American women's mission agency observed in 1866:

> The degradation of the female sex in many parts of the East is not sufficiently considered in Christian lands. . . . They are utterly destitute of nearly all those blessings which distinguish us, as rational and religious beings, and without which we should deem life insupportable.[3]

The "deplorable state of heathen women" . . . "utterly benighted" . . . "less favored sisters" . . . "pathetic, pitiable, downtrodden"—such phrases were common during the nineteenth century, the "Great Century" for missions in general and for women's missions in particular.

Certainly there were abused women in Muslim countries, as elsewhere. Even in loving Muslim families today there are millions of women who need schooling, health care, income-generating skills and, above all, the words of the gospel.

Yet when we focus on the weaknesses of another culture, we miss its strengths and beauties. We also miss the sins in our own culture. For example, Muslims are appalled at Western family life when they hear about abortions, promiscuity, disrespect for parents and neglect of the elderly.

In any case, even at the height of the Age of Empire, *women* missionaries often lived and worked closely with local women. Women's ministry never has been merely cerebral. It always has been holistic, involving body, mind and spirit. And as women have worked together, rested together, laughed together and cried together, de facto empathy has grown. Sisterhood has bonded women across cultures, whatever the missionaries' ideology.[4]

And some early women missionaries did see the difference between their culture and the gospel. In Iran in 1903, Dr. Winifred Westlake wrote, "We don't want to Anglicize the Persian women, do we? No, if we may be used to set them free from the trammels of Mohammedanism, placing them in the light of the Gospel of Christ, they will develop as God wills, and who can tell what they may do in His honour and glory?"[5]

Today there are new assumptions, new "myths" about ministry with Muslim women. Some focus on ministry strategy. Such myths can mislead us. They include

Myth 1. Muslim women are passive and submissive. They rarely think for themselves or exert much leadership.

Myth 2. Muslim women usually cannot come to Christ and grow in Christ unless their husbands become believers too.

Myth 3. A Muslim family will feel more threatened if a daughter or wife believes in Christ as Lord than if a son or husband does.

Myth 4. Muslim women and men can be evangelized and discipled together effectively, using the same strategies and the same Scripture texts.

Myth 5. Muslim women ought not to be evangelized until there is a Christian man available to evangelize the men. To do otherwise would be poor stewardship of personnel, since women will not lead a lasting fellowship.

This book will give us background for evaluating these myths. Consider myths 4 and 5. Can women be evangelized and discipled just like men? Should women's evangelism be subsumed under men's?

The short answer is "Sometimes." How beautiful it is when a household follows Jesus together. How natural it is in places where most important decisions are made corporately.

Unfortunately, Islam so resists the lordship of Jesus that even if a kin group initially hears the gospel together, members may hold each other back from moving closer. Then individual seekers have to pursue truth privately.

Sometimes the opportunities to speak to women arise before there are opportunities to speak to men. Sometimes Christian women are available to reach out before there are Christian men to do the same. Sometimes the abuses women have suffered or, alternatively, the richness of women's worlds call for a gendered approach.

Hagar surely would have resonated with this. Fiercely nurturant, desert-competent, spiritually alive, quiveringly vulnerable, Hagar went on to network a future for her boy. After they drank from God's well in the wilderness, they revived. The boy grew and became a strong hunter. In time Hagar got him a wife from Egypt, and he had sons and daughters. Some of those sons appear when the prophet Isaiah envisions a grand procession around the throne of God at the end of time. Descendants of Nabaioth, Hagar's first grandson, and Kedar, another grandson, march in that train. No longer are they outsiders. God accepts their offerings (Isaiah 60:7).

Hagar's daughters will be there too. Meanwhile, some of them are here in the pages of this book.

2

Every Woman Is an Exception

Camels grumble, forced to kneel in order to be loaded. Donkeys bray, horses whinny, cows low. It is sunrise. Saudah stretches her arms wide to fold the rough black goat-hair tent. Swaying in a makeshift hammock, her baby finds comfort in the familiar cacophony. Saudah has nursed him, but she makes a mental note to wipe and clean him before they climb up to perch on top of their riding camel. Boys strut around, swishing sticks, helping pack, jumping out of the way of their elders. Girls as well as boys clamber onto pack animals.

Not so long ago Saudah was one of that horde. Now a matron, she deposits three-year-old Fatimah and one-year-old Fazir in her camel's saddlebags. A quick glance around, a few odds and ends snatched up and stuffed in, and Saudah clambers onto the camel's hump, baby in her arms. The animal shoots its long neck forward, wobbles up onto its back legs, and struggles to lift its forelegs. Fazir snuggles down, never waking, thumb in mouth, head lolling. Fatimah peers out, wide-eyed. The baby nurses again.

A Bedouin camp is on the move.

In this chapter we will meet five kinds of Arab women—nomads like Saudah, settled village and town women, professional women, religious fundamentalists and political activists. These women are not interchangeable blobs behind veils. Every one is unique. Every woman is an exception.

When mission executives are not aware of this, they sometimes lump Muslim women into narrow categories. Then missionary women get squeezed into tight grooves too. "You just need to understand that in Muslim culture women don't have public roles," Joanna's mission team leader told her. "So you can't have one either if you want to be effective." But Joanna has met the head of the department of engineering at the local university. That department head is a woman. Joanna herself has been invited to teach a course there. *Who will reach these women with the gospel if leaders in important mission movements have little understanding of them?* she wonders.

As we meet different kinds of Arab women in this chapter, we will see that there is a need for variety in ministry. Citing classic and contemporary case studies, this chapter will focus on Arab women's public roles. Occasionally, complementary studies of non-Arab Muslims will be cited. Other dimensions of women's lives will be explored in later chapters.

Bedouin Women

The Bedouin life is the free life, idealized and enshrined in memory. Like Abraham and his entourage, a Bedouin group migrates in a regular pattern in order to find grazing for their camels, sheep and goats. Consider, for example, the al-Fadi and al-Hassanna Bedouin tribes, who surged rhythmically across the boundaries of Syria and Lebanon for generations.[1] The rainy season, the hot, dry season and the lambing season were some of their boundaries. Social patterns budded to blossom according to the way they fit into this arrangement of natural resources.

In the rainy season, women like Saudah churned butter and wove textiles. During the hot season migrations, they sold their products. It was also during that hot time that surrounding agricultural peoples harvested grain. Then the Bedouins could rake in hard cash for three months or so, transporting grain on their camels. In return, the animals were allowed to graze in the stubble.

At least that is how it used to be, before these tribes started buying trucks. As we will see, that changed women's lives as well as men's.

Traditionally, what did Bedouin women do? As a young wife, Saudah deferred to her husband's mother, Zohra, who was the *ahl-il-beit*, the leading woman of the camp. Administrator of domestic affairs, Zohra also held the purse strings. She bought from traveling peddlers and distributed the goods. At the end of the summer she planned the purchase of major provisions for winter and commissioned the men of the camp to do the buying.

If her husband was away, she welcomed and entertained any camp guests. An itinerant merchant, religious specialist or healer would present his credentials to her. Only then would he be free to offer his wares or services to the rest of the camp.

Zohra kept her eye on everyday meal preparations and personally carried food to her husband and his retinue. She planned domestic projects—sewing, weaving, food preservation and processing, animal care, visits and other outings, rituals—and shared out the jobs among the younger women, like Saudah. Although they had their own tents, all the kinswomen did a lot of the chores together. While the younger women baked bread, milked animals, cooked, washed clothes, swept, bathed children and sewed, the older matrons would keep the toddlers and infants in line, chuckling over their antics. When the older women needed a siesta, they might relax over a bubbling water pipe.

Nomad camps can be orderly, sometimes even elegant, and it is women who manage them much of the time. We glimpse this in the journals of Sa'eed, a Kurdish Christian doctor born in 1863. One day his medical services were requested by a chief of the Kashgai, a nomadic tribe in Iran. The chief's wife was sick. As Dr. Sa'eed records, the chief

> revealed his deep attachment to her, not only for her beauty, but for her numerous virtuous qualities and fine character. She was indeed a clever and capable lady, attending personally to much that went on in the large household. Occasionally, even in her husband's absence, she ordered and provided food for five hundred guests. She seemed to know every article in her huge pavilion, which took thirty-two poles to pitch. In this enormous tent were beautiful rugs—two of them seven yards by three, trunks of valuables in the chieftain's quarters, looms for weaving carpets in the women's section. Every detail bespoke the orderliness and industry of its mistress.[2]

The free life, the nomadic heritage: Women's life in the desert is by no means all bad.

Today, however, most Bedouin tribesmen buy trucks instead of camels. Camels' feet slip easily on paved roads, which makes camel transport increasingly hazardous. Camels forage widely. As more and more land along the migration routes is planted with crops, the Bedouin men have to sweat to keep their animals from gobbling up private produce. Even during regular travel through open country, camels tend to break formation. Rounding them up is a never-ending hassle.

And, of course, there is the prestige of owning a truck.

"During the dry summer season," an anthropologist among the al-Fadl and al-Hassanna reported, "there was not one day in which a truck, parked by a home, was not cleaned and dusted by the men and boys. Unlike other mechanical instruments (tape recorders, radios), these vehicles were constantly cared for. Scratches were covered, engines were kept in tune, dents were removed and the body of the vehicle was always gaily decorated. Talismans and proverbs to ward off the evil eye were always found somewhere on the vehicle, as were tassels, photographs, and mementos."[3]

Trucks may move Bedouins more efficiently than camels can. But when trucks replace camels, women's lives shrink. No longer do they have camels' milk from which to make butter and yogurt for sale. No longer do they have camels' hair from which to weave carpets for sale. No longer can they collect plants for dyes, medicines and foods as the caravan meanders slowly along its route. No longer can they look forward to reconnecting with kin, friends, buyers, vendors, and medical, religious and literary specialists on their slow migrations. Nor do they have the aesthetic outlet of designing, weaving and braiding decorative trappings as they did for camels. Men are the ones who decorate trucks. Instead of the leisurely migration, trucks now zoom from point A to point Z. Dumping off women, children and baggage, men hop back in and roar off to visit, buy, sell, learn, consult and worship. Women's lives are diminished.

In *Writing Women's Worlds*, anthropologist Laila Abu-Lughod traces these changes through three generations of Egyptian/Libyan Bedouin women who are living today.[4] Some of the younger women enjoy more education and more choices. Modernization does bring some blessings.

But there are also losses. With the passing of camels and the lifestyle they represented, treasured elements disappear. The richnesses of the traditional nomad woman's life should not be underestimated.

Village Women, Urban Women

What do settled village Arab women do? Most raise children and keep house. That's the dream. Quite a few also work for money. In one sample of a rural Moroccan village, 55 percent of the marriages evaporated in divorce.[5] Divorce, separation and widowhood propel women into the job market, especially if they have to support small children. But even in solid two-parent families, many mothers and young adult daughters must earn an income if the family is going to make ends meet.

Moroccan villagers. What jobs do these women hold? In the Morocco village mentioned above, women earn money in a variety of ways. The most desirable jobs are manager of the women's public bath, sewing teacher and seamstress. These jobs have high status and pay well. Two factors give these jobs status. They can be done inside the house, or at least inside the world of women. And they are the centers of communication networks.

Positions which have high status but pay poorly include religious leader, musician and midwife. At the other extreme, jobs which bring in enough money but have low status include field laborer and prostitute. Eight percent of the women sampled—the largest single group—are field laborers. Interestingly, school teachers and occult specialists hold ambivalent status.

A study of the Shahsevan people of Iran adds these high-status jobs for women: magician/medic, ceremonial feast cook, holy woman.[6] Women in these positions are invited to about thirty feasts a year, while ordinary women are invited to about ten. Like Muslim women in many cultures, Shahsevan women also gain in status as they age, or if they are the primary wives of important men and therefore placed at the center of a network with lots of management responsibilities.

The Shahsevan magician/medic combines the roles of midwife and occult woman. As in Morocco, she is viewed ambivalently. On the one hand, people want her help. On the other hand, they suspect her dubious supernatural connections. A different class of religious specialists are the "holy women." In Morocco these are *sherifas*, meaning that they trace their lineage back to the prophet Muhammad. "Holy women" among the Shahsevan are *Mashadis*, because they have made a religious pilgrimage to the shrine at Mashad. They are some of the few Shahsevan women who pray regularly. *Mashadis* are hired to perform religious rituals like laying out the dead. Both *Mashadis* and *sherifas* serve as religious consultants, private and public. People believe they have better connections with the supernatural than the average person does.

Cairo urbanites. Like their village sisters, many city women work outside as well as in the home. Some are educated middle- and upper-class women. We will discuss them in the next section. Among the less educated, some are recent immigrants from the countryside. Although they now live in the city, they still think and associate in rural ways.

But some are true urbanites, women from trading and laboring families who have made the city their home for generations. A study in Cairo finds these women working in factories and garment shops and as store assistants, shop managers, laundresses, nurses, government employees and traveling saleswomen who visit the homes of wealthier, more secluded women.[7] Back home at the end of the day, these women do the housework, assist in their husbands' projects and try to keep themselves pretty for their husbands.

These urban working women call themselves *bint al-balad*, daughter of the nation, *bint al-hitta*, daughter of the place, and *bint al-suq*, daughter of the market. Neither country women nor elite, they are proud of their lot in life. In contrast to the *fallaha*, or country women, they see themselves as alert, inquiring, acquainted with a wide variety of people, stylish, clean, streetwise and capable of protecting themselves. In contrast with elite women, they see themselves as hard working and ready to sacrifice for their family and neighbors.

Unlike what she perceives as the lonely and bored elite, a *bint al-balad* lives in a world rich in people. Because Cairo's population has overstretched its resources, sometimes as many as four families crowd into an apartment built for one. An urban working woman learns not to be too picky. She isn't too refined for physical experiences, like sitting on the ground, eating with her hands or relaxing in a coffee house. Nor is she too repressed to enjoy public emotional fireworks, whether *zar* spectacles of religious possession or ordinary loud joking and arguing. In short, she scorns what she perceives as the arid, antiseptic and lazy life of the upper-class woman, even while she envies her leisure and fine things.

A *bint al-balad* should know how to hold her own if a strange man accosts her. "Do you really fear men in the street?" said a man to a young woman in his community. "I am sure that if any man dares to bother you, you would immediately take off your shoe and beat him."

In fact, a twenty-year-old woman did just that. For weeks an amorous merchant had been following her around. He sent her presents. She returned them. Finally, when she ignored all his overtures, he started making dirty remarks when she passed.

"One day I became furious," she admitted, "and I followed him to the *baladi* coffeehouse, snatched off his glasses and beat him with my shoe. He tried to insult me again, but I answered back with a flood of insults. He even took a chair and tried to hit me with it, but I ducked and he fell and I fell on him and beat him. On that day I shocked the market; everybody heard about this incident, particularly since this man was known and feared as a tough guy. Since that day he has lost the respect of others. Had I not done what I did, he would have kept on saying I am a loose woman."[8]

A *bint al-balad* feels at home in her crowded city, and apparently she grumbles no more than the rest of us. For some other urban women, though, poverty is acute. Each day is a crucible of pain.

Ankara immigrants. In contrast to such established urbanites, immigrants from the countryside are the focus of a study based in Ankara, Turkey.[9] Some are young wives whose husbands prohibit them from leaving the neighborhood. They may sell handcrafts which they make, but their financial contribution remains relatively unrecognized. Another group of migrants are comfortable middle-class women who socialize with each other in formal receptions, rotating from one home to another. While rising in status, they have remained traditional. A third group are young women—responsible, contributing members of society—who rebel against patriarchal expectations.

A fourth group are most like the feisty *bint al-balad* of Cairo. When their migrant families faced discouraging dead ends, "it was the women's determination that kept their families in the city. . . . They took the initiative to build a squatter house or to buy an apartment for their families when their husbands failed to do so, and they put their physical labor into the process." When husbands couldn't find work, they couldn't object to their wives earning money. These women clean wealthy people's houses, run grocery stores or sell garments which they have machine-knitted at home. In so doing, they have "used the city as a place to develop and affirm new identities and ways of living."[10]

Settled village and urban women—glimpsed here in half a dozen microcosms—demonstrate resourcefulness and initiative just like their nomad sisters.

Educated Professionals

The Middle East boasts some of the richest countries in the world. Rich women don't work for money. If they work at all, it's because they want to serve their people. Or they want status. Or they want to express their creative energies. So they aim for the top. They have no interest in secretarial jobs. These women are bankers, doctors, professors, TV producers, real estate investors and business tycoons. In Tunisia, 25 percent of the judges are women, as are 20 percent in Morocco. In Egypt reportedly a higher percentage of the engineers are women than is the case in Germany.

Professional women are active even in restrictive countries like Saudi Arabia, where women can't drive cars or have direct business dealings with men who aren't relatives. More than 6,000 commercial licenses have been issued to businesswomen in just two Saudi cities, Riyadh and Jiddah. Some 78,000 women graduated from Saudi universities between 1995 and 2000.

Overall, the number of Saudi working women is estimated to be slightly more than 250,000. While formerly this work would have been optional, today many Saudi families need money due to an economic downturn in the 1990s.

How do these women manage if they must stay apart from male customers and contacts? They have brothers, sons, fathers, husbands, cousins, uncles, nephews or sons-in-law who can be employed to interface with the outside world. Some of these men may serve as sponsors, *mahrams* or "guardians."

While these businesswomen may not meet male contacts face to face, they can do vigorous commerce with anybody by telephone, fax or e-mail. Already they serve half the population—women who need women doctors, women lawyers, women teachers and women merchandisers. In 1980 an all-women's bank opened in Saudi Arabia. Since then, shopping malls for women only have appeared in Saudi Arabia, Pakistan and Abu Dhabi. To create the Saudi mall, women bonded together and invested ten million dollars of their own money. Besides regular outlets, the women's mall in Abu Dhabi boasts a cinema, gym, business center, mosque—and a video arcade, which is very popular with young girls. There are also women-only Internet cafes.

In some Middle Eastern countries, women who attend a university sit in an all-female classroom, watching their professor on closed-circuit TV. If they have questions, they phone from their classroom to the men's classroom. Once a week the university library is closed to men and open to women.[11] In other countries, like Kuwait, coeducation is the norm. And even staunch outposts of orthodoxy like the University of Al Azhar in Egypt have women professors of Islamic law.

Throughout history, skilled professional women have helped to fulfill the commandment "subdue the earth and have dominion" in the Muslim world. Long before there were modern medical schools, there were Muslim women doctors. Arab medicine was advanced during the Middle Ages. Years of training in anatomy, physiology and botany took place in reputable academies. Women as well as men attended. After graduating, a woman would apprentice herself to a male relative in the profession, and eventually she would take over the female part of his practice. Sometimes she would treat her patients' male relatives, too. In the treatises on Arab medicine which have survived from the Baghdad Caliphate, women surgeons and women medical professors are cited.

There were also a handful of women professors and judges of Islamic law in that period. Shuhda, for example, was considered one of the greatest authorities on the Hadith in twelfth-century Baghdad. "Prominent men came to her lectures and referred to her as 'the scholar.' "[12] And of course there have always been women saints.

Ironically, some of the best-educated women of the era were courtesans. "Though every educated woman of the day knew how to compose a good verse and strum a pleasant melody on the lute, most were amateurs compared to slave girls trained in the best conservatories since childhood by slave dealers who hoped to recoup their investment through the astronomical prices these artists fetched on the market. . . . Beauty alone was not enough, for many of the princes were poets and musicians in their own right and insisted on an artistic *dolce vita*, not a simple orgy with brainless sex objects."[3]

Consider Tawaddud, for whom Harun al Raschid (of the *Thousand and One Nights*) paid a fortune. Tawaddud is reported to have passed high exams in astronomy, medicine, law, music, philosophy, history, Arabic grammar, literature, theology and chess. (Incidentally, a courtesan had one other route to power: If she could bear her lord a son, she might become the freed mother of the next ruler of the realm.)

Today educated professional women salt the Muslim world. This is true even in Afghanistan, where, until recently, women have been suppressed more harshly than anywhere else. Even there, women professors who fled from the capitol in recent years helped set up a university in one region free from government control. There were three hundred students, sixteen professors and four different faculties. Classrooms were built from brick, mud and straw. There was no electricity. Yet families in occupied Kabul sent their girl children to study at this university.

Speaking in 1997, a professor explained their vocation as stewardship. "We detest the [governing] Taliban; they are against all civilization, Afghan culture, education and women in particular. They have given Islam and the Afghan people a bad name," she said. "The children of the Taliban are growing up with no education and only a knowledge of guns and opium. We are building a new generation of Afghans who will lead the nation towards peace and modernity."[4]

In Pakistan, although ordinary women may suffer harassment, there is an impressive line of educated professional women. This includes former Prime Minister Benazir Bhutto. Recently *Telegraph* magazine, based in London, interviewed several of these Pakistanis.[5]

"I never thought my identity was a problem until I was informed by others (in Britain) that it was," said one. "When I told my class teacher that I wanted to be a lawyer, her first question was, 'But surely your parents won't allow that?' I told her that my mother and my grandmother had both studied law in Pakistan."

"Muslim women throughout the ages have always sought knowledge and had professions," another commented. "In my grandmother's generation we were qualifying as doctors and teachers. In Egypt and Syria, women got the vote at the same time as women in Britain and long before they did in Switzerland."

In the book *Arab Women in the Field*, several female Arab social scientists describe how they conduct public research.[16] Some emphasize their professional role, finding that it is useful to be categorized by their occupation more than by their gender. They adapt to the culture by using courtesies and titles of address, even terms like *sidi*, "my master." When visiting traditional people, they wear veils. One brought her parents for a visit, and another brought her husband for a brief time. Meanwhile, they capitalize on their professional role.

Throughout history, sexually segregated society has meant a double set of job openings. Women at the top have had lots of opportunity to practice exercising power. Authority never has been seen as the antithesis of femininity. This is a heritage that flows from the Kashgai head lady out in the desert, running a camp and serving dinner for five hundred guests without batting an eyelash. There have always been Muslim women leaders, particularly in the world of women.

Religious Fundamentalists

Sally teaches English as a Second Language at an American college. Japanese and Arab young adults crowd her classes. This year a half dozen Arab women have enrolled. They aren't immigrants. They are wives of embassy personnel and airline employees, sisters of men students, and a few rare women here on their own.

A friendly teacher bubbling with curiosity and warmth, Sally invites her students to her home for a potluck dinner every term. This year she decided to have a coffee just for the Arab women too.

"My husband will be out visiting his sister from 3:00 to 6:00 on Sunday afternoon," she explained to the women. "Would you come?"

They did. They draped themselves around her living room, sipped her coffee, praised her brownies, tickled her children and chortled as escapades were recounted.

Then the time for Muslim afternoon prayer arrived.

Amal, a graduate in Islamic studies from Al Azhar University, rose, slipped a small prayer rug out of her handbag and rolled it out in the middle of the living room rug. Tucking her veil more closely around herself, she dropped to her knees, touched her forehead to the rug and, right in the center of the circle of conversation, began to murmur her prayer. When she swayed to her feet a few minutes later, a couple of other women followed her quietly, one after the other kneeling on the small carpet.

The rest of the Arab women kept their seats. Sally wondered why. Were they all having their menstrual periods? Did they think it was an inappropriate place for prayer? Were they simply not women of prayer?

As for Amal, why did she obtrude her religious practices so centrally, even in an outspokenly Christian home?

The winds of fundamentalism blow through the air today—around Muslims, around Hindus and even around Christians. These winds are powered not so much by theology as by the scary state of the world. Marxism has crumbled. In any case, it never was a serious option for Muslims, given its atheism. Yet Western-style democracy tastes less and less palatable. It seems to display a moral vacuum.

"Look at the West! What do you see?" Muslims groan. "Pornography. Beauty contests, displaying thighs and breasts. Weak families. Abused women and children. Disrespect for parents. Growing illegitimacy. Abortions. Sexually transmitted disease. Drugs."

From fundamentalist Muslims' moral perspective, Western culture no longer offers an attractive model. It has lost credibility. It is tarnished. Against this stands the Islamic vision of moral order. Given the collapse of alternatives, in their view the salvation of the world—physically and socially as well as spiritually—may depend on Islam.

If that is so, every Muslim's efforts will count, including women's. First of all, women can combat their own tendency to sexual allure. They can dress and behave modestly. This alone will help society take a step toward righteousness. Across the Muslim world, many young women are choosing to wear veils or headscarves—even women whose mothers went unveiled.

"We just went from being sex objects Oriental style to being sex objects Occidental style," says one woman, reflecting on the period of her life when she dressed in modern fashions. Turkish author Naila Minai comments, "Under such circumstances, the veil could be a tool for reasserting a woman's human dignity by forcing people to respond to her talents and personality rather than to her body alone."[7]

Beyond modesty, women can reach out from the sanctity of the home to protect society from moral degeneration. Since men have more contact with the outside world and don't have a lot of restraints, there will always be some who will get tangled in dubious behaviors or beliefs—sexual immorality, alcohol, pork(!), Christianity. Forewarned, women can take these aberrations in stride and wait them out. Whatever weird ideologies a few men may flirt with, if the women remain staunch Muslims, teach their children, and draw the family to participate in the community fasts, feasts, prayers, creed recitations, Qur'anic readings and visits to shrines—in short, if they by their behavior continually hold up for their menfolk the precepts of Islam—the heritage will flourish. Pious women can keep men from being shipwrecked on the temptations of freedom.

Clearly, then, Christian witnesses cannot take the gospel to men, introduce them to vital relationships with the Lord Jesus Christ and assume that their womenfolk will follow. Heads of households men may be; that doesn't make them the traditional conservators of religion. Without relevant communication of the gospel addressed specifically to women, a woman may decide to wait out this Christian phase. Or more radically, she may ask her father to arrange a divorce from the apostate husband.

Today many mosques have weekly Qur'anic classes for women. Religious sisterhoods, voluntary associations for laywomen, have sprung up. Members of a sisterhood may be identified by the specific way they wrap their headcloths. Some of these women's groups concentrate on religious study, others on social service and others on political activism.

At the university, too, when young men study business and technology, some of their wives and sisters are earning credits in Islamics. They are preparing to give moral guidance to homes and, in ripples, to communities and nations.

Some "fundamentalist feminists" adopt the most conservative dress recommended by the Hanbali school, adding black gloves to cover their hands and black stockings for their feet. With this clothing as a shield against slander and a testimony to their commitment to Islam, they speak out for women's concerns regarding jobs, education and children.

Educated or not, nearly all Muslim women are gripped by the conviction that salvation is not just an individual matter. It is a corporate responsibility. In this struggle, women play a key role. So Amal kneels on Sally's floor. As she does, she is proclaiming that she is more than a sex object and more than an economic producer. She is a human being with choices. She chooses to submit to God and to do it publicly.

Political Activists

For some women, the core issues are political. Solidarity with their people in political struggle is what grips them. Women's groups can serve this purpose. In Iraq today, for example, one and a half million women comprise 222 branches of the General Federation of Iraqi Women. "The Federation has become a strong force in implementing women's legal claims to land, assuring them access to education should fathers demur, and giving them rights to marry and divorce unheard of forty years ago."[18] In return, these women support Saddam Hussein's party.

In this section we will meet three historic role models honored for their political zeal.

Jamilah Buhrayd. "The young women of Algeria don't have time to discuss the problems of sex right now," says Jamilah Buhrayd, a nationalist leader. "We are still in a struggle to make our new country work, to rebuild the destroyed family, to preserve our identity as a nation. In the future, perhaps, we will arrive at a kind of life where men and women relate on a more friendly, equal and open basis. I hope so . . .

"[But] I don't think love is just sex. No. It's everything which is harmonious. It's deep feeling. It's the family. It's the country. That is love. If the younger generation forgets this, it is lost. The values are there. They search for peace, they say. But how can they see peace in a world where there is still Palestine? . . . Palestine will not get its freedom by utopian talking and imagining. They will have to fight. And this action and this justice must come from women as well as men, girls as well as boys."[19]

The woman who said that is the doting mother of three children. She spends her energies in neighborhood volunteer work. It was not always so, however. Jamilah was one of the heroines of the Algerian revolution in the 1960s. She carried bombs in her purse, and she threw them. She was arrested and tortured. She never broke. She never revealed her comrades' names. And she lived to see a free Algeria. In spite of sporadic fundamentalist violence, Jamilah's family lives peacefully. But she still thinks violently, at least where Palestine is concerned.

Political activism has a noble heritage among Arab women. During the nineteenth and twentieth centuries, alien powers rolled across the Muslim world. France took Syria and parts of North Africa. Britain took Palestine, Egypt and India. Italy took Libya. The Netherlands tightened its stranglehold of three centuries on Indonesia. Turkey chose the wrong side in World War I and lost its empire and the last great Sultanate.

Muslims found this much harder to stomach than Christians would have if the situation had been reversed. Admittedly, many Christians kick out a knee-jerk military response when they perceive a military threat. Yet Christian theology offers a framework for understanding suffering and subjugation as results of the freedom allowed by God in a sinful world. Muslim theologians are hard put to offer any such understanding.

After all, Christians follow Jesus, who went to the cross, despised. Muslims follow Muhammad, who experienced one victory after another. The Bible contains books like Hosea, Jeremiah and Isaiah, which trace the suffering of God's servants. The Qur'an, while it recounts stories of Adam and Eve, Noah, Abraham, Moses, and even ninety-three verses about Jesus, lacks parallels to the prophetic books' "suffering servant" passages. Muslims don't see victory growing out of defeat. So alien colonial rule made no sense. How could this be God's will?

To make matters worse, most Muslims don't believe in separation of church and state. A moral government is one based on God's law. Muslims resonate with the psalmist when he sings, "The law of the Lord is sweeter than honey, more precious than gold," because the law gives order to the chaos of our experience, and because the law comes from a Person who wishes well for us.

Naturally a society based on God's law will be a unified society. If alternative lifestyles are allowed, there will soon be immorality. If many points of view flourish, heresy won't be far behind. Yet colonial powers splintered godly communities when they introduced secular law codes. Since independence, a lot of the turmoil in Muslim countries has stemmed from efforts to reverse that split, to tie the law of the land to theology. Those who want theocracies battle against fellow citizens who want to maintain desacralized nation-states.

The struggle against infidel colonialists drew Arab women into the streets in the early 1900s. Throwing themselves into national resistance movements, they published newspapers, marched with banners, blew up railroad bridges, cut telephone lines and suffered torture. Jamilah the Algerian joined the battle.

Algeria had experienced one of the longest colonial rules in the Arab world—nearly a century. It was also one of the more intrusive: the French imposed their ways not only politically and economically but also linguistically and culturally. At school, for example, little Algerian children were taught to answer the question, "What is the capital city of your country?" by saying, "Paris." And on the playground during recess, if they lapsed into their mother tongue—"Tsk! Tsk! Not the language of barbarians. Speak French, please. Try to be civilized."

When she grew up, Jamilah joined the resistance bomb squad. That was what got her arrested and tortured. Today, although she is a model citizen, wife and mother, immersed in neighborhood affairs, she doesn't repent any of her violence. She feels her revolutionary work gave her life authenticity.

She remembers a fellow revolutionary being marched out of the jail to die. Housed far away from the other inmates, he wanted to let them know he was going.

"Allah-u-Akbar!" he shouted suddenly in a loud voice. "God is great!" Three times he shouted it before the guards could shut him up.

Then from the whole prison came a thundering echo: "Allah-u-Akbar! God is great!" Spontaneously the prison then burst into the forbidden national anthem of Algeria:

We have rebelled, it's life or death,

And we have determined that Algeria live,
So bear witness to our vow!

That was true community, Jamilah believes. That involvement has made her life ring true.

Huda Sharawi. If any woman could be called the mother of Arab women's liberation, it would be Huda Sharawi, founder of the Egyptian women's movement. Huda was born into a wealthy and socially concerned family in 1882.[20] She was educated in Turkish and French by tutors at home. But she crept into the study when her brother was having his Arabic lessons. In this way she learned to read her native language.

After that, nothing could stop her. She devoured everything in the family library, whether in economics, literature or philosophy. Throughout her life she never quit learning. Her consciousness continued to expand as she traveled, attended international conferences and talked with people in various countries.

In 1910 Huda founded a girls' school, the first of its kind. Vocational schools, such as midwifery training centers, had existed. But Huda's institution was for general education. Incidentally, all who enrolled had to take a letter to the local police station certifying that they were of good moral character.

Throughout her long life, Huda encouraged many women to sharpen their minds, whether they came from rich or poor backgrounds. She herself gave scholarships to promising writers and artists. She found them publishers. She arranged for their exhibits. Always she was known for her dignity, kindness, energy, active involvement and encouragement of creativity.

In spite of that, people remember her for the Egyptian equivalent of American feminists' "bra burning"! Coming back to Egypt from an international conference in 1923, Huda stopped dramatically on the gangplank halfway down from the ship, ripped off her veil and dropped it into the sea. Her assistant followed suit. Huda was the first woman known to do this. The furor was immense. Among other repercussions, Huda's husband divorced her. (Five years later he asked her to marry him again, which she did.) But an avalanche was begun. Veils came off right and left.

Veiling is a complex issue. The prophet Muhammad never required veiling of the face. Modesty was his rule, but not veils. With the hardening of Muslim institutions, however, veils became de rigueur, except for poor working women. Different degrees of veiling evolved in different countries.

In the 1920s and 1930s, modernizing Muslim rulers tried to release women from veils. Reza Shah of Iran progressively insisted on this through a series of edicts. Buses couldn't carry veiled women. Taxis couldn't transport them. Various stores couldn't sell to them. Eventually all the elite were summoned to a command performance ball, and they were commanded to bring their wives unveiled. It was nearly enough to cause heart attacks. These officials had known each other for decades. But they had never seen their friends' wives unveiled. It seemed like a naked orgy. For many of the women, the sin and shame was immense. "Today they tell you to bare your head; tomorrow they will make you eat pork," a little Algerian girl was told by her mother, when the French-oriented schoolteacher wouldn't let the girls wear head scarves in class.[21] The girl was pulled out of school and did not leave home alone until she was thirty-five years old. She was the mother of journalist Fadela M'rabet, author of several fiery books arguing for greater freedom for women in Algeria today.

In Turkey, the prime minister traveled throughout the country with his wife unveiled beside him in the 1930s. In 1980 the Turkish government still was attacking veils. Women were prohibited from wearing coverings on their heads in school except during Qur'anic classes. But Turkish women have not accepted this. Recently some female members of government have shown up for work in head scarves.

At the opposite pole, veils—but not face veils—have been required by law in Iran since 1979. When the decree first appeared, five thousand Iranian women took to the streets in protest. One hundred thousand people marched out in counterprotest, in favor of veils.

While Huda Sharawi, that great Egyptian educator, is primarily remembered for ripping off her veil, her life contributions were much more substantial. In the 1920s Egyptians were hammering away at independence from Britain. Huda wrote strong public letters to British leaders whom she had met socially.

In these sorrowful times that my country is passing through, I would like to remind you of our conversation last summer. . . . What do you think, Madam, of your government giving itself the right to impose curfews in a time of peace and to banish persons who have committed no crime?

She authored petitions.

If you rely on power alone, Your Excellency, to destroy our rights, I ask you to reconsider this point of view as well. For power passes, but right remains.

She spearheaded marches. The sight of hundreds of veiled women striding through the streets for their country gave Egyptian men new energy to struggle on.

A political activist named Sa'ad Zaghlul was arrested without publicity. The British hoped that his case would sink into oblivion. They had not counted on Huda. She organized the women of the nation to gather in homes every afternoon and to write on every piece of paper money, "Long Live Zaghlul!" The British effort to avoid publicity took a nosedive.

In 1920 the first women's association in Egypt was founded, with Huda at the head. In 1924 she established the Women's Union. This formalized activities that some wealthy, benevolent Egyptian women had pursued for a long time, adding some modern dimensions. Orphanages, job centers for unemployed women, abolishment of prostitution, equal job opportunities, education for women and raising the minimum age of marriage were central causes. A school, a magazine, a club, a work center and government lobbying were activities of the Union.

Huda was not merely a feminist nor merely a nationalist. One of her last acts was to attend a conference on atomic weapons in 1946. She was one of the first women to call for their abolishment.

Zaynab al-Ghazali. Huda's liberalism did not please everybody. Zaynab al-Ghazali, one of Huda's young colleagues, split with Huda at age eighteen. Huda was too secular, in Zaynab's opinion. Zaynab went on to found the Muslim Women's Association, which was the complement of the militant Muslim Brotherhood.[22]

Her goal? To see Egypt ruled by the Qur'an, not by secular civil law codes. And eventually to see all Muslim countries united in one great federation. "The Islamic nation possesses one-third of the world," Zaynab mused. "Geographically, we are richer than the rest of the world, in oil we are richer than the rest of the world. So why are we backward? Because we are not following our religion. . . . If we return to our Koran and to the Sunna of our Prophet, we will live Islam in reality, and we will control the whole world."

Huda was a nationalist. Zaynab was not. Her vision was more encompassing. Many Muslim activists like Zaynab view nationalism as Western-imposed fragmentation. The true political entity is the people of God, the people of Islam. (Other nationalists are able to generalize from their national loyalty to a larger Muslim world loyalty, as Jamilah did when she spoke about Palestine.)

Zaynab's father was a successful and devout cotton merchant. Even when she was small, he urged her to take her life seriously, to become a leader. Referring to various famous women, he would ask her, "Which one would you choose to be?" The more thoroughly Muslim heroines were the role models he recommended.

By 1955, Zaynab recounted, "I found myself drafted into the service of the Islamic call without an invitation from anyone. It was the cries of the orphans who lost their fathers to torture, and the tears of the women who were widowed and whose husbands were behind prison bars, and the old fathers and mothers who lost their heart's delight."[23]

After work with various social organizations, Zaynab felt compelled to take a binding oath to the Muslim Brotherhood. It seemed to radiate a spiritual authority that was missing everywhere else. Thereafter she edited publications. Some of these were virulently anti-Zionist, anti-imperialist and anti-evangelical. She organized women's activities. She headed up men's study groups as well. These were part of a thirteen-year intensive training program in true Islamic lifestyle. Because it was so disruptive, the Muslim Brotherhood was outlawed. Zaynab was arrested, tortured and jailed for six years.

Was she a "battle axe"? Glimpses of her marriages, provided by Valerie Hoffman, soften the picture. Zaynab was married twice.

"I found that my first marriage took up all my time and kept me from my mission, and my husband did not agree with my work," Zaynab explained. "I had made a condition that if we had any major disagreements we would separate [the legal possibility for such conditions in marriage agreements was partly the result of Huda Sharawi's lobbying], and the Islamic cause was the essential. My second husband knew that I left my first husband because of the cause. He gave me written agreements that he would not come between me and my mission, but that he would help me and be my assistant. And in fact we had an enjoyable married life in which there was cooperation, love, faithfulness to God, and purity of soul and conscience. We separated only when I was sent to prison, and he died twenty-one days after I was sentenced."[24]

Prior to that, when the situation first began to appear dangerous, Zaynab's husband warned her. Not involved in the Brotherhood himself, he asked, "Are the Muslim Brothers having meetings in our house?"

"Yes," she told him.

"What kinds of things are they actually discussing and organizing?"

"Husband . . ."

"Zaynab, things are getting rough. I'm afraid you're going to get hurt."

"Husband, do you remember what you promised me when we married?"

"Of course. I know I promised not to interfere with your political work. I remember it well. When I asked you what you wanted for a dowry, you said, "No gifts. Nothing material. Just your promise never to keep me from the path of God.'"

"Yes," said Zaynab. "And I remember what else I told you. I said, 'You are proposing to a woman who gave herself to the struggle in the path of God to establish the Islamic state when she was eighteen years old. If there is a conflict of interests between marriage and the call to God, then the marriage will come to an end, and the call will remain in my whole being.'" Zaynab paused. "Do you remember?"

"Yes."

"Today I ask you to keep your promise. Don't ask with whom I am meeting. I ask God to give you a portion of the reward of my struggle as a grace from Him if He accepts my work. I know that you have the right to give me orders, and it is my duty to obey you. But God is greater in our souls than ourselves, and His call is dearer to us than our own selves. We are in an important phase in the life of the cause."

"Forgive me," said Zaynab's husband. "Do your work, with God's blessing. May I live to see the day that the Brothers achieve their goal and the Islamic state is established."

Activities multiplied. Young men came knocking at the back door day and night. Zaynab's husband would roll out of bed, unbar the door, escort the strangers to the office, go to the maid's room and wake her, asking her to prepare food and tea. Then he would shake Zaynab gently. "Some of your sons are in the office."

While she dressed and he drifted back into sleep, he would murmur, "Wake me if you pray the morning prayer together, so I can pray with you, if that's no bother."

Zaynab concluded: "And if we prayed the morning prayer together, I would wake him so he could pray with us. Then he would leave, greeting those who were present in a fatherly way, full of warmth, love and compassion."

For some Arab women, political solidarity with their people is what gives meaning to life. Ironically, after the struggles for independence, women—as in the United States after World War II—often were expected to leave the business world to men who needed jobs, and to spend most of their working hours at home.

Nowhere have women's post-revolutionary limits been pointed out more succinctly than at a conference of major North African resistance leaders on the brink of Algeria's freedom. One leader was Jamilah Boupacha, who had been arrested, tortured and raped by the French.

As the conversation ranged over various possibilities for the new government, Jamilah broke in, "And what about us women? Our situation must change now—"

She was cut off by Muhammad Khider, a major figure. "Women after independence?" he shrugged. "Why, you will return to your couscous, of course."[25]

Politically active women, religious fundamentalists, professional women, settled village and town women, and nomads—the world of Arab women is a rich mosaic. But in the end, every woman is an exception. How we present Jesus to a woman will be shaped by who and where she is.

3
Arab Sisters

Mommy, why am I doing this?" Eight-year-old Habiba rubbed her bleary eyes with her knuckles. Half-asleep, hair tousled, nightgown rumpled, she could hardly stand up straight.

"We simply have to do it, little one," her mother answered, as she unrolled the prayer rugs. It was barely dawn.

"If I'm praying, there should be somebody listening," Habiba murmured, struggling to consciousness. "He should answer. God should be like Daddy. When I talk to him, he answers. I respect God. I honor him. Why doesn't he talk to me?"

Habiba: "The Man for Me"

At age seven little Habiba had been veiled. In her very orthodox Muslim home, she prayed five times a day. Her mother was her mentor.

Yet in the bubbling, swirling maelstrom of Egypt, other influences flowed over Habiba. When she was ten, she went to a movie with her sister. Afterward, as they ambled down the sidewalk, a woman called to her from a passing car. When Habiba approached, the woman smiled at her and held out a small booklet. "Please take this book, daughter," the woman said softly.

Startled and intrigued, Habiba received it. The woman drove on her way. What was the book? The girls puzzled out the title. *The Gospel of John.* Oh. A religious treatise. Worthy of respect, of course. But hardly interesting. Furthermore, it looked like a Christian book. Her family would not be happy about that. When she got home, Habiba hid the booklet in a drawer. Then she forgot all about it.

But as she grew, she kept on asking questions. Once in college, Habiba studied philosophy more seriously. What was the basis of order in the world? How did the physical world hold together? What was the meaning of history? How could society be just?

The result was that Habiba became a Communist sympathizer.

From an orthodox Muslim to a Communist—just through studying philosophy? How could that be?

Egypt was bursting at the seams. Cairo's population had exploded. Sewage was inadequate. Transportation was inadequate. Basic postal, telephone, water and electrical services were inadequate. Housing was inadequate: two, three or four families crowded into a small apartment, whether they knew each other or not. Health services were inadequate. Schools fell further and further behind in providing places for the children who needed to attend.

In the 1956 war with Israel over the Suez Canal, Egypt suffered great loss of reputation. In the 1973 war, Egypt lost more. In spite of a couple of great leaders, and in spite of trying several alternative political and economic strategies, conditions continued to deteriorate. What humiliation for the descendants of the Pharaohs, the keepers of the Nile, the heirs of great civilization.

Clearly a new approach was needed. Marxists at the university actively propounded one. Habiba even attended a course in Islamics and Christianity taught by a Marxist professor. Marxism explained that workers should own the results of what they produced. Profits should not be skimmed off for absentee owners. A cooperative Marxist society would reward workers equitably.

So, longing for a healthy Egypt, longing for the justice that she studied abstractly in her philosophy courses, Habiba got caught up in the whirlwind of Marxism. She marched barefaced in the streets with the Marxists.

But when a march was over, she would put her veil back on, go home, kneel down and say her prayers.

Somehow it all would *have* to fit together.

This was her life when, at age twenty-five, Habiba stumbled on an outdoor Christian music concert on the outskirts of the university district. There were lutes and zithers. Ancient psalms and new songs. Haunting minor key melodies. Habiba was moved.

Before the concert, however, the lead musician prayed to "Father," and that confused Habiba.

Who is his father? she wondered. *All these people in the audience look younger than he does.* The simple question nagged her like a sore tooth. *Could he have been praying to God? But how does he dare to call God "Father"?*

Then she remembered her early morning prayer times as a small child with her mother. She remembered protesting,"Why am I doing this? If I'm praying, there should be somebody listening. He should answer. If God is true, he should be somebody like my Daddy."

Did these Christians really know God as a father?

Back in her room that evening, Habiba was restless. Was it possible to know God more personally? Did the Creator actually care about relating to ordinary individuals in the chaos of Cairo? Suddenly she remembered the *Gospel of John* in her bottom drawer. She hadn't given it a thought for years. Of course by now she knew it was part of the Christian Scripture, the *Injeel*, the life of the prophet Jesus.

Habiba crossed the room decisively, yanked open the drawer and rummaged among the mementos and outgrown clothes. Was it still there? Hmm . . . no, that was her graduation program. How about this corner? Yes! She gazed at the little book, then recrossed the room to curl up on the bed. She opened the booklet thoughtfully and began to read.

In the beginning was the Word. . . .
Through him all things were made. . . .
In him was life, and that life was the light of men. . . .

He was in the world,
and though the world was made through him,
the world did not recognize him.
He came to that which was his own,
but his own did not receive him.
Yet to all who received him . . .
he gave the right to become children of God. . . .
The Word became flesh and made his dwelling among us.
We have seen his glory. . . .
No one has ever seen God,
but God the One and Only, who is at the Father's side,
has made him known.

Wow. The power of the poetry socked her. Blasphemy, probably. Son of God and so forth. True prophets don't get sidelined—"His own did not receive him"? And certainly the Eternal doesn't take on flesh. Still, what a radical concept. Appealing too. The Creator visiting his planet in human form to show us his glory and share with us his power.

She read on. The stories were so human. A party, a wedding, recorded in chapter 2. She pictured the men dancing in their slow and stately way, the prophet Jesus among them. Mary, a mother calling on her son: "Pssst! We've got a little crisis here. They underestimated the supplies and the gatecrashers! Anything you can do to help?"

But then, in the cool garden under the stars, amid the fragrance of the night-blooming flowers, the prophet Jesus advises the spiritual seeker Nicodemus, "You must be born again."

What?!

Nicodemus retorts—very sensibly—"How can a man be born when he is old? Surely he cannot enter a second time into his mother's womb?"

"No," Jesus answers, "Be born of the Spirit."

After painting word pictures of the Spirit, Jesus sets the "new birth" in context. "God so loved the world that he gave his one and only Son, that whoever believes in him should not perish but have eternal life. . . . [But for those who ignore God] this is the verdict: Light has come into the world, but men loved darkness rather than light, because their deeds were evil."

Hmm, thought Habiba. A lot of truth here about men loving darkness rather than light. Even some Marxists. Even religious leaders sometimes twisted power in dark ways. What did it mean to "come to the light"?

It was connected with God's Son as an object of faith, apparently. And with spiritual birth.

Habiba read on. Here in chapter 4 was a woman who had had five husbands and now lived with another man! What *was* she, a nymphomaniac? Or had she been maltreated in a dysfunctional relationship and bounced onto a downward spiral? Habiba thought about women she had known who had been beaten, or abandoned, or even raped. What were they to do? Especially if they had no relatives nearby.

The prophet Jesus treated this strange woman with amazing respect and took her theological opinions seriously.

He also, in the course of the discussion, claimed to be the Messiah.

Habiba continued reading. What compassion she saw in Jesus. What elegance in his philosophical arguments. "I was beginning to fall in love with Jesus," she says now.

Then she came to chapter 8.

> The teachers of the law and the Pharisees brought in a woman caught in adultery. They made her stand before the group and said to Jesus, "Teacher, this woman was caught in the act of adultery. In the Law Moses commanded us to stone such women. Now what do you say?"
>
> They were using this question as a trap, in order to have a basis for accusing him.

Suddenly Habiba's stomach began to churn. What *could* the prophet Jesus say? Of course the woman had sinned. But where was the woman's partner? Did these bigots think she had been committing adultery with herself?

How unfair men were. And sometimes religious men were the worst. Religion had sanctioned legal injustice and even brutality against women. She had seen it in her own community. It had disgusted her. It had pushed her toward Marxism or some other alternative.

Now this beautiful gospel story would be ruined because of these hypocrites. The prophet Jesus couldn't ignore adultery. In the end he would have to agree to stoning the woman, wouldn't he?

With a snap, Habiba closed the Bible. "I can't bear it. If he stones her, I don't want him. But if he lets her go, I don't want him." If Jesus approved the woman's destruction, he would be no better than the Muslim clerics. On the other hand, if he approved the woman's behavior, he would confirm the common belief that Christians were immoral.

She strode across the room and shoved the Gospel back into the bottom drawer. *I don't want to read any more.* She went out to the lounge to watch TV with the rest of the family.

But that night Habiba couldn't sleep. Finally she got up and rummaged around in the drawer until once again she held the *Gospel of John* in her hands. She thumbed through the book. *What sura was I reading?*

Ah, yes, chapter 8. Yes, here are the Pharisees. Here is the woman, dragged along. Here is their challenge. And here is the prophet Jesus . . . stooping down unconcernedly and writing with his finger in the sand, of all things.

> When they kept on questioning him, he straightened up and said to them, "If any one of you is without sin, let him be the first to throw a stone at her." Again he stooped down and wrote on the ground.
>
> At this, those who heard began to go away one at a time, the older ones first, until only Jesus was left with the woman still standing there. Jesus straightened up and asked her, "Woman, where are they? Has no one condemned you?"
>
> "No one, sir," she said.
>
> "Then neither do I condemn you," Jesus declared. "Go now and leave your life of sin."

Habiba sat quietly. *This is the Lord I want to follow,* she told herself at last.

That night she opened her heart to the possibility that Jesus was Lord, on the basis of what she had read in the first eight chapters of the Gospel of John. She had learned that Jesus could be an object of faith. A person could be "born again" through the Spirit. God offers eternal life. And God calls us to live in the light. So as an educated woman of Cairo, Habiba went out and found a pastor. She confided in him. He led her into a relationship with the Lord Jesus. For a year they met once a week.

Only then did she tell her parents. Very angry, they brought in a sheikh to deprogram her. Her pastor advised her to get theological training outside the country, then come back. She went to Lebanon, where she lived with other believers of Muslim background and attended Bible school. Georges Houssney, a Muslim-background Lebanese, mentored her, as did his wife, Joy. In time Habiba met a believer from Europe who fell in love with her and married her. Today they minister to Muslims and to whomever else the Lord sends.

But the Man who will always matter most to Habiba is the beautiful Son of Man whom she met in the Gospel of John.

Nawal: The Girl Who Lived in Books

Books were Nawal's best friends. At home, drunken violence spewed over everything.

"Ptui!" Nawal's father roared, as he spat a mouthful of couscous onto the floor and pushed his chair back from the table.

"Indeed, Hamid, the eggs were bought fresh today," Nawal's mother fluttered. "And the grain is from Daud, just as always. Here—" she nervously adjusted the dishes—"have some more pepper—"

"I resent that," Nawal's father enunciated carefully. "Trying to cover up putrid food. Palming garbage off on me—"

Flinging out his arm, he swept the dish off the table. On the floor tiles the pottery broke and the grains scattered.

"Hamid, please—"

"—on *me*, the head of this house," he intoned.

"I'm so sorry—"

"Yes, you say that now, you useless slut. But what do you say behind my back? Eh? Eh? Worthless baggage. Can't even serve a meal—"

Cowering in the background, Nawal covered her ears and scooted out. A quiet corner and a book—that would be her comfort. She had learned early to take refuge in books. First it had been schoolbooks. Then she looked for books wherever she could find them. In the end she discovered more than she had dreamed. Not just alternative worlds where she could escape from the misery of her existence, books became doors which opened onto real life. Books pointed her to the Lord Jesus Christ.

As a teenager, Nawal began dropping into a lending library next door to her school. Each afternoon she would slip shyly through the shop door. The smell of paper, glue, ink and dust assaulted her nostrils. She inhaled greedily. To her it was the smell of comfort, the smell of adventure, the smell of different worlds, better worlds. Her furrowed brow relaxed as she shrugged off her school bag, handed in yesterday's borrowed book and scanned the shelves for something new. So many books. So many friends.

Mrs. Jones, the American woman who ran the store, was a friend too. Each day when Nawal came to exchange her book for a new one, they talked.

"Why don't you try this book?" Mrs. Jones suggested one day.

It turned out to be stories of Old Testament prophets from Abraham to Joseph. Many Bible references cluttered the pages.

"This is the first time I've read this kind of book," Nawal confided when she brought the book back. "It's very nice. But what is this Genesis 1, John 1 stuff?"

Mrs. Jones laughed. "You want to know? If you have time, come to my house."

What a tumult Nawal tumbled into when she entered the Jones house. There were six children, five boys and one girl.

In one corner, twelve-year-old Stephen sat hunched over the radio.

"Altorki has the ball," intoned the announcer. "He's running clear. Five yards. Six. Wait. He's— "

In another corner, eight-year-old Bernard conjugated French verbs. From the piano came the clear and distinct notes of Bach's Minuet II, where ten-year-old John was practicing. On the sofa sprawled one-year-old Simon, flipping through a picture book, cuddling his teddy bear, sucking his thumb and softly humming a tune of his own invention.

A banana peel decorated a lampshade. A lifelike rubber snake lay on the floor. A trail of discarded toy swords and capes led to a blanket-draped dining table. Squeals and giggles emerged from underneath. Nawal lifted a corner of the cloth and peeked into the depths of the makeshift tent. Well, who would have guessed? A tea party was in progress.

"Come in!" Two glowing preschoolers wriggled over to make room for her. "Have a cookie!"

In the background the radio droned on. "It was outside. There'll be a penalty. Yes, that's a penalty on Altorki . . ."

And Bernard plowed on through his conjugations. "Nous valions, vous valiez, ils vaillent . . ."

What energy vibrated through the Jones house. Yet it was a happy tumult. In fact, the love in this home shocked Nawal. She had never seen such joy in her own family. *Her* family shouted and cursed, then turned sullen.

Nawal visited the Joneses almost every week, and she and Mrs. Jones became good friends. Depositing her books, Nawal would help prepare coffee or tea and cake. Then they would sit and talk.

Gradually Mrs. Jones talked about the Lord Jesus Christ. When Nawal compared the love in the Jones household with the lovelessness in her own, Mrs. Jones explained, "My love isn't mine. It comes from the Lord Jesus. He gave me the desire to love others."

The music in the Joneses' house soothed Nawal too. While she prepared tea or washed up, Mrs. Jones often sang in Arabic, "God so loved the world—come to him . . ." Nawal could listen to that song over and over and never tire of it.

When Christmas came, Nawal found herself going with Mrs. Jones to the Feast of Noel at the church. At Easter she was there again. Once she began to study English, she went to church frequently in order to improve her language skills.

How did I fall into this routine? she would ask herself on the way to church. *Well, I find church attractive,* she admitted.

"What do you think about our lifestyle?" Mrs. Jones asked her one day as they inhaled the fragrance of mint over the rims of their teacups. "What do you think about the Lord Jesus? About his crucifixion, for example? What does it mean to you personally?"

"You surprise me!" Nawal burst out, spilling her tea. "I don't know. I can't answer." She swabbed up the spill. "Give me some time to think."

For two weeks she pondered. Riding the bus, bandaging children's scraped knees at the hostel where she worked, stirring a pot, she asked herself, *What does this love and peace mean to me?*

This is the truth of life, an inner voice whispered.

But it was too alien to think about.

She went back to visit Mrs. Jones and told her truthfully, "I'm happy to be with you. But I cannot say Jesus is the Son of God. It's against our culture. I can't say it. It's impossible. It's blasphemy."

Mrs. Jones shrugged and smiled. "Okay. If that's a problem for you, don't say it. You accept that God loves you. That God is our priest. The Spirit of God will help you."

"The Holy Spirit came on me gradually," Nawal says now. "Gradually I came to accept Christ as God. One day I prayed in the name of Jesus the Son of God. Without the Holy Spirit, I could never have pronounced those words."

That was twenty-five years ago. Today Nawal is a professional woman who works with children. She has matured spiritually in the company of a handful of local believers. As the oldest of eight children in a dysfunctional family, and as a motherly single woman who longs to marry but finds no Christian husband available among the few believers in her country, Nawal has not had an easy life. Had she had less education, had she not had a good job, had her family been stronger, they might have persecuted her more. Though they did reject her for years, today they welcome her. She is a blessing to them in many ways, and they have come to appreciate that.

Books were signposts on Nawal's pilgrimage. While she is still a reader, she has found that life is much more than books. She doesn't have to hide in alternate worlds anymore.

Latifa: "Show Me!"

A beach is a beach. Why did it feel so special to be here on this beach with these people?

Latifa shrugged and rolled the ball back to two-year-old David. Sand stretched in both directions. Out on the blue Mediterranean, tiny fishing boats bobbed.

"This ball is big," David chortled, as he tumbled into the sand.

"Yes," Latifa agreed.

"And also fat," he crowed, righting himself.

"Yes," she smiled.

"But not as fat as me, right?" He grinned, kicked the ball and came running to flop down beside her.

Latifa ruffled David's hair as the evening breeze caressed hers. How she enjoyed this child. And this beach. A rocky promontory embraced the north shore. Wisps of cloud streaked the sunset with color. White wavelets laced the sea. Wood smoke curled up from the beach fire where David's parents, Zach and Maria, roasted mutton. David's sister Susan dabbled at the water's edge. Sand which had baked and shimmered in the heat of the day now felt cozy as Latifa burrowed her toes in it.

This is the life, she sighed. *The kind of weekend teachers need.*

But, she groaned inwardly, *why do I have to have such a good time with* Christians?

Latifa and Zach taught at the same school. Zach was a foreign teacher, an American. Their friendship had not blossomed easily. It was getting to know Maria and, even more, Susan and David that had drawn Latifa to spend more and more time with this family.

Latifa's family were ordinary Muslims. But she was not. Large, quick-thinking, managerial, Latifa was anything but medium. She aimed for excellence. As a child she had longed to fast like her parents. Proudly she had abstained from food, even if just for a few hours. As she had grown older and had imbibed modern French culture, her ideas of excellence had broadened considerably. By the time she was a self-supporting professional, she considered herself a free thinker within Islam. She had an apartment of her own. She was not ashamed to sit in cafes drinking coffee with men. Although both nominally and by deep conviction a Muslim, she welcomed new ideas.

Among Latifa's fellow teachers was Daphne, a British woman who was passionately anti-Christian.

"Watch out for Zach!" Daphne warned Latifa. "He's a missionary in disguise."

"How could that be? Why, what does he hope to accomplish?" Latifa wondered.

"He wants to change your minds and your culture," Daphne snorted.

That made Latifa mad. She was sick of colonization. First it had been political. Then it was economic. Now it was religious? *Who do these people think they are?* she fumed. *What right do they have to overrun us?*

To combat the enemy, she got herself invited to a Bible discussion at Zach's place. But there she met Maria, Susan and David, and she was disarmed.

Summer vacation arrived, and Latifa found herself going to parks with the foreign family. They played sports and games. They helped her practice speaking English. The children's antics amused her. Over the course of the summer, as Zach and Maria had to make various decisions, they were transparent and open. So Latifa got an inside view of the way they operated. It seemed to her that something extra was present in everything they did.

When they prayed in the name of Jesus, though, Latifa hated it. "It was against my identity," she says. "It reminded me that I was there to attack them—whereas really I was having fun!"

In the fall they started a Bible study on Christian ethics. This subject intrigued Latifa. "What *do* Christians actually think about anger, forgiveness or holding a grudge?" she wondered. "I accepted a Bible because I wasn't going to be stupid and not know what was in that book," she admits now.

At first she just looked up the references recommended for each topic study. Then she got hooked and began to read the Bible from cover to cover.

Consistency was what she found, both in Jesus and in Zach and Maria. "That was rare in my world," she comments. "That started my problem. This guy Jesus was saying things I admired. The teaching was beautiful. But you couldn't have that and throw out the teacher."

Soon her conscience began to nag: *If this is true, you ought to try it.*

"I felt sick," she says. "Before I was even awake each morning, Christ was in my mind. The Bible attracted me so much. At the same time, I loved the Qur'an. The chanting of the Qur'an was so beautiful. Sometimes I'd hear it on the radio and my whole being would go into turmoil."

Every day when she prayed as a Muslim, she would recite the Qur'anic words. *Show me the way.*

Don't let me be among those who are lost because of the blindness of their hearts.

One day she gritted her teeth and added, *Okay. Show me. If Jesus*

Christ is the true way, show me.

Not long after that, Latifa came home one afternoon to find a note under her door:

> Come to the beach with us tomorrow. We're going to have a Christian com-
> munion service. This is something you won't want to miss. We'll stop by at
> 10:00. Zach and Maria.

But Latifa already had an invitation to go to the beach with some local friends. What to do?

She was tempted to break the first date and go with Zach and Maria. They and their Christian fellowship had become very important in her life. Should she go with them? Or should she go with her other friends? She couldn't decide.

"I'm tired," she shrugged. "I'm going to bed. Whoever comes first I'll go with. Anyway, one way or the other, I'll get to the beach."

The next morning both parties arrived at her door at exactly the same time.

"God didn't make it easy," she comments. "God was saying, 'Don't let circumstances decide for you. Always follow me.' "

Latifa decided to go with the Christians. "Do you mind?" She asked her other friends. They acquiesced amiably and went on their way. She turned to Zach, Maria, Susan and David and experienced a rush of great joy. But why? A beach is just a beach, after all.

Once at the sea, they paddled in the water. They played ball. Finally they began their Communion service. Latifa was asked to read aloud the traditional verses from 1 Corinthians 11:

> The Lord Jesus, on the night he was betrayed, took bread, and when he had
> given thanks, he broke it and said, "This is my body, which is for you; do this
> in remembrance of me." In the same way, after supper he took the cup, say-
> ing, "This cup is the new covenant in my blood; do this, whenever you
> drink it, in remembrance of me." For whenever you eat this bread and drink
> this cup, you proclaim the Lord's death until he comes.

"As I was reading," Latifa recalls, "I was in the Spirit. I was transferred to the upper room. I could see Christ. I could hear Christ. I could sense him saying, 'This is my body, broken for you.'

"I don't know how I looked. Everybody disappeared. Time stopped. I was there with Christ, with the awesome presence of his holiness. I started looking at my life with his eyes. Suddenly my life, with which I'd been content, looked terribly dirty. I wanted to run away. Then I heard him say, 'Eat. I came not for you to run away, but, on the contrary, for you to come close to me.' "

Latifa began to cry—a deep, cleansing cry. "Joy replaced everything I felt was wrong," she says. "At that time I knew all my questions about the Trinity had no meaning because I had met Jesus personally."

That beach Communion service happened twenty years ago. The beach is much the same today. But Latifa is dramatically different. Two decades of pruning have shaped her.

Cigarettes were one of the first branches to be lopped off. The week after her experience on the beach, Latifa read 1 Corinthians 6:19-20: "Do you not know that your body is a temple of the Holy Spirit, who is in you, whom you have received from God? You are not your own; you were bought at a price. Therefore honor God with your body."

When she read that, Latifa was a slave to cigarettes. But by the grace of God, that pollution stopped.

Although she had her own apartment when she came to Christ, Latifa felt God sending her home to live with her family. Her dad was sick, and they needed her salary. Living at home meant harassment, though. Whenever a Christian meeting was scheduled, her parents would stand at the door and forbid her to go. She would go out crying, but she would go. Since they needed her income, they didn't expel her. Looking back now, she is thankful for that period of persecution because it helped her mature spiritually. It brought out the fruit of the Spirit in her life.

Even before Latifa became a follower of the Lord Jesus, she had critiqued her parents' religious gullibility and naivete. Once Latifa's mother had wanted to send Latifa's clothes with someone who was going on a pilgrimage to Mecca, so the clothes could get blessed. "If God can't bless me here, I don't want a blessing," Latifa had stormed.

Another time her mom had consulted a fortune teller regarding Latifa's future. "You aren't a true Muslim!" Latifa had protested then.

So Latifa's family members were somewhat used to her religious critiques. They weren't completely unprepared when she began to worship in a new way. In time, especially after her most fundamentalist sister married and moved out, her family quit grumbling about her love for the Lord Jesus Christ.

For twelve years after she came to Christ, Latifa refused marriage proposals, both Muslim and Christian. Finally she heard her biological clock ticking. She saw the value of creating a Christian home and family, rare in her society. So she married a believing man, also from Muslim background, also from her ethnic group and nation. Today she is the busy mother of several children.

That doesn't slow her down, however. As well as being a public school teacher, she actively disciples others in her small Christian fellowship. This little body is precious to her, notwithstanding its squabbles and shortcomings.

When she began to follow Jesus, the only Christian fellowship group in her city was three foreigners. Several years later she had a chance to go to Egypt. "I was so hungry to *see* a church!" she remembers. Visiting an indigenous church was the high point of her international trip. Naturally, then, the church growing in her own country is of great value to Latifa. She makes it a priority to give time in its service.

"I am a teacher," she says, "so I teach new believers how to read the Bible." She also visits people in her country who respond to Christian radio broadcasts beamed from overseas.

A beach is just a beach. Yet as Latifa stood on that beach twenty years ago, on the edge of the immense Mediterranean, she discovered that the ocean of God's grace in Jesus Christ can touch us at any point on earth.

4

What Is Liberation
for Muslim Women?

Susan! Give me your daughter Mary for my son Fazlur!" Farza called across the room.

It was a wedding. Susan, plump, pretty, extroverted, wife of an American engineer and mother of four children, had been looking forward to this day. She didn't have a Dior or a Balenciaga. She didn't have any diamonds. Just one gold chain. And that was only fourteen-carat gold.

But Susan was a party person. So she washed her hair with henna, for highlights. She even splurged and had her hands decorated with red designs. Depilated, perfumed, she tucked her two youngest children one under each arm and set out to enjoy herself with her Arab neighbors.

Crunchy roasted mutton, a whole sheep of it, reposed on a tablecloth spread on the floor. But not for long. The guests squatted down in their finery and tucked in to meat, rice, fruit and pudding, with no utensils or napkins. Tidy eating here was an art form. Afterward, servants brought water for hand-washing. Perfume was handed around. Each woman took a turn standing over a sweet-smelling brazier, letting the smoke billow up under her skirt and on up through her neckline.

Then they adjourned to the roof garden where it was cooler. Thirty carpets had been spread out across the expanse. Women musicians played. Individual women took turns performing dances. In the courtyard below, visible through latticework, the men shuffled gravely through circle dances, arm in arm. Up here among the women, the bride sat silent, waiting for her groom. Turn by turn, women offered her congratulations. Endless refills of coffee and tea circulated.

Then, to liven up the party, a woman named Farza called out, mostly joking, "Susan, give me your daughter Mary for my son Fazlur! Let's be coparents-in-law!"

Women cheered. Something new to while away the hours . . .

How could Susan respond gracefully, especially in front of a couple hundred women? A shyer person might have been intimidated. But outgoing Susan wasn't fazed. "Great!" she called back. "We would be honored. And—to sweeten the tie—you give me your daughter Fatimah for my son John!"

Pounding the floor with approval, women chortled. One up for Susan. Muslim men are allowed to marry Christian women, but Muslim women aren't allowed to marry Christian men.

Farza laughed good-humoredly and shrugged, admitting that she had been bested.

But Susan had sunk her teeth in. "I'm serious, " she called. "Why not give me Fatimah for John? Being coparents is a wonderful idea. Being doubly coparents would be even better."

Farza mumbled, smiling.

"Why not?" Susan persisted. "Is there something wrong with us?" Susan knew her friends delighted in satire and overstatement, so she pressed on. "Haven't you taken your shoe off and rubbed your bare foot on my floor to see that we're a clean family? Aren't we god-fearing? Aren't we moral? *Why* would you not marry your daughter into my family? Are we not good enough for you? I'm insulted!"

"Susan," Farza placated, "you know Fatimah can't marry John."

"Why not?" Susan insisted.

"Because . . . John is not a true believer," Farza explained.

"And neither could Mary be given to Fazlur!" Susan announced firmly.

"Why not?" Farza asked mildly.

"Because . . . Fazlur is not truly circumcised!"

Suddenly a deathly silence fell on the roof garden. Susan had blurted out fighting words. Every Muslim man is circumcised. To say Farza's son was not circumcised was like stabbing her. There was a hiss of indrawn breath.

"What do you mean," Farza said evenly through her teeth, " 'Fazlur is not circumcised?' "

"Because there are two kinds of circumcision," Susan continued, chin up. Every woman in the room now was listening intently. "There is the circumcision of the body. For that we women must stand aside. Our brothers have circumcision feasts. Our sons have them. Being connected to men who are circumcised makes us more pleasing to God, in traditional belief. But we ourselves are left out. We can only stand at the edge of the crowd and look on."

"So?"

"That's the circumcision of the body. That's a surface matter. But there is another kind of circumcision, a deeper kind, the circumcision of the heart. And that circumcision is available to every woman in this room. Not through our fathers. Or our brothers, or our husbands, or our sons. But for us, ourselves."

"How do you know?"

"In the Torah given to the prophet Moses, God promises to circumcise his people's hearts, so that they may love him with all their heart and with all their soul, and live. But did the Jews do that? No way. And so a later prophet, Jeremiah, says to them, 'All the nations who are circumcised only in the flesh are really uncircumcised, and even the whole house of Israel is uncircumcised in heart.' And later on, the prophet Paul, a follower of the Lord Jesus, says, 'True circumcision is circumcision of the heart, by the Spirit, not by the written code. Such a man's praise is not from man, but from God.' "

"That's good, Susan. Obviously you know the prophets. But Jews— what do you expect? Of course they're uncircumcised in heart."

"And how about ourselves?" Susan persisted. "Do we love God with all our heart and with all our soul? Or do I not overhear women taking God's name in vain with every other breath? Do I not see women going to shrines to consult spirits, instead of trusting in the one true Allah? Do I not see women tying charms on their children to ward off the *jinns*—"

"We are far from perfect, Susan . . ."

"God knows. And so, visiting us in the prophet Jesus, God provided the power for us to have circumcised hearts. So the prophet Paul says—" and here Susan began a sort of liturgical chant:

> In Christ all the fullness of the Deity lives in bodily form,
> and you have been given fullness in Christ,
> who is the head over every power and authority.
> In him you were also circumcised,
> in the putting off of the sinful nature,
> not with a circumcision done by the hands of men
> but with the circumcision done by Christ,
> having been buried with him in baptism
> and raised with him through your faith in the power of God,
> who raised him from the dead. (Colossians 2:9-12)

Pausing for breath, Susan added, "That's not a surface matter. That's deep circumcision. And sisters, it's for us."

Farza sighed, "You quote religious thoughts beautifully, Susan."

The women drifted quietly, thoughtfully, on to other subjects. When they went home, some discussed circumcision of the heart with the rest of their households.

The next day a schoolteacher appeared at Susan's front door. She introduced herself. "I was not at the wedding yesterday," she said. "But I heard that you spoke about a circumcision of the heart available even for women. Could you tell me more?"

For two hours they sat at Susan's table and pondered God's gift of grace to those who are children of Abraham by faith.

Today Susan's challenge is being repeated around the world. Muslim women are being invited to consider the Lord Jesus Christ. That is the topic of this book.

In this chapter, we explore some theological themes. What are the implications of the gospel for Muslim women? Does it liberate? And what does that mean? If Muslim women come to know God through Christ, will they choose their own husbands? Drive cars? Expect equal pay for equal work? Or are those secondary questions?

Liberation begins deeper, rooted in truths like these:

☐ Muslim-background women are created in the image of God.

☐ They are redeemed by Christ.

☐ They are capable of being empowered by the Holy Spirit.

☐ They are called to active service in God's world.

Muslim Women Are Created in the Image of God

> When God made the earth, he could have finished it. But he didn't. He left it as a raw material—to tease us, to tantalize us, to set us thinking and experimenting and risking and adventuring. And therein we find our supreme interest in living.
>
> He gave us the challenge of raw materials, not the satisfaction of perfect, finished things.
>
> He left the music unsung and the dramas unplayed. He left the poetry undreamed, in order that men and women might become not bored but engaged in stimulating, exciting, creative activities that keep them thinking, working, experimenting and experiencing all the joys and durable satisfactions of achievement.[1]

Eve, along with Adam, is created in God's image. Both are charged with the responsibility to take care of the earth—to sing the music and dream the poetry. As God is Creator, so Eve and Adam are to exercise creativity, reflecting the image of God. Muslims and Christians both affirm this calling. In Christian Scripture humans are told, "Fill the earth and subdue it. Rule over the fish of the sea and the birds of the air and over every living creature that moves on the ground" (Genesis 1:28). In Muslim terms, Adam and Eve are commissioned to be God's managers, or *khalifa*. In both cases, humans are not owners but overseers. We hold delegated authority. It is *under God* that we administer and develop the earth.

Muslim civilizations. Fulfilling that mandate, Muslims have spread civilization from the Arab world to Persia to West Africa to India to Indonesia. Wherever Muslim rule has appeared, so too have monotheism, literacy

and ethics rooted in scripture. Muslims have pioneered medical, mathe-
matical, scientific, architectural and engineering breakthroughs, like the
Taj Mahal. Muslim peoples enjoy sophisticated philosophical, theological
and literary heritages. The poetry of Hafiz of Iran, for example, is exquis-
ite. Equally noteworthy, poetry is not left on dusty shelves in Iran but is
seen as an essential part of life for a civilized person. School children learn
long passages without objecting. Even the Ayatollah Khomeini, stern
father of the Iranian Revolution, composed passionate poetry (which had
to be interpreted spiritually, of course).

During Europe's "Dark Ages," Muslims kept the wisdom of Greece and
Rome alive. Muslim Cordoba in 950 boasted seventy libraries, three hundred public baths, street lights and a university to serve its half-million people. During Europe's Middle Ages, the Mali empire in Africa was
exchanging commerce and culture regularly across the Sahara.

Finally, through their ordinary family structures, Muslims help to order
God's world. Families differ from culture to culture. Yet throughout the
Muslim world, parents and children, brothers and sisters and extended relatives often enjoy strong ties. Frequently they will sacrifice for one another
without a second thought. Surely these patterns bless God's world.

Image of God. In the end, however, although Adam and Eve are God's
khalifa, they are *not* made in his image as Muslims understand it. "Orthodox belief is that man has no God-likeness. God breathing into man His
spirit is explained by some scholars as the faculty of God-like knowledge
and will, which if rightly used gives man superiority over all creation."[2]
Allah simply is too transcendent, too totally other, to share his image.

Who is Allah? For Muslims, God is holy, just, all-powerful, all-knowing,
creator, sustainer, final culminator of history. He is the single ground of
being: He is one, not a profusion of spirits or saints, nor even a trinity.
Muslims like to meditate on the "ninety-nine names of God." He is, for
example, *Al-Rahman al-Rahim*, the Compassionate and the Merciful. He
is *Al-Haqq*, the Real. He is *Al-Wali*, the Friend, the Patron, the One alongside. *Allah*, a word related to the Hebrew *Elohim*, is the term by which
Muslims refer to God.

Such a God is achingly lovely. This is expressed in the prayer of a
seventh-century woman mystic, Rabia:

"Oh God, if I worship you from fear of hell, burn me there.
If I worship you from hope of heaven, exclude me from that.
But if I worship you from love of your own self, then withhold not from me
your eternal beauty."[3]

Sadly, such a God remains distant. Allah reveals himself through prophets and through scriptures. But he would never lower himself to take on human form, as we believe God has done in Jesus. In Islam, then, "revelation is . . . of law, not of personality. God the Revealer remains unrevealed. . . . Revelation is not a personal self-disclosure of the divine. It is for this reason . . . that the Qur'an does not use the term 'Father' in relation to God, or 'children' in relation to believers. It allows only *Rabb* (Lord) and *'abd* (servant)."[4]

What good news the gospel adds! What an awesome privilege it is to affirm that women are created in the image of such a great God. It is enough to make us shiver. Eve has magnificent dignity.

Jesus and women. Women are affirmed even more, though, when God becomes personal in Jesus. His story begins with the faith of a woman, Mary. Soon after his birth, Anna the prophetess confirms Jesus' uniqueness. Upon coming of age, Jesus commends his friend Mary for giving herself to the study of spiritual things. Later, when their brother Lazarus dies, Mary's sister Martha is commended for giving a christological confession almost identical to some words we associate with the apostle Peter. Martha affirms, "You are the Christ, the Son of God" (John 11:27). She says it authoritatively. The Gospel writers take her witness as seriously as they do Peter's.

Another Mary anointed Christ's feet, and he commended her audacity. Several women traveled with him and helped support him. He in turn served women: the widow of Nain; a woman crippled by a spirit for eighteen years; the Samaritan woman at the well; Peter's mother-in-law; the woman taken in adultery; Jairus's daughter; the woman with a hemorrhage of blood; the Syrophoenecian woman.

Among the Jews, as among Christians and Muslims, when religion became institutionalized, various restrictions were placed on women's worship and religious study. Jewish men often thanked God that they were not born women. But in his teachings, Jesus never offered a low view of women. He never deflated women. Rather, his stories sparkle with women making choices: the lost coin; the widow's mite; the persistent widow; the wise and foolish brides; the woman using leaven; the queen of the South who will rise in judgment on this generation; two women grinding grain together when Christ returns.

Women were important figures at the cross. They were the first to receive the news of the resurrection. In sum, "making a clear break with custom, Jesus had women learning from him as disciples and traveling with him in service. He engaged in theological dialogue with women. He helped women in need and in sin without demeaning them. He treated men and women alike with regard to their failings. He encouraged both men and women in their faith. He was absolutely pure in his relations with women."[5]

Muslim women are created in his image. That is our Christian testimony. Whether weaving carpets or running computer programs, Muslim women reflect the image of their Creator as they express their God-given creativity.

Muslim-Background Women Are Redeemed by Christ

Who is Jesus? For Muslims, he is one of the greatest of the prophets. His birth was unique, comparable only to Adam's. His end was unique: he is the only man in history who never died, according to traditional interpretations. He will play a key role at the final judgment. He is mentioned in more than ninety verses in the Qur'an, generally with reverence. Titles awarded to Jesus in the Qur'an include prophet, messenger, servant, sign, witness, example, mercy, spirit of God, word of God and—eleven times— Messiah, anointed princely messenger.

Speaking about Jesus as the word of God, renowned Muslim commentator Baidawi says Jesus is called a word "because he came into existence by God's command without a father, so that he resembled the new creations, who are the world of command." Razi, another commentator, says Jesus is called a word from God because he was the fulfillment of the word spoken to the prophets.[6]

A prophet but not God. Yet for Muslims Jesus is not God. To say he is God is blasphemy. God is high and holy. He reveals himself through prophets and through scriptures. But he could never lower himself to take on human form. How could God become a baby, crying and colicky, diapered and nursed? How could the Ultimate become a point in time? How could he take on the features of a particular race?

There is also a gross misunderstanding of Mary, Jesus' mother. When Christians speak of Jesus the Son of God and the son of Mary, some Muslims think we believe God had sex relations with Mary. Naturally this repels Muslims. Some also think the Christian Trinity includes God, Christ and Mary.

If Jesus isn't God, who is he? Jesus was a prophet, according to Islam. In fact, he was one of the greatest of the prophets. More particularly, he was a Muslim prophet. His witness buttressed the final witness which came through Muhammad, the seal of the prophets. Muhammad was not God. He was a messenger. Most certainly, Jesus was not God either. That is the Muslim view.

The great mystery. How different is our experience. Consider these pictures of Jesus:

> God, who at sundry times and in divers manners spake in times past unto the fathers by the prophets, Hath in these last days spoken unto us by his Son, whom he hath appointed heir of all things, by whom also he made the worlds; Who being the brightness of his glory, and the express image of his person, and upholding all things by the word of his power, when he had by himself purged our sins, sat down on the right hand of the Majesty on high. (Hebrews 1:1-3 KJV)

> He is the image of the invisible God, the firstborn over all creation. For by him all things were created: things in heaven and on earth, visible and invisible, whether thrones or powers or rulers or authorities; all things were created by him and for him. He is before all things, and in him all things hold together.

> And he is the head of the body, the church; he is the beginning and the firstborn from among the dead, so that in everything he might have the supremacy. For God was pleased to have all his fullness dwell in him, and through him to reconcile to himself all things, whether things on earth or things in heaven, by making peace through his blood, shed on the cross.

. . . the mystery that has been kept hidden for ages and generations . . .
Christ in you, the hope of glory.
   We proclaim him, admonishing and teaching everyone with all wisdom,
so that we may present everyone perfect in Christ.

My purpose is that . . . they may know the mystery of God, namely, Christ,
in whom are hidden all the treasures of wisdom and knowledge. . . .

For in Christ all the fullness of the Deity lives in bodily form, and you have
been given fullness in Christ, who is the head over every power and authority. (Colossians 1:15-20, 26-28; 2:2-3, 9-10)

Is Jesus only a prophet? These texts tell a different tale. The story is bizarre,
of course. It recounts how God—Creator, Sustainer of the universe, Culminator of history, Conqueror of the powers of darkness—looks at us in
our human dilemmas, with our ozone depletion, our threat of nuclear
holocaust, our international economy tottering, Afghanistan a smoldering
volcano, Central America in tatters, Africa facing famine again—the
Christian story holds that God looks at us and announces that the answer
to the human dilemma is a crisis pregnancy.
   Absurd.
   Yet it goes right to the core of our human paradox. God reminds us that
what really matters in the universe is personal.
   How *do* we handle human conflict, selfishness, pride? It's a cosmic
problem. But it needs a personal solution. Microsoft can't program selfishness out. The president can't veto it. A Pentagon printout can't give speci-
fications for love. It's only when God fills us with his love, when God is
willing to get involved in our mess, that we find the power to change.
   Even more than Christians, Muslims emphasize that God is all-powerful. For Christians, God's omnipotence is defined in terms of his whole
character, crowned by love and mercy. For Muslims, God is not so limited.
He does whatever He wills. The phrase *Inshallah*—"if God wills"—continually salts Muslims' conversations. So when a Muslim protests, "God
can't take on human form!" we can ask, "Who are we to limit God's sover-
eignty? Do we dare to say the Creator of the universe *can't* visit his creation
in human form if he so chooses?"
   We should avoid the phrase "Son of God." Jesus' neighbors thought it

sounded wrong, just as it does to Muslims today. For the Jews it had well-defined messianic overtones. So when the Pharisees challenged Jesus about his identity, he usually didn't answer them directly. Instead, he created word pictures about himself—the door, the bread of life, the light, the living water, the vine, the good shepherd, the cornerstone. Similarly, when the apostles preached to pagans, they usually didn't call Jesus God's Son. Often they called him Lord. That may be a good term to use with Muslims: *Rabb na Isa*, the Lord Jesus.

The Trinity is, in J. I. Packer's words, "perhaps the hardest concept that the human mind has ever been asked to grasp." It took Christian theologians three centuries to find words to talk about it.

Basically, God is love. Love is essential to his nature. Even before anything was created, God loved. But whom? Or what?

Love flowed between the three persons of the deity. From the beginning they existed in relationship, in community, in love.

Theologians talk about three personal centers within one essence. None is subordinate to the others. "These are not three roles played by one actor or three relationships to us sustained by one agent, but three coequal and coeternal entities within one entity, each being God in just the same full sense as the other two."[7]

All three are present in creation, in redemption and in sanctification. Biblical teaching on the Trinity is found in the baptismal formula in Matthew 28:19; the accounts of Jesus' baptism (see Mark 1:9-11); Jesus' teaching in John 14—16; "triadic" theological passages such as Romans 8; 1 Corinthians 12:4-6; 2 Corinthians 13:14; Ephesians 1:3-14; 2 Thessalonians 2:13-17; 1 Peter 1:2; Jude 20-21; Revelation 1:4-6; and all the general teaching on the unity of God, the deity of Christ, and the Spirit's divine personhood.

So what? Why does it matter? Everybody agrees that it remains a mystery, even when we've put some words around it. Those inadequate words are important, however. This concept ultimately helps us understand God better, helps us worship God better and protects us from falling into false beliefs.

To communicate with Muslim thinkers, a Christian might say, "God is the one and only Divine, eternal and infinite Spirit with Unity of Essence in a Trinity of Personalities as Father, Son, and Holy Spirit, perfect in wisdom, power, holiness, justice, goodness, truth, and love."[8]

In the end, of course, nobody will be convinced of the Trinity by sheer logic. Jesus' disciples confessed him as God after they got to know him. In the same way, Muslims' intellectual questions about the Trinity diminish as they get to know Christ personally.

Why Jesus came. "Who is Jesus?" is the first question. "Why did Jesus come?" is the next. He didn't come as a great prophet simply to publicize God's message. That is not the witness of the Gospel record. Jesus came to show us what God is like. He came to conquer the powers of darkness that terrify us. He came to reconcile us to God and to others. He came to pay for our sins, to clean us from pollution and to justify us before God.

Jesus came to conquer the powers of darkness. These enslave Muslim women. Most don't know Muslim doctrines well. In life's crises they turn to charms, mantras, spirit mediums. Mothers pass the lore to daughters. Whole communities depend on these dark powers for grassroots spiritual protection. Jesus came to liberate people from dark powers. In this book we will explore several examples.

Jesus came to reconcile women to God and to others. The prophet Muhammad was right when he insisted that God is more than the sum of the saints and folk deities. God is qualitatively other. He is high, holy, pure, just, omnipotent, omniscient, eternal. Unfortunately, without Jesus he is also almost unreachable. He is seen as one who can't be bothered with the trivial crises of individual lives. But those clutch at women's hearts. Will my husband love me? Will he take another wife? Will my child die?

In desperation, women turn to spirit mediums for assurance. But Jesus came to bridge the gap between God and women. He came to show them that God is not far. Coming alongside, cutting through the fear, the alienation, the estrangement, Jesus reconciles women to God.

Jesus also reconciles women to others. Khadija is one Algerian who came to Christ because she hated her mother-in-law. Anger was eating her up. She knew it wasn't healthy. She needed help from outside. Jesus, she learned, could explode her hatred and reconcile her to her enemy.

Jesus came to pay for our sins. He came to die in our place. The Qur'an doesn't support this reasoning. Regarding Jesus on the cross it says, "[The

Jews] did not kill him, nor did they crucify him, but it appeared so to them" (4:157). Most Muslims believe Jesus didn't die on the cross. God couldn't allow his holy prophet to die the shameful death of a criminal. So at the last minute something miraculous happened. Maybe God whisked Jesus off the cross and substituted an angel. Maybe God substituted an apparition. Or maybe God put Judas on the cross in Jesus' place. All of these are popular interpretations. In any case, Jesus didn't die. Naturally, then, he didn't rise from the dead either.

This fits with Muslim scripture, Muslim experience and Muslim theology. The Bible and the Qur'an tell different versions of many of the same Old Testament stories: Adam and Eve, Noah, Abraham, Moses. They also both say something about New Testament characters like Jesus and Mary. But the Qur'an has nothing like the later prophetic writings—like Isaiah, Jeremiah and Hosea—which describe the suffering of God's people in a sinful world. It has no "suffering servant" passages. Instead it tells of one victory and vindication after another. This was, in fact, the experience of the Muslims for many centuries. Muhammad was more a "Constantine" than a "Christ" figure. So Jesus' sacrifice seems strange and shameful—*if* it happened. And most Muslims don't think it did.

Some Muslim scholars have tried to build bridges to Christianity. But at the crucifixion and the resurrection, they balk. Abbas Mahmud al-Aqqad wrote a book in 1952 entitled *The Genius of Christ (Abqariyyat-al-Masih)*. Though he gives honor to Christ, he draws back from the cross. Nothing historically certain is known after Christ's experience in the garden of Gethsemane, he maintains. "Thus he bypasses the Cross and Resurrection and attributes the spread of Christianity to the zeal of the disciples and the suitability of their message to the world of that time," Kenneth Cragg comments. "The work . . . represents a sincere and reverent attempt to comprehend Christ within a Muslim frame of reference. It is an interpretation of the Gospels without the climax that brought the teaching to its consummation and generated the Gospel that made the Church. It is a tribute that nevertheless insists: 'Come down from the Cross.' "[9]

Another Muslim writer, Khalid Gauba, in his biography of Muhammad, *Prophet of the Desert*, comments: "Poor Jesus Christ expressed the

noblest sentiments on charity and forgiveness; thus upon the Cross, persecuted and crucified, he forgave his enemies—'They know not what they
do.' But it was never in Christ's good fortune to have his enemies reduced
to impotence before him."[10] However Muslims view Jesus on the cross,
"the supreme glory of Christ has become something that renders him
pathetic. It is not simply that Christ goes unrecognized in the hidden majesty of redemptive love, but that the criteria of majesty are devalued and
'good fortune' given precedence over 'great grace.' "[11]

Death is not success. When Muslims object to the crucifixion, they
have a point. In the ordinary course of affairs Jesus charted a course for
disaster. He alienated a lot of potential networks. Look where it got him:
crucified. Most of us wouldn't want a colleague to behave like that. It
could wreak havoc with our carefully honed and prayed-over five-year
plans. Surely that would be irresponsible stewardship?

The law of sacrifice. On the other hand, there may be something
strangely true in the paradox that unless a seed falls into the ground and
dies it doesn't produce anything, but if it is buried it can produce much
fruit. John Seamands talks about this giving of self:

> The law of sacrifice runs through life, from the lowest to the very highest. In
> any realm of life those who save others cannot always save themselves from
> trouble, sorrow, yes, sometimes even death. The seed gives itself and dies in
> order to produce a harvest. The mother bird throws herself into the jaws of
> the serpent in order to save her young. The human mother goes down into
> the valley of death to bring a child into the world. The young patriot, with all
> his life before him, takes his one life into his hands and marches out against
> the bayonets of the enemy, in order to save his home and country. . . .
>
> Now if this is a universal law—and it seems to be—then when we come to
> God, the highest Being, we would expect to find in Him the greatest and
> noblest expression of sacrificial love in the whole universe. Otherwise the
> creature would be greater than the Creator. A worm would be greater, a bird,
> an animal; they give themselves, but not God. It is unthinkable that God
> would write a law of saving by sacrifice throughout the universe and be
> empty of it himself. . . .
>
> But the cross shows that there is such a God.[12]

Jesus came to pay for Muslim women's sin. In one sense his death may be seen as demeaning. In another sense it is glorious. Heroes who give their lives for their people palely reflect this kind of glory. It may not be the quickest route to success. But it can be the most effective.

God's grace is not cheap. A moral God doesn't overlook injustice with a wave of the hand and a shrug of the shoulders. We can't wipe out the stain of our selfishness by our merits. We can't bridge the gap between our polluted selves and a holy, eternal God by our good works. No, penalties must be paid. In Christ they *are* paid.

Muslim women understand blood sacrifice. Once a year all the Muslims in the world commemorate Abraham's sacrifice of his son and God's provision of a substitute just in the nick of time. Family by family, a sheep is sacrificed ritually, meat is distributed to the poor and the family and friends celebrate, enjoying God's good gifts in the context of the larger blessing of his care and provision throughout history.

While Muslims believe that it was Ishmael and not Isaac whom Abraham stretched out across the altar under the point of his knife, the fundamental truth is the same for both Christians and Muslims: God himself can provide a sacrifice.

A woman's life is measured by the recurrence of such feasts. As a small girl she may help keep an eye on the spitted mutton to make sure that it is turning evenly. On the brink of womanhood, she may have a major part in lugging the bloody carcass, washing it, coating it with herbs. Or, if the men preside over the sheep, she will be shaping other festive foods. In her prime, a woman may supervise the overall preparations. Making couscous, counting utensils, nursing an infant and shooing toddlers out of trouble will distract her from spiritual contemplation. But she knows the story behind the party.

Muslims treasure the stories of many Old Testament heroes who approached God by way of sacrifice. Cain and Abel. Noah offering sacrifices after he came out of the ark. The Passover lamb.

Is it any wonder, then, that when Muslim women hear about Jesus, our sacrifice, God's provision, it makes sense? Having sweated over fires and ovens for so many years to enact the shadow of Jesus' sacrifice, they resonate with the idea that Jesus is God's lamb. "A lot of them accept that Christ died for them, bore their sins, was a lamb," reports one missionary.

"Now here's my problem: Shall I teach them what Islam really teaches, so they can make a choice?"

Jesus died for Muslim women's sins. It boggles the mind. It confounds reason. Yet, paradoxically, it rings strangely true. God is indeed a God of moral absolutes, a God of law. He is also a God of love. Habiba, reading about the woman caught in adultery, recognized the need for both law and love. "If he stones her, I can't respect him," she said of Jesus. "But if he lets her go as though nothing had happened, I can't respect that either." Jesus did neither. In his answer he magnificently combined law and love.

"The cross reveals that God is not only zealous to uphold the moral order of the universe and to do something about wrong action and sin, but He is also zealous to uplift the one who has gone against the moral order and to redeem the sinner. So in the cross the justice and the love of God meet. There we see that God loved justice too well to forgive lightly, and loved man (and woman) to well to be indifferent."[13]

In one sense Muslims know a lot about Jesus. In another sense they don't. What a privilege to be able to fill in the missing episodes. "Consider the Qur'anic Jesus alongside the New Testament," says Islamics scholar Kenneth Cragg. He continues,

> How sadly attenuated is this Christian prophet as Islam knows him. Where are the stirring words, the deep insights, the gracious deeds, the compelling qualities of him who was called the Master? The mystery of his self-consciousness as the Messiah is unsuspected; the tender, searching intimacy of his relationship to the disciples undiscovered. Where is 'the way, the truth, and the life' in this abridgment? Where are the words from the Cross in a Jesus for whom Judas suffered? Where the triumph of the Resurrection from an empty grave? There is in the Qur'an neither Galilee nor Gethsemane; neither Nazareth nor Olivet. Even Bethlehem is unknown by name and the story of its greatest night is remote and strange. Is the Sermon on the Mount never to be heard in the Muslim world? Must the story of the Good Samaritan never be told there? Must the simple, human narrative of the prodigal son never mirror there the essence of waywardness and forgiveness? Is 'Come unto me all you who are weary . . . and I will give you rest' an invitation that need not be heard, and is Jesus' taking bread and giving thanks a negligible tale? Should not all humankind be initiated into the meaning of

the question: 'Will you also go away?' In sum, must not the emasculated Jesus of the Qur'an be rescued from misconception and disclosed in all his relevance?[14]

Muslim-Background Women Can Be Empowered by the Holy Spirit

Blood dripped down Aliya's arms as she hurled herself into the center of the room. Tambourines throbbed. Torches blazed in the darkness. A dozen men swayed in a line dance, each gently turning circles. Rhythmically, hour after hour, they chanted the name of God.

Against the measured, melodic rise and fall of their voices, Aliya screamed and propelled herself into the arena. Down her arms her fingernails sliced, drawing blood. Gouging, incoherent, she danced—jaggedly, erratically, electrically. Her hair, unbound for the occasion, tumbled violently. In the corner stood a carton of poisonous snakes for the snake-handling ritual. Next to that were tins of kerosene to baptize the torches before fire eating. In the background, levelheaded and steely eyed, was the spirits' pimp, the master of ceremonies, who kept order. When Aliya was ready to fall, he would lead her to the sidelines. In the next room was the sick little boy for whom this seance was being held in the mountains of Morocco.

Christ is victor over the powers of darkness. He died to demonstrate that victory. He rose to seal it. He sent the Holy Spirit to fill the places that are left empty when evil powers are banished.

Deliverance from demonic power is recounted more often in Asia, Africa and Latin America than in the West. A great cloud of cases could be cited. But what does this have to do with Muslims who worship the one God?

In fact, great masses of Muslims dabble in the occult. This is especially the case for women. Amulets are pinned to children, poked into crevices above door lintels, strapped to the arm beneath outer garments, swung from rearview mirrors in taxis and trucks. Curing ceremonies, magic, sorcery, fetishes, propitiation of spirits and saints all are common.

This is not true Islam. While orthodox Muslims believe in angels and demons, they know that God is not a plethora of spirits. Nor can a person manipulate God by magic. Yet many women aren't well grounded in Muslim doctrines. They learn by rote, without understanding or seeing the applications. At best, they discover a God who is lofty. But they crave a God who is near. When a baby is sick—or when there is no baby—when a husband is thinking of taking another wife, when crops fail, when the streets erupt in riots, when traffic accidents cut swathes through the city, what help is a God who is far off, however pure and magnificent? Lots of women turn to traditional ways to get in touch with the supernatural, as do many men.

Exorcism. How do Christians relate to all this? Sometimes through exorcism, framed by discerning prayer, fasting and Christian community. In this book we see Fatma set free through exorcism. We see Simin confronting a spirit of death. *Christ Supreme over Satan,* a clear, practical book first written in the Urdu language for Pakistani believers, explores some of the questions we might ask about exorcism:

☐ How do we know if someone is demon-possessed or not?

☐ If so, what can be done about it?

☐ Can a house be haunted by evil spirits?

☐ If so, what needs to be done to cleanse it?

☐ How does one distinguish between what comes from human perversity and what is directly satanic?

☐ Where does superstition end and the demonic begin?

☐ How does one distinguish between mental illness and satanic obsession, or depression, oppression and possession?

☐ What underlying animistic practices affect the Christian community in Pakistan?

☐ Why do Christians visit Muslim pirs or saints?

☐ How can Christ's victory over evil be manifested through his church?[15]

Different Christians will evaluate the "demonic component" in an event differently. "I love to go to weddings and funerals," says Joan. "But I won't go to a circumcision or a naming party. A sheep is sacrificed there on behalf of the child. And the festival that is the equivalent of our Christmas or Easter—*Id al Khabir*—has the same thing: a sheep sacrificed for the people. Many Christian women married to nonbelieving men cook the sacrificial sheep, but they won't eat it. The Christians in our fellowship have a lentil picnic that day, while all the other Moroccans have a mutton feast." Women like Joan believe that demonic powers may have been invited into the sheep.

Donna, a member of the same team, equally as evangelical, equally as concerned for holiness, equally as aware of spiritual warfare, says, "Name day feasts? *Id al Khabir?* I love to go. Sure, like everybody else, I receive some of the mutton from the sacrificial sheep. And I eat it with a good conscience."

Regardless of how we view a specific event—whether our concern is to avoid demons or dysentery—we know that Christ is victor. Throughout the world Muslim women are being set free. Sometimes it happens through healing or exorcism. Whole groups of Muslims come to Christ in this way.

But it would not be honest to suggest that this is the whole story.

Oppression. Laila is an Arab follower of Jesus who is ensnared by demonic influences. She met Christ as a teenager and grew through Bible study, prayer, occasional fellowship with a missionary and a few other believers, and the experience of God's presence. When she came of age, her parents married her to Hamid, a Muslim. Seeing no alternative, she cooperated. She moved in with her in-laws, who live in a four-story building, one family to a floor. They all cook and eat together.

"I can't meet with you anymore," she whispered when she saw her Christian friends. "In fact, in my living situation, I hardly have the privacy to read the Bible or pray!"

When Laila didn't get pregnant after a couple of years of marriage, gynecologists and herbalists were consulted. In her room Laila prayed fervently. "Oh Lord, Creator of the worlds, oh Lord Jesus Christ, you gave a baby to Sarah when it seemed impossible. You gave a baby to Hannah. You gave a baby to Elizabeth. You took on human form yourself as a baby. Oh Lord, as the psalm says, 'Children are a heritage of the Lord . . . like vines curling their tendrils around our table.' My table has nobody, Lord. I am so empty. Please give me a baby."

But Laila's blood flowed out month after month.

"No growth yet?" The neighbors patted her on the stomach and clucked, shaking their heads.

"It's a shame," nodded Taiza, Laila's mother-in-law. "We'll have to take her to a shrine after all, never mind the expense."

"No!" Laila breathed silently. But finally, as a last resort, her in-laws took her to a shrine. Here Laila sacrificed a chicken to the saint of the shrine and begged for a baby.

When she got home, she got pregnant.

But she was also in bondage to make a sacrifice to that saint annually for the rest of her life.

Now when believers visited her, she sometimes wanted to hear about the Lord but at other times heard a voice telling her not to listen. Although she prayed in the name of Jesus and claimed the blood of Jesus, sometimes she would tell Christians, "Don't talk to me about the Lord today. I can't stand to hear it."

Later she miscarried the baby. She has never gotten pregnant again.

At this writing, some Christian believers like Laila are making annual pilgrimages to saints' shrines, where they offer sacrifices. Some experience degrees of spiritual oppression.

Love of battle. However, even if we are called to exorcism, we must beware of a fascination with battle. Missionary anthropologist Paul Hiebert, admittedly a Mennonite pacifist, reminds us:

☐ Satan is not independent, and he never wins.

☐ Human beings are responsible, not pawns of higher forces.

☐ The central issue is not power but holy and loving relationships.

☐ The way to victory is not primarily battle but the cross followed by resurrection.

We have been raised with a bias toward battle, Hiebert argues. He suggests some background:

> Central to the IndoEuropean worldview was the myth of a cosmic spiritual battle between good and evil (Larson 1974; Puhvel 1970). . . . In IndoEuropean battles, the good characters become like their enemies: they end up using violence, entering without warrants, lying, committing adultery, and killing without due process. All of this is justified in the name of victory. Righteousness and love can be established only after the victory is won, and are second in importance. . . .
>
> Relationships in the cosmos are based on competition. . . . Battle is the center of the story. When it is over the story is done. The final words are "and they won (or were married, or beat out a rival) and lived happily ever after." But there is no story worth telling about the "happily ever after." The

adventure and thrill is in the battle, and to this we return again and again.[16]

Is this our hidden heritage? Do we delight in battle? If we focus on war more than on reconciliation, belligerent attitudes may come to dominate our daily life. Love, peace and justice may become secondary.

After hundreds of Indonesian churches were burned by Muslims in 1997-1998, Christians gathered for an annual conference. While comforting the bereft, the conferees asked, Did we ourselves fan the flames in any way? They reviewed their worship practices. In some churches right in the heart of strong Muslim neighborhoods, Christians had sung loudly about the battle as the Lord's. Now the conferees asked themselves, "What were the neighbors supposed to think? Did our songs' focus on battle fuel an antagonism that ended in burning?"

Exorcism is an occasional exercise. Love is an everyday essential.

The Holy Spirit. The spirits Muslim women know are spirits of rebellion, not spirits that give homage to the Creator. How about the *Holy Spirit?* What can women expect from this Spirit as they become new in Christ?

At Pentecost, when the Holy Spirit came in power on the disciples, the apostle Peter quoted the prophet Joel: "I will pour out my Spirit on all people. Your sons and daughters will prophesy. . . . On my servants, both men and women, I will pour out my Spirit in those days" (Acts 2:17-18; see Joel 2:28-29).

The Holy Spirit is God's presence with his people. The Spirit empowers us with "gifts" and "fruits." Gifts of the Spirit include wisdom, prophecy, teaching, administration, hospitality, healing, speaking in tongues, discernment and whatever other gifts God may choose to give (1 Corinthians 12; Romans 12). Fruits of the Spirit include love, joy, peace, patience, kindness, goodness, faithfulness, gentleness and self-control (Galatians 5:22-23). All these gifts and fruits are the birthright of Muslim-background women who are in Christ.

How desperately Muslim-background women need the Holy Spirit! Can a woman love a husband who takes another wife? A mother-in-law who controls and spoils her children, and sends her off to do the grunge work? Family members who beat her, drug her and lock her in when she wants to attend a Christian fellowship? Empowered by the Spirit, she can.

Suffering. Life in the Spirit, a life of love, is not natural. Throughout Galatians, the apostle Paul's essay on "walking in the spirit," he shows how the way of the cross is the opposite of our ordinary inclinations.

Luci found this out. She and her husband and children were part of a team ministering to an unreached Muslim people group. The work was hard but exhilarating. They knew they were on the cutting edge. For fourteen years they poured their lives into this service. Then, unexpectedly, the team fell apart. The breakup was ragged and painful. Now all the missionaries are home, wounded.

Recently Luci was asked to speak at a conference on the topic "Why I Am a Missionary." She gave us a glimpse of her pain and confusion. "Why *am* I a missionary?" she began. "Sometimes I don't know at all." Suffering was no surprise, she told us. "When I came to Christ, I was taught that the one who follows Jesus must take up a cross. So when I was called to mission, I was prepared to suffer. I was willing to pay the price."

What she wasn't prepared for was failure. "I was willing to pay the price—*but* I wanted results commensurate with the cost."

Amid the ashes of her dreams, Luci explained that walking in the Spirit doesn't mean walking according to North American values of efficiency, goal achievement and success. "I had to learn that being a follower of Jesus is worth utter, total failure in all the ways I define success." Nevertheless, she added, she will go on ministering to Muslims. "Eating at Jesus' banquet is so delicious that I could never stop inviting people to the dinner."

Life in the Spirit includes suffering. But in the providence of God, shouldering pain can lead to new life. A cross can lead to a resurrection. Jesus endured, not as a martyr but "for the joy that was before him" (Hebrews 12:2). In many parts of the world, when local believers have suffered, other Muslims have come to Christ.

Freedom. Life in the Spirit means more than submission and suffering. It also means power, freedom and courage to do new things.

That sounds good. In reality, however, we may find ourselves immersed in the "tyranny of the urgent." Husbands have needs, the boss makes demands, neighbors expect certain standards, children clamor, messes pile up. We often feel overwhelmed by other people's expectations.

Yet the apostle Paul insists in a great passage on the Spirit that we are "called to be free" (Galatians 5:13). "It is for freedom that Christ has set us free. Stand firm, then, and do not let yourselves be burdened again by a yoke of slavery" (5:1).

Paul wrote this out of his own experience. He felt propelled to the "unreached peoples." God had not called him to a life of established programs but to life in the Spirit, not for self-indulgence but for creative service (5:13-14).

One of the brightest periods in women's mission history was dynamized by this same sense of God's liberating love. Like Paul, nineteenth-century North American women across the spectrum of denominations discovered that God's love empowers us to serve.

> Submission to God . . . provided women with the means of their own liberation from fear of public speaking, financial management, and travelling alone. Submission to God for the cause of missions empowered women to serve as educators, lay preachers, and lay theologians. . . .
>
> Submission to God's will obtained through an experience of "perfect love" . . . gave women the confidence they needed to travel around speaking and organizing on behalf of missions and other social causes. . . .
>
> As women across Methodism experienced holiness, they felt freed from the silence imposed on them by American society and they began to speak out in church and to commit themselves to social service and mission work on behalf of others. . . .
>
> The prominent healing and compassion ministries of Pentecostals in the twentieth century were largely the product of women, an indirect offshoot of the missiology of divine love.[7]

And it is this experience of God's love mediated through the Holy Spirit that enables Muslim-background women to love creatively. Like Hagar, they discover that they are not nobodies. They are not alone. They are loved. And as they are filled, they can become conduits of that love to others.

Jesus sends the Spirit to Muslim-background women to comfort them, to lead them into truth, to empower them and to enable them to blossom with the first fruit of the Spirit, which is love (John 14—17; 1 Corinthians 12). Through the Holy Spirit, Muslim-background women are learning to love the Lord their God with all their heart, soul, mind and strength, and to love their neighbors—and their mothers-in-law—as they love themselves.

Muslim-Background Women Are Called to Service in God's World

Christ calls us to be "salt" in our societies. We are to remind the world continually that God is king. He reigns over nature since he created it and maintains it. So we care about deforestation. We care about water management. We care about public health—nutrition, immunization, family planning programs. In the same way God reigns over people since he has created and redeemed us. So we care about schools and jobs and our national heritage.

Every country, every neighborhood, desperately needs such citizens. People who neither condemn nor condone their culture but creatively work to transform it. People who know that evil is powerful but that God is even greater. People who can look sin in the eye without losing sight of grace. People who can affirm that beyond every cross there is the possibility of resurrection.

Muslims believe in taking care of the earth. Adam and Eve were commissioned to be God's stewards, or *khalifa*. So Muslim women's associations teach hygiene and literacy classes. They lobby for better marriage laws. They form Mothers' Councils in various neighborhoods. They set up shoebox libraries. They prepare relief supplies for disaster victims. These are noble efforts that deserve our cooperation and support.

Some Muslim women model spiritual leadership. There are women in *Hamas*, a political party in Israel and the West Bank, who, in a recent meeting, "modestly attired in *hijab*, answered *sura* for *sura* the men's pronouncements about what was or was not proper Islamic behavior. The women had . . . the authority of their dress but also their education."[18] There are women in Saudi Arabia who subscribe to total body covering, even of hands and feet, to legitimize their right to argue for greater opportunities in work and education. "They claim erudition in Quran and *hadith* as a means of advancing feminist interests. . . . Through their ability to refer to Quran and *hadith*, they can engage in dialogue with conservative men, drawing on examples of independent women from the life of the Prophet as their models."[19]

There are women in Pakistan who are "developing performance, social and leadership skills, experiences with diverse people and situations, and a growing awareness of their capabilities," learning to think differently about themselves and about women's place in society. Ironically, this happens as they participate in very fundamentalist women's groups. "*Majales* brought women *both* fundamentalism *and* freedom."[20]

There are women in West Africa who are Sufi leaders, mostly for women followers. They must know written Arabic and must be "ordained." They guide initiates through various levels of formulas, prayers and practices. They interpret doctrinal questions. They teach songs of praise to the prophet Muhammad and local Sufis. They advise on legal matters. They dispense herbal and Islamic medicine. They foster members' children, receiving in return the benefit of the child's labor in their households. They may be mystics. They may perform miracles. One has written many books. Another has read *tafsir*, exegeting the Qur'an for the whole community in the emir's palace during Ramadan. Although this is frowned on elsewhere, one woman leads major community worship for both men and women.[21]

Wali Sulayman (1890-1939) was a northern Nigerian who encouraged this development. He himself was surrounded by four spiritually thirsty women who took advantage of every opportunity to learn—his mother, his sister, his wife and his emir's wife. Wali Sulayman's wife taught in the emir's household, handling classes of 100 boys at a time. For many of the current titleholders in the Kano Emirate, she was their first teacher. After her husband's death she taught Qur'an, Arabic grammar, *fiqh* (Islamic jurisprudence), *hadith* (Sayings of the Prophet), and *tafsir* (exegesis) at the Kano Women Teachers' Training Centres.

Women are called to active service, called to be *khalifa* who care for God's domain. Yet many women in every culture forfeit this birthright, due to ignorance, selfishness, fear or externally imposed limits. What a waste of human resources. What potential lies undeveloped. Here Jesus' women can be a breath of fresh air. In the Muslim world they can join with other women—artists, politicians, mothers, saints—to strengthen the community. But they can do more. They can so live that people realize that Saudi Arabia is the Lord's—it belongs to the God who showed his love in Jesus. That Bangladesh is the Lord's. That the markets and universities and multinational corporations are the Lord's. These women can be channels of God's love to the crowded warrens of the cities, the transient guest workers, the broken marriages, the confused children, the atheist young adults, the government leaders scrambling for moral guidance. Their lives can show the beauty of righteousness, the wonder of grace, the power of godliness. As we will see in this book, women who are believers in Jesus are doing that.

How the Muslim world—like every other part of the world—needs a praying network of contented older women, role models with lifetime testimonies to the grace of God. What power such a network could generate. How the Muslim world needs the vitality of Spirit-filled young mothers. How it needs the challenging example of chaste and passionately caring single women. Today the energies of Muslim women often are squandered. Very few know that they are created in the image of God, redeemed by Christ, capable of being empowered by the Spirit, and called to active service in God's world. So old women gossip. Young women experiment with cosmetics and intrigues. Yet who knows how many human needs could be met if God through Jesus Christ would dynamize such women?

5
Iranian Sisters

Ladan's family were not fanatics. An international banker and import-export broker, Ladan's father was fluent in French, Russian, Persian, Turkish and Arabic. Her mother had a French education in local convent schools. They were Muslim, but ethics tended to overshadow theology in their circles. With a high view of women, Ladan's father insisted that her two brothers respect their only sister. He gave her a fine education, culminating in a master's degree in England. He also saw to it that she was happily married.

Ladan's mother was known for her kindness even to servants. She ensured that they had regular time off to visit their families. She checked that they had extra food to take with them and good clothes. "Far too liberal," scoffed her neighbors. But Ladan remembers her mother being "like a saint," although she never talked about religion.

It was from the servants that Ladan learned the basics of Islam. For people of her class and generation this was commonplace. Their parents were cosmopolitan and broad-minded. It was the servants who transmitted the traditional heritage.

Ladan: A TV Show, a Stolen Bible, a Persian Church

When Ladan went to England for university studies, she began to make her faith her own. For six years she lived in that cold northern country. Often she was lonely. Letters from home were too few. She had brought with her a translation of the Qur'an in the Farsi language. Now for the first time she read the scripture through. She tried to approach God in the only way she knew, by praying and following the way of Islam.

Today she says, "If you're hungry and you have only popcorn, you eat it."

Over the next decade Ladan would discover dozens of books on Islam written in the Farsi language, and she would read all that she could. Still, when she married and had children, Ladan wished she had something more to offer them. "I wanted to learn a bigger truth so I could give it to my children and it could be the foundation for their lives."

Instead, the Iranian revolution exploded. The traditional government of the Shah was ousted. In its place rose a strict religious regime. To Ladan this was a tragedy. Her country, which had been on the brink of playing a significant role in the modern world, slipped backward.

"After the Revolution it would appear we had been hurt greatly," she says. "I was angry with God. I got involved politically, trying to stop Khomeini."

This was somewhat dangerous. Ladan's family decided that she and the children should move to the United States temporarily. Her husband would stay behind to see what developed. Many Iranian families were following this route if they could afford it.

In the United States Ladan would have to start out poor. That frightened her. "When you're raised with lots of money, you think if they take your money away you're going to die. I didn't know you could live with just a plate and fork and spoon. But I've since learned."

Yet even in the United States Ladan found herself drawn into politics. Elite Iranian exiles like herself gathered frequently to plot the overthrow of Khomeini and the future of the nation. She came home from these sessions weary from the scheming and political machinations.

Then she discovered an oasis: Christian TV. Regardless of the hype associated with some of the shows, it was these programs that confronted Ladan with the Lord Jesus Christ. Against all the backstabbing among her

Iranian colleagues, against the political gossip and intrigues that made up her world, Jesus stood apart, a perfect person. "Jesus was such a good man that, if he had five daughters, he could get them all married," she says. To find peace, she turned on the TV and reveled in Jesus.

One day the anchorman of *The 700 Club*, Ben Kinchlow, asked his viewing audience, "Would you like to know Jesus as your personal Savior?"

Would I? Ladan asked herself. *I don't know what that means. But yes. Of course. I'd like to be as close to Jesus as possible.*

Ben Kinchlow invited responsive members of the audience to pray the "sinner's prayer."

"Fold your hands—"

Ladan did.

"—bow your head, close your eyes—"

Ladan did.

"—and repeat after me, 'Lord Jesus, I admit that I'm a sinner. I need you to forgive me. I need you to clean me up, to transform me, to renew me, through the power of your death and resurrection.'"

Ladan prayed sincerely. Yet if someone had asked her after that if she was a Christian, she wouldn't have said yes. In fact, that is what happened. Some time after praying with Ben Kinchlow, Ladan was enjoying a beautiful afternoon in a city park. A woman sat down beside her. She turned out to be a homeless "bag lady" who carried her possessions with her. They fell into conversation.

"What's your religion?" the bag lady asked after awhile. "Aren't Iranians Muslim?"

"Oh, I've left that behind," Ladan answered. "I'd like to follow Christianity. But I don't know how to go about it."

"Do you have a Bible?"

"No."

"Well, I have one that I stole from a hotel," the bag lady announced. "Here—" she reached down into her bag, fished out the Bible and handed it to Ladan. "You might as well have it."

When she got home, Ladan put the Bible by her bed. Every night for the next two years she read the passages underlined in red—the words of Jesus—and committed many verses to memory.

Then once again Ben Kinchlow reached into her life. "Would you like to find a church near you?" he asked.

That was a new thought to Ladan. She had never considered a church.

"If you want a church and you don't know where to go, call this number and we will find you a church close by," Kinchlow continued.

Do I want a church? Ladan mused. *Well, if he could find me an Iranian church . . . but that could never be. So—what do I have to lose? I'll give him a call.*

Two days later *The 700 Club* returned her call with the addresses of *two* Iranian churches in her immediate vicinity.

At last she got plugged into a network of people with whom she could talk freely about the Lord Jesus. Ladan's understanding of the Christian life began to mature. Surprising things happened in her daily life too. When Ladan was baptized, for example, her craving for cigarettes evaporated. For ten years she had smoked ten cigarettes a day. Several times she had tried to quit. The day she was baptized, she returned home late, only to discover she was out of cigarettes and all the stores were closed. The next day she didn't light up until noon, and then only out of habit. "What happened to my craving?" she asked herself. Little by little her smoking disappeared totally, without effort on her part.

Prayer became power. "Because I know God can hear me, I feel like I have a lot of strength," she says. Praying, she was delivered from worry about finances. Sure enough, soon she got a source of income. Praying about her daughter's lousy boyfriend, she found that he dropped out of the picture.

"Mom, please don't pray for us," her children plead, only half joking.

"It's gotten to the point that my children are afraid of the power of my prayers," she chuckles.

Christian doctrines began to make more sense. Teaching on the Trinity had bothered her for a long time. If Christ is God, how was the earth sustained when Christ was on earth? she wondered. Yet, if Christ has done so much for me, how can I think he's anything but God? The analogy of water has helped her. Water is in the ocean. Water also is in the faucet. One quantity of water is vast, one is specific and limited. Yet they can be from the same source of water, both parts of the whole.

Some of Ladan's efforts to share her faith with her husband over the international telephone lines have been humorous.

"Look, Massoud, if you have any trouble, talk to Jesus."

"What? Who? What agency is he in?"

Ladan revealed how she had experienced salvation in Jesus and how she longed for Massoud to be saved.

"Saved?" he retorted. "You're saved? From what? From me?"

"Oh Massoud, cast out those bad thoughts. They're from the devil."

"What! Now I'm possessed," he groaned.

With these communication mixups, Ladan is praying more than she is witnessing. She is looking forward to seeing Massoud face to face.

Meanwhile she is enjoying God. "To find Jesus is like someone who has never eaten anything sweet. When he does, he says, 'I've found it!' God is wealthy and generous. He's not jealous of us being happy. Just like I want my children to be happy, so God wants us to be."

And Ladan prays for Iran. Her ethical, socially conscious parents raised her to care not simply for her own needs but also for those of others. Today she does not simply pray for herself, or simply for the needs of other individuals, but also for the Iranian people as a whole. "Every night I pray a long time for Iran. I feel for the Iranian people because I know the suffering that I went through without God. I don't want my people to die without the Lord. I know we're bad people. Hardhearted. Lacking concern for others. Superficial. Clever, but using our cleverness against others to manipulate them. But we have suffered a lot now . . ."

Ladan owns three pieces of land in Iran. A few years ago they were confiscated by the revolutionary government. Miraculously she regained title. When conditions change she dreams of starting a low-cost Christian clinic on one of the locations. In the meantime, she plans a Bible cassette distribution program to spread the gospel in the rural areas. "The people of Iran are my people," she says.

Zohre: "You Mean All This Time It Was You, God?"

"If your bad deeds tip the scale, you'll end in hell. You'll be buried under the ground for millions of years. You'll burn. You'll suffer . . ."

It was a warm, sultry afternoon. Dust motes shimmered over hard wooden desks. Heads nodded and feet shuffled as the fourth-grade teacher droned on.

Suddenly Zohre's hand pierced the class's lethargy. "Yes?" Looking over the top of his glasses, the teacher nodded at her.

"What if they're equal?" Zohre asked.

"If *what* are equal?" the teacher echoed.

"Our good deeds and our bad deeds. That God weighs on his scale. What if they're equal?"

Religion was Zohre's favorite subject. She often argued with the teachers. By now they were used to her questions. In particular, she was concerned about death.

"What if your deeds are equal?" the teacher mused. "In that case, you'll go to hell. Because goodness is your duty."

"Well, then what's the use?" Zohre wondered. "If goodness is our duty, it doesn't matter whether we have slightly more good than bad. Any bad deeds at all will disqualify us. We can never measure up."

Later in life Zohre would storm at God, "If you were to come down as a man yourself, you couldn't keep your own laws. I can't perform all the prayers. I try and fail, try and fail. You expect too much. You create me fallible and then demand that I be perfect. You place me in a world full of sensory arousals, and then I find that music will send me to hell, pork will send me to hell. It seems that happiness itself will send me to hell."

Zohre also hated God's apparent male chauvinism, equating the witness of two women to that of one man, for example.

Zohre's mother reminded her, "You shouldn't perform your prayers just because you want to go to heaven. You should do them because you love God."

"I'd like to love God," Zohre answered, "but God isn't lovable. He seems to have created us just so he can send us to hell. He's an unrighteous judge. He plays with us like puppets on a string." Here Zohre was paraphrasing lines from *The Rubáiyat of Omar Khayyám*, lines which express the sentiments of many Iranians. God ordains our fate. We are his toys. He is the puppeteer. We are the puppets.

"God's will" is a phrase Muslims use frequently. "Inshallah"—"If God wills"—is an expression common throughout the Muslim world. But the thought of God's will made Zohre want to vomit. Years would pass before she would believe that God's will for her was love. At this stage of her life, she was deeply frustrated. On the one hand, she longed to keep God's standards. On the other hand, she couldn't. She was unable to measure up. And since it was impossible, God was unreasonable to demand it. Later, when asked her favorite Bible text, Zohre would quote John 1:17: "The law was given through Moses; grace and truth came through Jesus Christ." She would add, "God used Islam to show me that I was a sinner. But for a long time all I had was the 'bad news.' "

And yet there were glimpses of something more. As a child she was fascinated by the stars. She wanted to be an astronaut. She used to ponder the greatness of the Creator of the universe and wonder, *In this immense pattern, where did I come from? Where am I going?* She was the only one in her family to ask such questions. "God had his hand on my life from childhood," she says now. From an early age Zohre had a love-hate relationship with God. Her very anger grew out of her longing.

While still a child, Zohre also glimpsed something of Christ's giving his life for the sins of the world. Her family had many international friends. From time to time she saw crucifixes on the walls of some of her friends' houses. And Zohre's mother, who had attended a Christian elementary school, got her theology mixed up. She taught Zohre that Christ had been crucified, thinking this was orthodox Islam. Later God used this confusion.

Zohre grew up outwardly serene and successful, inwardly often in despair. She practiced Islam because she feared death and hell. Yet she saw no real hope of escaping them. Conflict between her parents deepened her gloom. As early as age seven, she toyed with the idea of suicide. When the Iranian revolution erupted, she considered joining the rioting crowds, since the one and only way she could be sure of going to heaven was if she was killed in a holy war.

Instead she ended up being sent to college in Utah, surrounded by Mormons. Suddenly the world was full of questions as diverse and practical as "Which way do I face to pray? Where do I get *halal* meat?"

But before long those questions faded. Back home in Iran under her father's scrutiny Zohre had been a straight-A student. Now, like the other Iranians around her, she began to party. Grades slipped to the background. Even God slipped out of sight. "I forgot about God, but he didn't forget about me," she says now.

When she did think about religion, that too was from a more liberal perspective. Meeting and talking with Baha'is, Jews, Mormons and evangelical Christians, she became more cosmopolitan in her views. "I made up my own way of communicating with God," she recalls. "Many Muslims do." She still recited the regular prayers from time to time. But after the set words, she would add her own personal longings.

Open to new ideas, open to new friends, open to fun, she began to fall in love with Joe, a renegade Mormon.

Meanwhile, the Lord Jesus Christ was being presented to her, though not in ways that would fit any evangelism manual. First, Mormons tried to convert Zohre. As always, she enjoyed arguing about religion. Ironically, the Mormons' view of Jesus was too high for her.

"Show me that Jesus is God!" she challenged them.

"Pray," they responded, "and ask God who he is."

She took up the challenge and added this request to her personal prayers.

A second witness to the Lord Jesus was Sarah, Zohre's roommate. Sarah was a committed evangelical Christian. She cared for Zohre. She longed for Zohre's conversion. She got her Bible study group to pray for Zohre regularly, though Zohre knew nothing of this for months. Sarah took every opportunity to put in a word for the Lord Jesus.

One day, for example, they discovered some ants in their room. Sarah turned it into an object lesson. "If you were God, and these ants were people, and you wanted to communicate with them," she mused, "wouldn't the best thing be for you to become an ant?"

This struck home. As a child, watching ants on the ground, Zohre sometimes had pretended to be God. Her "godlike" action had been to stomp on all the ants!

Nevertheless, for all Sarah's winsome witness, there was a major block. Sarah slept with her boyfriend nearly every night.

"How can you aim for godliness and do this?" Zohre asked.

"It's okay," Sarah answered, "because Jesus died on the cross for my sins. He forgives me in advance."

God uses surprising witnesses. In Ladan's case, a woman stole a Bible and gave it to her. In Zohre's case, a roommate witnessed while practicing sex outside of marriage. In Simin's case, as we will see in the last chapter, an old man visited her every day to read the Bible in a language and version—King James English—that she couldn't understand. Yet all of these irregular witnesses were links in the chain that drew these Iranian women to the Lord Jesus.

Shall we be fools, then? Is rational strategy irrelevant? By no means. We are to worship God with our minds. We are to be stewards of all the resources available to us, including our knowledge of effective communication principles. It seems that God used these foolish people not because of their foolishness, but because they loved in spite of their imperfections. They reached out in spite of their faults. They didn't wait until they had it all together before they dared to care. Their love was greater than their pride. God honored this.

In time it became apparent that Zohre's boyfriend, Joe, was a bad bargain.

Ever-ready Sarah turned the knife in the wound. "Have you ever thought that your relationship with Joe might not be God's will?"

"God's will!" Zohre stormed inwardly. "Can't I ever escape? Yes! I will! I'm going to show you, God. No matter what your will is, I'm going to control my destiny. I chose this relationship. I'm going to go through with it."

The more the relationship deteriorated, the more stubborn Zohre got. Soon she and Joe were talking marriage plans.

Two weeks before their wedding date, Joe got kicked out of school and fired from his job.

"Sorry, Baby," he told Zohre. "I guess there's no future for us after all." He rode off into the sunset.

Whew! was Zohre's unspoken first reaction.

Anger was her second, when good old Sarah piped up, "See, I told you Joe wasn't God's will for you."

Zohre went aside for a tête-à-tête with her Maker. "Okay, God, you win," she told him. "You're the Puppet Master. You pull the strings. But," she added, "that doesn't mean I have to like you. In fact, I don't want to have any more to do with you than is absolutely necessary."

Enter Al. A member of Sarah's Bible study, Al had met Zohre in registration on the first day of school. Unknown to Zohre, Al had been praying for her ever since. Now that Joe was out of the picture, Zohre and Al began to do things together, not romantically but as friends.

The more Zohre saw of Al, the more impressed she was. He seemed to have his life together. The Mormons didn't, in Zohre's opinion. The Muslims at her university didn't. The Baha'is didn't. But Al had the whole picture. He attributed it to his relationship with God through Christ.

Al also seemed to care about Zohre.

Al's and Zohre's friendship is not an ideal model for evangelism. As a rule, cross-gender witness to Muslims is counterproductive. Misunderstandings (and worse) result. Generally, men ought to witness to men and women to women. An exception is an older woman talking with a younger man. In the role of mother or aunt, an older woman can touch a younger man profoundly.

Yet Al's witness to Zohre turned out to be one of God's happy surprises.

"God loves you," Al began. In the back of his mind were the "Four Spiritual Laws" developed by Campus Crusade for Christ.

"No way!" Zohre retorted, to Al's surprise. "God is great. But he isn't love. God is a killjoy."

Nevertheless, Al and Zohre started praying together. Zohre discovered that Al's prayers got results. "You gotta pray through Jesus," Al told her.

He tried to explain how Christ died for our sins.

"How could someone else die for us?" Zohre scoffed. "Everybody has to pay for their own deeds. That's common sense. It also happens to be what the Qur'an says."

"Really? I thought Christ was a great prophet in Islam. Don't Muslims believe Christ died for the sin of the world?" Al questioned, not knowing.

Suddenly Zohre experienced a flashback. Her eighth-grade class had been studying world history around the time of Christ. Zohre had been called to the front of the class for her turn at recitation.

"What happened to the prophet Jesus?" the teacher had asked.

"He was crucified," Zohre had answered, parroting her mother's mixed-up theology.

"No," the teacher had explained patiently. "History books may teach that. But we Muslims know Judas was substituted in Jesus' place —"

Zohre now repeated that to Al.

"You believe that? That Judas was substituted for Jesus? On what evidence? Just because your teacher said so?" Al shook his head in wonder. "Sounds shaky to me. That's even harder to believe than that Christ gave his life for us."

Zohre was quiet. Slowly she said, "You're right. It does sound shaky."

Another day they discussed hell. "If you died tonight, do you know where you'd go?" Al asked her.

"Yes," she answered.

"Where?"

"To hell. And there's nothing I can do, and I don't want to talk about it," she answered.

Yet through Al she was beginning to experience a degree of peace in her life.

Ironically, once again the Christian witness had feet of clay. Al took Zohre to horror movies. Afterward she would have nightmares. Sometimes, while she lay half-paralyzed, a red, ugly demon would grab her and drag her toward a deep tunnel where fire roared.

"I'm going to hell, and I'm taking you with me," the apparition would croak.

She couldn't scream.

She began to be afraid to fall asleep.

But when she prayed in Jesus' name, God took the dreams away. Still she resisted submitting to God. Sometimes when they prayed, Al would tell her, "Don't tell God what to do. Let him do it his way." But Zohre didn't want God's will.

On the other hand, she was getting tired of fighting God. Sometimes she would pray privately, "Help me. Do what you want." At such times, she would feel a big load lift off of her.

Once again the scene changed. The school year drew to a close, and Al was moving on. "Well, Zohre. It may be now or never. The Lord Jesus Christ stands in front of you . . ."

"I want what you have," Zohre answered, "but I don't want Jesus."

"Zohre, I know God has brought me into your life for a purpose. It's time for me to go to Colorado. But you're so stubborn. You won't let Christ save you—"

"Save?" The only time Zohre had heard the English word *save* was at a baseball game.

Al turned to 2 Corinthians 5:17: "If anyone is in Christ, he is a new creation; the old has gone, the new has come!"

It sounded so good. "If only I *could* start over again," Zohre thought. "God, you made me once. You could make me again. . . . Well, maybe I should try Jesus. Oh no, if God finds out I asked Jesus for help, I'm going to hell! Hey! I'm going to hell anyway."

Zohre threw out a challenge: "God, you have to prove this to me."

Again she flashed back to her eighth-grade classroom and her teacher contradicting the history books. *Who ever proved to you the things you believe now?* she asked herself. *Don't you take them on faith?*

Reluctantly—like C. S. Lewis, who described himself as "dragged through the doorway kicking, the most reluctant convert in all England"—Zohre prayed with Al, asking Christ's forgiveness, asking Christ into her heart, asking for a new birth.

"You're a Christian now!" Al beamed jubilantly.

"No, I'm not!" Zohre snapped. The change of nomenclature was just too much. Her faith wavered immediately. "How can I keep on believing this?" she wondered. "Maybe if I concentrate on the words, 'Lord Jesus Christ'. . ." She tried that. It wasn't much help.

"I know I don't practice my Muslim religion now," she admitted ruefully, "but whether I believe it or not, whether it's true or not, it's part of me. For me to pray to Christ and believe in the Bible, it's going to take a miracle."

The next day that happened. The miraculous love of God thawed her frozen heart. She and Al were sitting under a tree, talking about his family.

"Why did your mom marry three times?" Zohre asked.

Al described how his first dad had been an alcoholic. As he talked, Zohre remembered Joe. She began to see how her life might have developed had she married him. The past few years of her life swam through her consciousness as if on film. While Al shared his mother's heartaches, Zohre thought, "That could have been me."

Suddenly she was talking to God. "*I've* made foolish choices. And you've protected me from the consequences. I'm a sinner. I've hated you.

Why have you helped me?"

"God loves you." Al's words reverberated in her brain. All at once a veil was torn from her understanding, and the things Al had been saying to her over the months clicked into place.

Again she prayed with Al. This time she asked Christ to take full control. "And I don't even mind being called a Christian," she laughed. "Let's read the Bible together every day that you're still here. Starting in Genesis."

That was twelve years ago. "God started changing me from the dark person that I was," she recalls. Zohre was a journalism student and a bit of a writer. Before her conversion, she wrote about pain, darkness and death. Sometimes she would sit in a cemetery to get into the mood for writing. But now hope and purpose sparkle through her prose.

"How do I tell my parents about the Lord Jesus Christ?" Zohre wondered. Eight months later God showed her through a dream how to do it. When she finally told them, her mother was hurt. Her dad said, "Just so long as you get good grades—that's the bottom line." Her parents stuck with her, and they remain close.

What else has happened? More character growth. "I was always a very selfish person. And I still am. But I know it now," she says. "I'm freer from fear. I'm learning not to idolize people—pastors, boyfriends. I'm learning to come to God not for what I can get, but to worship him."

For so many years, Zohre feared God's will. God was great, but he was cruel. He would never will any good for her, she suspected. Whenever she glimpsed any loveliness in God or in the Lord Jesus Christ, she ran away. Such hints of caring and beauty were deceiving and not to be trusted. If anything good did happen, she took the credit herself or attributed it to her parents or her friends, never to God. When the Lord Jesus revealed himself more and more through Sarah, Al and others, Zohre remained suspicious. It was only later that she was able to look back, to recognize the many evidences of God's loving providence in her life and to say in wonder, "You mean all the time that was you, God?"

Esmat: The Woman Nobody Wanted

Looking up at the stars, Esmat lay on the board sleeping platform that her family always placed over the garden pond on the hottest nights of the year. Three-year-old Naqi snuggled close. For how much longer? Thumb in mouth, he lay content and secure. How would he sleep when his father, Esmat's ex-husband, took Naqi to his new wife's home? Would Naqi revert to wetting the mattress again? What would his stepmother do? Legally his father had the right to take Naqi. But oh, it was intolerable!

Esmat fled her country, slipping Naqi out with her. Like Ladan, she was married and a mother when she came to Christ. Like Ladan, she came to the United States. But there similarities end. Whereas Ladan was from an influential family, with wealth, networks, and a supportive husband and brothers, Esmat had nobody. New Iranian acquaintances shunned her when they learned of her divorce. So did old friends. So although Esmat thought she was losing her Iranian heritage when she came to Christ—before she met another Iranian believer—she thought she didn't have much to lose.

It was in a Presbyterian church in San Mateo, California, that Esmat stumbled on people who cared for her alone. Although she was proud of being a Muslim and insisted on it for a long time, there came a day when she said, "I don't care about doctrines about God, Christ, heaven or hell. Just give me what is in these people. They care about me, and they care about God. I want to be like them." Today Esmat radiates competence and peace. Far from looking lost or lonely, Esmat looks like a woman who knows where she is going—and who knows that she is loved.

An eighty-two-year-old man was the first Christian to reach out to Esmat. Irving was sitting on a park bench when Esmat and her little boy came to play in the park one afternoon. Irving joked with Naqi and tried to talk with Esmat. He invited them to church. But she spoke little English and didn't understood anything that he said.

Six months later Esmat happened to be walking down the street past Irving's church. For some reason, in the middle of the service Irving got up and went out onto the front steps. He saw Esmat, remembered her, and called out. "Esmat!"

She was startled. Who was this who knew her name? She had forgotten Irving. When he reminded her of their casual encounter and invited her into the church, she stepped in out of politeness and stayed for about ten minutes. That was an appropriate amount of time to spend to repay his kindness, she thought.

Somewhat to her surprise, she found herself back at the church the next Sunday. Well, she told herself, she was lonely. The church seemed to be a clean, well-lighted, warm and happy place. She enjoyed being with all of the nice people there.

She drew clear boundaries, though. "I'm a Muslim," she smiled as she shook the pastor's hand. "I come to church only to learn English."

"Excellent!" he exclaimed. "This is a fine place to improve your English. Let us know how we can help."

Orville and Margaret, retired missionaries in their seventies, took her under their wing. When Naqi got chicken pox, Margaret stayed with him for a whole week while Esmat was at work. Frequently Orville would sit with Esmat while she read the Bible aloud. He critiqued her pronunciation and explained the things that she did not understand.

One sentence in a Sunday sermon stood out: "God is love." That shook her up. She understood the words. But the meaning remained unclear. Yes, God is Creator and Judge, omnipotent and holy. But loving? Not in Esmat's experience.

Some things that the church people did puzzled Esmat. Single women like herself asked for prayer and counsel about their dates and romances. To her, they seemed to view themselves as sex objects. Other church people drank alcohol. Didn't they have respect for their physical bodies? Still, Esmat loved the church and the Bible readings more than she would admit.

"Don't forget that I'm a Muslim," she would remind her fellow parishioners.

Nobody objected. Nobody criticized her. Some Iranians in other churches have heard their culture disparaged and their people dismissed as terrorists. That wasn't Esmat's experience.

During Bible studies and fellowship meetings, she would offer her perspective: "The Qur'an says this—" or "Islam teaches that—."

"That provides some helpful insights, doesn't it?" her fellow discussants would respond.

Margaret invited Esmat to everything going on at church, and she always volunteered to take care of Naqi. Esmat felt so at home. Yet as she increasingly glimpsed Jesus Christ as Lord of the universe, she became increasingly uncomfortable. The more Esmat learned, the more squeezed she felt. "It is hell," she says now, looking back, "from the time when a person starts to believe until the time of their decision." For effective outreach, she counsels, we need to respect people's beliefs and give them time and space.

One night Esmat had a dream. Earlier that day a church member had prayed for her. His words had been beautiful, and his eyes had been kind. *Why couldn't the eyes of the mullahs back home look like that?* she had asked herself. *Why couldn't they convey that kind of love?* That night she dreamed she was in Iran, going down the street dressed in her *chador*. She had to go through a narrow passage. It was lined on both sides by rows of armed guards. Like walls, they hemmed her in. "I want to be free!" she cried to the Lord. At once the walls fell down, and the face of the man who had prayed for her that day showed through the broken wall.

During this period Esmat attended a Communion service.

"This table is for people who want to be healed," the pastor said. "Jesus came for the healing of the brokenhearted. He died for the healing of the nations. He burst out of the category of death, rising to life again, in order to bring us to health. Our wholeness is in him."

Esmat knew she was a walking wound. She hurt. She wanted to be healed. She began to cry. Then she felt something special in that room. She went forward to the table and knelt down. When she touched the table, the warmth of God filled her. The pastor prayed for her. Later she would trace a new integration and sense of wholeness and well-being to that therapeutic incident.

But the God she had known so far in her life was a lawgiver and judge. Who was this God who healed?

Some time later, she was attending a prayer meeting. Suddenly she opened her eyes and looked around. *What am I doing here?* she asked herself. *These aren't my people. This isn't my religion.*

"Someone here is not trusting God," said a man.

Esmat was pierced. God had spoken to her. She felt a weight and began to cry. As she did, it seemed that an invisible man came, touched her and fell down alongside her.

"I'm so tired. I'm in hell," Esmat said to God. "Who am I? Where should I go?"

A verse flashed into her memory: "Jesus answered, 'I am the way and the truth and the life. No one comes to the Father except through me' " (John 14:6).

Esmat fought it. She didn't want to admit that something was changing her. It took her a year to make a decision for Christ. Even when she found herself following Jesus and experiencing his transforming presence, it was some time before she could acknowledge that, even to herself. She didn't want to be a Christian. Yet the only peace she experienced came through the church—nowhere else.

When Esmat was a Muslim, God seemed very strict, always watching what she did wrong. When she met God through Christ, he changed from a strict master to a loving, constant Father. Esmat still gets lonely and tired, weighed down with all the decisions facing a single mother in a strange land. But she says that when she feels most like a leper, when no one wants to get close, God comes and touches her sores. This gives her the confidence that she radiates today.

Parvin: "Daddy, You've Broken My Heart"

Soft folds of aqua-green fabric shimmered in Parvin's full skirt as she floated through her dance. Her arms rippled, all the way to her fingertips. Her chin was balanced, her eyes controlled as she circled and swayed. Behind an easy-looking grace, her pirouettes hid strength built through years of dancing lessons.

That's how I first saw Parvin, during an Iranian cultural evening.

But that loveliness was not the grid through which she viewed herself. Parvin has burned in the special hell which sometimes engulfs poor little rich girls. Now in her mid-twenties, she stands amazed at how God's grace has rescued her. She stands grateful that Christian friends and the Holy Spirit have helped her grow up toward responsible adulthood.

"I never wanted for anything as a child," Parvin remembers. Her father was a physician who owned his own four-story hospital. The family had lots of maids, so she never had to clean up after herself. She and her father were very close. He had high standards for her, but he also flooded her with nice things. She depended on him absolutely. By her own estimation, she was a spoiled, pampered darling with no practical skills when at the age of fourteen she moved with her parents to the United States.

One day two years later everything changed.

Her adored Dad called her into his study. "I have to go back to Iran to manage the hospital," he told her. "You're a grown-up woman now. Take care of your mom. Take care of the house. I'll see you—"

He bought them a house. And he gave them about $100,000 to start a business. So who knew anything about running a business? Parvin's mother couldn't drive. She hardly spoke English. Parvin herself was still playing with Barbie dolls, learning how to load the dishwasher and how to write a check.

That was the situation when Dad left the country. They wouldn't see him again for seven years. By that time he would have married another woman, since it is legal in Iran to have more than one wife. And he would have a new daughter.

In the meantime, his phone calls would become unbearably superficial. "Hi. How are you? I'm fine. Gotta run—"

Pain twisted through this family in still other ways. Parvin had been her father's pet. Whenever her mother had tried to discipline her, her father had butted in, "Leave her alone." So Mom had become the enemy, the killjoy.

But Mom had an alternative. Parvin wasn't an only child. She had an older brother, Sharouf. For some reason, Sharouf and their father never had hit it off. The father alternately disciplined his son, then neglected him. As Sharouf grew angrier, their father grew more disappointed and disgusted. Their mother, on the other hand, idolized Sharouf, and he in turn was close to her. What a family dynamic: Mother and son united against father and daughter!

When Parvin and her parents came to the United States, Sharouf had stayed behind with relatives. At that time he had abandoned all thought of college because he had developed into a chess master. Chess was his life. Teenage Parvin, on the other hand, entertained vague ideas about going to medical school. Naturally this pleased their physician father. Let his son be a washout; his daughter would succeed. So he brought Parvin to the

United States to give her the best educational foundation. Sharouf he left behind.

Imagine, then, how Parvin and her mother felt when both the men in their lives were back in Iran, leaving them stranded in America, stuck with each other. *If it wasn't for you, I wouldn't have to be here at all,* Parvin's mother said to herself as she looked at Parvin. The unspoken words vibrated in the space between them. *If it wasn't for you, I could be back in Iran with my son and husband. Then he wouldn't seek out the company of another woman—*

Who are you to tell me what to do? Parvin said to herself as she looked at her mother. *You never had any authority over me before. Besides, now I have to take care of you. I have to interpret for you. As soon as I get my license, I'll have to drive you everywhere. Why, oh why, can't you be like an ordinary American mom?*

Parvin tumbled down an emotional roller coaster. She started skipping classes in high school, forging her mother's name on written excuses. Although she had begun a premed track, she dropped that. Her grades crashed. Previously she had been an A student. In the end, she barely squeaked through with enough credits to graduate.

Sometimes Parvin and a girlfriend would slip out of school, drive around aimlessly and end up parked under a tree, crying the afternoon away. Parvin even considered suicide.

Sometimes she prayed. Since her early years she had performed the *namaz* in Arabic. Sometimes God seemed close. But prayer was not a blessing to her. It didn't help anything.

Then her brother, Sharouf, arrived in the United States. Their mother was overjoyed and lavished attention on him. Now Parvin felt like the odd one out.

Sharouf was a powder keg of anger. Often he wouldn't say anything to Parvin for days at a time. When he did notice her, it was worse. Her free-wheeling American behavior offended his more conservative Muslim Iranian standards. "Where are you going at this time of night?" he would demand. "What? No, as your elder brother, I can't permit that. I forbid you to go. And take off your coat. What! Look at your blouse! Mother, how can you allow your daughter to dress like that? Have you no shame—"

But Sharouf changed. It was because of Peter, an Iranian follower of Jesus who befriended Sharouf, surly, uncommunicative and bull-headed though he was. Little by little, Peter got him to uncurl, to become more human, to look at the world around him. The day came when Sharouf cared enough to begin to follow the Lord Jesus.

Parvin knew nothing of this. All she knew was that when Sharouf came home now, he would put his arm around her and hug her. "How did your day go?" he would ask. And he would listen. On Valentine's Day he gave her a card in which he had written out the first chapter of the Gospel of John in Persian.

Of course Parvin had talked to Peter over coke and pizza while the family sat around watching TV. Now she began to pay attention. So did her mother. Like Ladan, Parvin had questions about the world in general. "If Christ is the only way, what about the people in Africa?"

Sharouf's communication skills had mellowed only so far. After Parvin had peppered Peter with questions for awhile, Sharouf would yell in exasperation, "Don't you get it *yet?*"

Finally Peter rested his case. "Ask God to show you," he urged.

That night in her bedroom Parvin cried for half an hour. "I don't know what's true," she sobbed. "I want to get close to you, I want to do what's right. I'm going to pray in your name, and I want you to tell me what's true."

The next day, in the course of her nurse's training, she found herself praying in Jesus' name for a seriously sick patient. That night she found herself asking her brother to pray for the man too. A couple of weeks went by, and she discovered that she had slipped into a new worldview and lifestyle. "I didn't know I was born again," she says, "but I was praying in Jesus' name."

So began a pilgrimage of changes and miracles: physical healings, emotional healings, financial healings and relational healings.

A car slammed into the vehicle in which Parvin was riding, and her back was injured. For months she wore a neck brace. Still, over the next two years the pain got worse. Sometimes she couldn't even sleep.

"Not much more we can do," both her orthopedist and physical therapist shrugged. "You'll just have to try to manage the pain."

Nursing requires a strong back. Patients must be lifted, turned over and assisted to walk. Parvin was training to be a nurse.

One day Peter had a vision. Parvin was lying down. Peter was at her feet. Her brother was at her head. They prayed. The Holy Spirit healed her.

So Peter said, "Sharouf, let's pray." And that's just about how it happened. As they prayed, Parvin heard her back crack. She felt a release of pressure. It felt good.

"Did you hear that crack?" Sharouf asked Peter.

"Yes—"

Ever since then, Parvin has had no back pain.

She also has been healed from painful menstrual periods. Every month she had experienced agony. Sometimes she would vomit. Sometimes she had diarrhea. She hurt so much that she would cry and pound on the floor.

An inflamed ovary was diagnosed.

One evening in a Vineyard Fellowship meeting, women with painful menstruation were invited to come forward. As these women were prayed for, Parvin felt warmth flow through her body. Her ovary area quivered.

She had come into the meeting with a prescription in her pocket for a powerful painkiller. That prescription never has been filled. It has not been necessary. Parvin still has discomfort and takes mild medication, but the great pain is gone, thank God.

Even more important, Parvin's relationships with her mother and brother are being healed.

Perhaps Parvin's biggest healing has been in her relation to her dad. Seven years after he left for Iran, her dad returned. Both Parvin and her mother had dreamed of this reunion so often. They had idolized the man. His faults had been swept out of their memories. They had imagined that their life together would pick up right where it had been when they parted. Maybe he too had dreamed of something like that.

In any case, the reality was jarring. Too much water had flowed under the bridge. They all had built new lives. None of them had stayed the same. Also, Parvin's dad may have felt guilty for having abandoned his wife and daughter. To cover his guilt, he lashed out.

"What have you done with all the funds I left for you to invest in a business?" (Of course their business efforts had not been successful; they had no training or experience to build on.) "Why are you living from paycheck to paycheck? You should have profits and interest and dividends rolling in by now. Of all the stupid incompetents—"

Two months later Parvin's dad left for Iran. There was no talk about his ever coming back again.

Parvin's mother was devastated. No longer could she cover her emotional nakedness with illusions. Her man was gone. Once a cherished daughter, loving wife, faithful mother, she was now an abandoned woman. Oh, the shame of it. The loneliness of it. To this day, six years later, she still suspects that people everywhere look at her with scorn and disgust.

Parvin was appalled too, but not just at her father. She was shocked by herself. When her dad had come back, he had treated her like Daddy's little girl. She had missed that so much. She had fallen right into the old routines. Once again they were a sweet twosome. Then, after two short months, he had left. Parvin was furious.

"I had so much anger against him, and against myself for not telling him how angry I was for the way he abandoned me and my mom the first time."

Paradoxically, while Parvin was ashamed of herself, she also was proud when she compared her reaction at her dad's leaving *this* time with her reaction the previous time. "When my father left me at age sixteen, I was like a three-year-old. I didn't know how to do bills, drive or speak to people," she remembers. But now she was able to cope much better. The comfort of the Lord Jesus Christ, Christian friends and many classes at the Vineyard Fellowship had helped her grow up.

Coping skills were needed, not least in the area of their finances. When her dad left this time, he cut off any hope of further support. Parvin had two more years of nursing school. The family had hardly any regular source of income. What to do?

Parvin's mother filed for divorce. The house was awarded to her. Parvin's dad had paid $150,000 in cash when he had bought it. Now they were able to sell it for $350,000. With this money they settled their debts and established a nest egg. Sharouf and Parvin pitched in. Iranian Christian friends helped them with money. The months flew, and in God's good time she had her diploma and a nursing job.

But kids don't get divorced from their dads. Parvin still cared for him. Over time she discovered how to handle her feelings better. She practiced writing letters to her dad, though she didn't mail them. She worked on expressing her true feelings and convictions.

Recently she has had a chance to reach out to her dad. Not long ago he called on the phone. For the first time she was able to say, "Daddy, I'm really upset with you. You've broken my heart. I've lived through hell. I love you. But I need to let you know what I've been through."

He started to cry. She started to cry. Together, ten thousand miles apart, they began to communicate honestly as adults. Letters now are making that communication more explicit.

When I first watched Parvin swirl and pirouette, I had no idea about all these turns in her life. Only later did I discover why this poor little rich girl has so much reason to dance.

6
Family: Sex, Singles, Husbands, Children

Women have very great sexual desires, and that's why a man is always necessary to control them, to keep them from creating all sorts of disorder, to keep them from leading men astray. Why else do we call women *hbel shitan* (the rope of Satan)?" Abdullah was describing human nature to an anthropologist in Morocco. His views are not held by every Muslim, but many would agree with him.

"There are three fundamental elements of which human nature is composed: *ruh*, *nefs* and *aqel*," Abdullah continued. *Ruh* is the soul that comes from God and returns to God. *Nefs* is passion. It corresponds somewhat to the *id* in Western psychology. *Aqel* is "reason, rationality, the ability to use our heads in order to keep our passions from getting hold of us and controlling us. . . . God gave man the freedom to act as he pleases, but he also gave us reason so we would not be completely at the mercy of our *nefs*."[1]

Sex: "The Rope of Satan"

Women have strong *nefs* but weak *aqel*, Abdullah explained. Partly this is due to their feminine nature. Partly this is because women don't have as

much opportunity to develop their reasoning powers and moral discernment, since women have less chance to study Qur'an and pray without
interruption.

But why lump all women together as "the rope of Satan"? Women distract men from God. Such distraction is evil. Also, sex involves physical
messiness. Just like all the other dirt which people must wash off before
they can pray, sexual secretions bar people from God's presence.

Even married sex is a kind of evil, according to Moroccan Fatima Mernissi in her book *Beyond the Veil: Male-Female Dynamics in a Modern
Muslim Society.* Because sex is polluting, the couple having sex should
keep their heads turned away from Mecca. "The symbolism of spatial orientation expresses the antagonism between Allah and the woman. . . .
During the coital embrace, the male is actually embracing a woman, sym-
bol of unreason, disorder, the anti-divine force of nature and disciple of the
devil."[2]

To guard against being distracted from God and idolizing a woman, a
man should pray during sexual intercourse. "It is advisable for the husband
to start by invoking God's name and reciting 'God is one' first of all and
then reciting the *Takbir* 'God is the greater' and the *Tahlil* 'There is no
other divinity but God' and then say, 'In the name of God the very high
and very powerful, make it a good posterity if you decide to make any
come from my kidney.' "[3]

Women are distracting. Women are dirty. Women can be tools of Satan.

Is this low view of sex and of women necessary to orthodox Islam? Not
at all, many would argue. The Qur'an itself teaches positively that God
created people male and female so that they might find mutual affection,
tenderness and love together (Q 30:21). Marriage is an arena of sexual freedom ordained by God. Marriage is "noble and universally necessary
because it brings quiescence, progeny, and continuation of life with purity
and responsibility . . . and facilitates constructive participation in society's
corporate life and mission through socialization of the children," according to an essay in the *Cultural Atlas of Islam.*[4] This essay goes on to contra-
dict Abdullah's and Mernissi's views cited above when it observes, "Islam is
free of the preconception of woman as temptress, as source of evil and
death, or as cause of the fall of humanity."

Whether or not they believe sex glorifies God, Muslim women talk about it a lot. Attracting and keeping a man's attention is the main road to success and security. Breeding and birthing are frequent and focal. Sometimes the women in an extended household may have to compete with one another for material goods or freedoms doled out by their men. In this competition sex is a factor, whether in the form of attractive appearance, sex technique or the ability to bear sons.

On the other hand, Muslim women probably don't see themselves as sex objects as much as men do. Whereas some Moroccan men classify talking with a woman as structured by *nature* (rational man talking with emotional woman), the women who join them in those conversations say that talking with a man is *socially* structured (individuals are using their bargaining skills to negotiate).[5]

Overall, how does a Muslim woman's femaleness shape her destiny? And what are the implications if she comes to Christ? In this chapter we explore these questions. Specifically, we wonder

☐ What did the prophet Muhammad teach about gender, sex and marriage?

☐ What did his successors teach?

☐ Can a single women who follows Jesus thrive in the Muslim world?

☐ If a woman comes to Christ when she is already married to a Muslim, can that marriage thrive?

☐ Can she raise her children in the Lord?

Wives of the Prophet

As an orphan, the prophet Muhammad was shifted around among relatives. He had the good fortune to marry a loving, well-to-do, older widow, Khadijah. For twenty-five years they enjoyed a happy marriage. She capitalized his business ventures and was one of his first religious followers when his teaching began to emerge.

After Khadijah's death, the prophet Muhammad married almost a dozen women. Some were widows of his followers who had been killed in battle. "Although he never established with any of them as deep a spiritual rapport as he had enjoyed with Khadijah, he gave each wife freedom to develop her own talents," according to Naila Minai, a Turkish female scholar.[6] "Saudah, the middle-aged widow of an early Muslim convert, earned a good income with her skill in fine leatherwork. Zaynab, the widow of Muhammad's cousin who was killed at war, was devoted to charitable work and was revered as Mother of the Poor." Umm Salama was an astute political advisor and a religious leader for women's worship. Aysha was deputized to give religious counsel in Muhammad's absence. "A model husband to all of his wives, he helped with the household chores and mended his own clothes," Minai says.

The prophet recommended marrying older women and women of different races. Yet Aysha was only six or seven when they were betrothed and ten when she moved in with her toys. Aysha and Umm Salama, both lovely and both strong, quickly polarized the other wives into opposing camps centered around the pair. Nervous fathers-in-law watched these domestic intrigues as if they were the Dow Jones average. It was during this "overchoice" period, this period of domestic strife, that the prophet Muhammad is thought to have spoken the Qur'anic passages which seem to demean women:

> Men have authority over women because Allah has made the one superior to the others, and because they spend their wealth to maintain them. Good women are obedient. They guard their unseen parts because Allah has guarded them. As for those from whom you fear disobedience, admonish them and send them to beds apart and beat them. Then if they obey you, take no further action against them (Q 4:34).
>
> Your wives are fields for you to plow (Q 2:223).

Various interpretations of these passages have been put forward. Some say the injunction on beating limits a husband's violence: only a light beating is allowed. Whatever the interpretation here, in other areas the prophet Muhammad's teaching seems to have helped women. He prohibited killing baby girls, a common practice where resources were scarce. He insured that daughters receive a regular inheritance. He regularized the divorce process, so that a man could not throw his wife out one week and take her back the next without any cost to himself. Theologically, the sexes were seen to be equal in origin, equal in error and ignorance, and equal in their reception by God.

On the other hand, while a daughter inherits, she inherits only half as much as a son. A woman's testimony in court is worth only half a man's. Women may be subject to corporal punishment in the house. Men have unique rights to concubinage and more rights in divorce. In case of divorce, children go to their father's family after a certain age, which varies from region to region.

This is as far as the prophet Muhammad went in his restrictions. He required modesty but not veils. In the earliest days some women were worship leaders for mixed groups. Muhammad's wives were canonical consultants, helping to formulate the Qur'an and Muslim laws.

Like Muhammad, many strong Muslims have happy marriages. Akbar is a Kuwaiti importer who does most of his business with Iran. Whenever he travels to Tehran he takes his wife, Khadija. Their idea of an evening out is to go to a religious study center and listen to a radical mullah lecture on revolution.

Often they take the children on their trips. Akbar takes a turn minding them in a hotel room, while Khadija enjoys activities at one of the Islamic women's colleges.

"When Khadija decided to do postgraduate work in London, her husband readily rearranged his business to accommodate her," says reporter Geraldine Brooks.[7]

Brooks asked Khadija why their marriage worked so well. "My husband is a good Muslim. He knows what the Quran actually says about relations between men and women, and that is what he lives by. It's as simple as that," Khadija answered.

"The two of them never showed any physical affection in the presence of outsiders," Brooks comments. "But there was electricity in the looks they exchanged and warmth in the way they spoke to each other that made the intensity of their relationship quite obvious."

"Fields For You to Plow"

But don't women suffer under Islam? What about Betty Mahmoody's popular book-turned-movie, *Not Without My Daughter*? What about Jean Sasson's book *Princess*?[8] What about Afghan women under the Taliban regime?

Yes, there are restrictions. In countries like Saudi Arabia, a woman must wear a veil when she goes out. She can't drive a car. If she wants to travel abroad, the government requires her husband's permission. She can't manage a business without men as intermediaries. She can be divorced on a whim, no matter how good a wife she's been—and she may lose her children in the process. She has to accept second wives and concubines, unless she ruled this out in her marriage contract.

In some countries she may be killed with impunity. A BBC documentary entitled *A Matter of Honor* features interviews with rural Pakistani men who have killed their sisters or daughters because a girl was alone with a man, or because a girl wanted to marry for love. The killers defend their actions calmly. Their neighbors stand firmly behind them. Even some village women support them. This documentary was aired in the United States on ABC's *Nightline* on February 16 and 17, 1999. To be fair, the documentary also includes interviews with urbane Pakistanis who hate and deplore such practices.

Sometimes a woman has no choice in her husband. This varies, depending on the "school" or type of Islam, and on the customs of the group. Take the case of Zahra.[9]

"Mother, the Altorkis! They live three days' journey away. If I married Fawzhur, I'd almost never see you. Or Lila. Or Fatimah. Or—"

"Hush, child, look on the positive side. At least they have cousins here. So they do visit—"

"Besides, what do I know of Fawzhur?"

"Of course you remember him as a child, when they would stay with Sheikh Rahman?"

"As a child!"

"He's not a stranger, girl. We know his kin. They vouch for him."

"Hamid and Farouk talk about wild parties in Lebanon—"

"Lebanon isn't here. Even if true, it's by no means uncommon. What men do overseas is a fact of life we have to endure. But here Fawzhur is attentive to his family and causes no shame."

Zahra and Fawzhur were engaged. A marriage contract was signed.

Before the wedding, Zahra panicked. "Mother, I'm sorry. Dad, I'm sorry. I know it's an incredible amount of trouble for you. But I can't go through with it."

They argued. They cajoled. They shut her up in her room. They scorned her. No luck. Zahra wouldn't budge. So, embarrassed and angry, Zahra's father made an appointment with Fawzhur to cancel the marriage contract.

Then he discovered that two could be stubborn. Fawzhur wouldn't budge either. "She agreed. I won't be shamed. I won't release her."

Zahra's father trudged home to persuade his daughter to accept the inevitable.

She wouldn't.

Back again to Fawzhur. "Young man, you have a great future ahead of you. You come from an honorable family. You have charisma, and skills. Nothing should stand in your way. Why entangle yourself any longer with this foolish, unwilling girl? Forget her."

No such luck. Months passed. Zahra's father was chagrined. Here was his beautiful daughter in full bloom. Wearily he tried again. "Young man, to ease the parting, I am prepared to sweeten the deal. Not simply with the return of the betrothal gifts. That of course you will have. But beyond that, I am prepared to add a substantial sum of money—"

Still Fawzhur would not release Zahra from the contract. Eventually he married someone else. Allowed four wives, he could do this without letting Zahra go. Five years later, she remains in never-never land—never truly married, but not unmarried either.

How did the prophet Muhammad's teaching sink to this level? How did such restrictions emerge? It is not uncommon for women to be marginalized as a bureaucracy develops, religious or otherwise. Pioneering movements have room for workers of any gender. But when a movement institutionalizes, positions of power are consolidated and organized hicrarchically. Men tend to step into these positions. Women shift down to being decorative assistants. Their schedules may be full, but their activities become peripheral to the centers of power.[10]

In her book *Womanpower*, Nadia Hijab describes this shift in Jordan. She includes the words of Elizabeth Fernea: "When labor demand was high, ideologies which discouraged women from working outside the home were dismissed as unimportant. But when labor demand was reduced, the ideology re-surfaced and women had less success gaining ground in the workplace."[11] And as we noted earlier, when Jamilah Buhrayd asked about women's opportunities after the revolution she was told, "Why, you will return to your couscous, of course."

How an expanding movement empowers women is evident in the recent history of northern Nigeria. In the 1940s, traveling teachers of the Sufi Tijaniyya order conducted mass initiations. Many of the new members were women. While those with male relatives could learn the faith at home, others needed women teachers. It was this movement that precipitated selected women into Islamic leadership roles as *muqaddama*.[12]

Sidelining women is not unique to Islam. Hindus, Buddhists, Jews, Christians and Muslims all have pigeonholed and stereotyped women at times. It has been argued that Hindu women's status declined after the *Code of Manu* was formulated. Theravada Buddhist women pin their spiritual hopes on their sons' monkhood and on their own rebirth as males. Jewish women who tried to sing the Hallel at the Western Wall in Jerusalem in June 1999 were pelted with large pieces of wood hurled by Jewish men who were praying. In the Christian tradition, Scripture shows that the Lord Jesus clearly championed women. But during the centuries that followed, esteemed theologians such as Aquinas, Augustine and Tertullian categorized women in markedly limiting ways:[13]

> A woman is something defective and accidental. . . . She is a male gone awry. . . . A woman is dominated by her sexual appetite, whereas a man is ruled by reason; and a woman is dependent on the man for everything in life, whereas he depends on her for procreation only. (Aquinas)
>
> A good Christian is found to love in one woman the creature of God whom he desires to be molded again and renewed, but to hate in her the corruptible and mortal sexual connection, i.e., to love in her what is human, to hate in her what pertains to a wife. (Augustine)
>
> You (woman) are the devil's gateway, *you* are the unsealer of that (forbidden) tree; *you* are the first deserter of the divine law; you are she who persuaded him whom the devil was not valiant enough to attack. You destroyed so easily God's image, man. On account of *your* desert, that is death—even the Son of God had to die. (Tertullian)

Given this tendency in religions, it is no surprise that the Hadith and Sharia limit women more than the earlier Qur'an. Today some Muslim

women call for a return to the broader teaching in place of the later restrictions. "Go back to the prophet Muhammad," they say.

In Islam, two reasons for limiting women emerged. First, women are
polluted and polluting. In the face of a God of dazzling purity, bodily processes which secrete substances are unclean. Men, after urinating, defe-
cating, ejaculating semen or touching something ritually unclean, must
wash ceremonially. Women do more: they menstruate, give birth, suckle
infants and clean up children's messes. Menstruating women cannot pray:
God will not hear them. Pregnant and nursing women do not fast. Given a
high birth rate, a woman may miss fasts for years. But every missed prayer
and fast adds to a person's spiritual indebtedness. All in all, then, women
are always "behind" spiritually. And "this (required) abstention from worship is a proof of their deficiency in faith."[14] Even though they may try to
"make up" days of prayer and days of fasting, they never really catch up
with what God requires.

Second, women are passionate, not reasonable. And with their passions,
women ensnare men. They incite men to lust. They distract men from reason and righteousness. It is because of their imbalance of emotions that a
woman's testimony is worth only half a man's. Both biologically and mentally, then, women are less suited to lead, especially religiously.

How do these views of her femininity affect a Muslim woman when she
comes to Christ? Can she flourish as a single woman? as a married
woman? Practical applications will make up the rest of this chapter.

How to Thrive as a Single Woman

"What issues trouble African Muslim women who come to Christ?" I
asked Tokunboh Adeyemo, director of the African Evangelical Association.

"Singleness," he answered. "When a Muslim woman believes, she
sometimes loses a chance for a husband. How can she live in a society
where there are virtually no unmarried women? Can singleness be a calling?"

Most Muslim women are married. Their families and friends help
them find husbands. Occasionally the ruler has required all women to
marry, as in the Kano region of Nigeria in the 1950s and 1960s.[15]

But there are exceptions. A succession of women in some Iraqi tribes have stayed single to preserve ethnic purity, since marrying anyone outside the kin group would have mongrelized the gene pool. In Lebanon, there are communities where some women have stayed single for economic reasons, to keep their landholdings in the family.[16] Many other Muslim women once were married but now are single, either divorced or widowed.

Today a minority of women deliberately choose to be single. Some want to pursue a profession undistracted. They feel life is freer without a husband. Personal taste or even a sense of call to singleness may be factors. Although their families may want them to marry, some women manage to evade that tie.

A flourishing and fulfilled single life in the Muslim world is not impossible. Single women can function successfully. For both local women and missionaries, six principles may help.

☐ Be professional
☐ Fill your mind with godly role models
☐ Develop a network of friends
☐ Nurture children
☐ Recognize that no role is perfect
☐ Welcome the desert of loneliness

Be professional. In *Arab Women in the Field: Studying Your Own Society*, six social scientists tell what it was like to carry out their research in Middle Eastern communities. Although some were married, all lived and worked in the field alone.

To some extent the local people viewed them more as professionals than as women. "It was expected that an educated city woman . . . would be used to sitting and conversing with men," says Camillia Fawzi El-Solh of her work with migrant Egyptian communities in Iraq.[17] Among Circassians in Jordan, where Seteney Shami worked, the tribal council announced, "Until the end of her research, we will treat Seteney as a man."[18] In her classic work "The Woman Fieldworker in Purdah Society," Harriet Papanek found the same acceptance among South Asian Muslim communities.[19] So a single woman who is a teacher, medic, artist, writer or other professional may want to emphasize that role rather than her gender.

Even a woman who gives herself to prayer may be seen as a professional—a saint in the making!

Nevertheless, women and men are not interchangeable in Muslim society. Even those women researchers who talked with men extensively had to adjust to many nuances. Modesty remained crucial, however it was defined. There were suitable times and places for such "professional" conversations, and unsuitable milieus. Coffee shops, for example, tended to be a man's world in many communities.

"The same settler who conversed with me at length in [the public area of] his own home would, if he met me on the public road, confine our contact to a friendly but brief greeting, and hurry off. . . . It was inappropriate of me to linger in a public place and engage someone in a lengthy conversation," according to Fawzi El-Solh.[20] In other societies, other settings and other rules apply.

It was important to be introduced not only as a serious professional woman, but also as a godfearing woman of good family. One researcher took her father along on her first field visit. Another took her mother. A third took her husband. A missionary woman can show photos of her family, mount such photos conspicuously on the wall in her home, and talk frequently, warmly and respectfully about her parents, brothers and sisters, nieces and nephews, and uncles and aunts.

However, some of the researchers described in *Arab Women in the Field* were less free to make contacts with men. They had to seek access to men through the women in the community or through the men in their host family. To brazen their way into the men's world on their own would have been seen as ill-bred and immodest.

Fill your mind with godly role models. Single women have enriched the world and the church through the ages. Nowhere has that been more true than in the Muslim world.

In the 1880s, the gently educated Lilias Trotter went to Algeria to pour out the rest of her life. She witnessed to women and men, nurtured new believers, and wrote, illustrated and distributed Christian publications. She traveled deep into the desert, where she found spiritually hungry people. She cried with those who suffered and even with those who apostatized. She loved Algeria, its people, its cultures and its natural setting. As an artist, she decorated her manuscripts with sketches of the faces and flowers of the desert. She filled her journals with sunsets, rock formations, oases, questions and testimonies of men and women, and promises of God.[21]

Five times early in the twentieth century, Mildred Cable and two single friends crossed the Gobi Desert. They took the gospel to Chinese Muslims who lived in an area, thick with bandits, that lay beyond the Great Wall. The women themselves were kidnapped and held briefly by a famous brigand. Through their efforts, people believed in Christ. Congregations were formed. Today even secular feminists are rediscovering and promoting this brave explorer's books.[22]

Maud Cary was one of the very few missionaries to stick it out in Morocco all through World War II. She was still opening new mission stations at the age of seventy-two, and when a Bible school finally was begun, half the students were fresh believers from her newest station![22]

Long before there were antibiotics and jet travel and diplomatic immunity, single women missionaries and local Bible women were traversing jungles, deserts and mountain ranges to enter the harems and purdah rooms of many countries in order to bring good news to the women inside.[24] Lilias Trotter, Mildred Cable and Maud Cary are role models. So are the Arab and Iranian and Indonesian and African sisters whose stories are told in this book. Scripture is full of women, from the virtuous woman in Proverbs 31 to the women who talked with Jesus face to face. The single woman must nourish her mind with these companions.

Develop a network of friends. Build trusting and caring relationships. Mutually encourage each other to stretch in creativity and service. In *Surviving Without Romance: African Women Tell Their Stories* by Mary Lou Cummings, the reader meets Christian women divorced because they were childless.[25] Yet their lives radiate joy. They took in children, worked to generate income, banded with other church women to serve and to sing, and like one woman named Priscilla, they testify, "Nevertheless, I am praising God! I look back over my life, and I think how I have given up a marriage, my body desires, and having my own children. But God has given me such joy. I am at peace in my old age."

Some churches and missions encourage single women to develop their gifts. Look for such groups. Then follow these strategies:

- [ ] Develop a specialized and needed skill.
- [ ] Set up strong women's groups, so that together you can accomplish something significant .
- [ ] Produce and administer economic resources as women.
- [ ] Find wise older women and men who will mentor and "sponsor" you.
- [ ] Aim to mature into a wise old woman.

And don't forget to play! In her book *Purity Makes the Heart Grow Stronger*, award-winning reporter Julia Duin recommends a range of work, play and rest activities for single people:

- [ ] praise
- [ ] a healthy asceticism (fasting; a simple lifestyle)
- [ ] intercession
- [ ] study
- [ ] artistic creativity
- [ ] sports
- [ ] service to the poor
- [ ] and—surprise!—a good cry now and then[25]

You and your single friends can demonstrate that a chaste life is a fulfilled life. This can be a powerful testimony in the Muslim world.

Nurture children. Nawal is a round, soft, motherly woman who came to Christ at age twenty because of the love she saw in a Christian home. Now she is postmenopausal. She has never married. She has never borne a child. She has never had a home of her own. In her small network of Christians, there was no husband for her. How has Nawal coped? She works as a dorm mother in a government school, surrounded by children. All her stored up mother-love is poured out daily where she works.

Most people need children in their life. Ask the Lord to guide you to some children to whom you can become an "auntie." Everyone will benefit. The harried parents can use a breather. The children themselves will be richer because you have provided another adult role model for them.

Recognize that no role is perfect. Do singles idealize marriage? Sometimes. If a woman's father prohibits her from attending church, she may groan, "If only I was married! If only I had my own home . . ." Yet if she were married, her husband might keep her from church. A single may daydream, "I wouldn't be lonely if I was married!" But many married people are lonely. Marriage can bring great blessings. It can also bring great problems. Every role has strengths and disadvantages. Our call is to love God and our neighbors with all our powers *wherever* we find ourselves.

Welcome the desert of loneliness. Jesus hiked into a desert for forty days at the beginning of his ministry. Paul camped in the backside of Arabia for three years at the beginning of his. They went away to be alone with God. They sought emptiness in order to be filled.

Emptiness makes filling possible. Thomas Merton has defined *celibacy* as "vacancy for God." Many married women crave this space. There are mothers who are alone with God only in the bathroom. There are mothers who can read Scripture only because they keep a Bible open to the same chapter in every room in the house. As they run from one crisis to another, they make it a point to read the next verse in the chapter.

"I understand why the saints were rarely married women," Anne Morrow Lindbergh wrote. "I am convinced it has nothing inherently to do, as I once supposed, with chastity or children. It has to do primarily with distractions. . . . Woman's normal occupations run counter to creative life, or contemplative life, or saintly life."[27]

The apostle Paul warned that distractions would be the bane of married life. All of us, married or single, clutter our lives with idols. Emptying ourselves for God is an ongoing spiritual discipline. If "purity of heart is to will one thing," as Kierkegaard suggested, where does that leave the mother juggling a dozen agendas "with eyes in the back of her head"? Here singles have an edge. The modern world may view singleness as freedom for pleasure. We can see singleness as "vacancy for God." While children may not be tugging at our skirts every waking moment, God is tugging at us. Every day is an opportunity for us to give him delight.

How to Bless a Muslim Husband

"Why do you want to study the Bible with my wife?" the well-dressed Arab man asks Vanessa as they sit in the parlor of his home.

A man who cares for his family *should* ask questions when an outsider wants to begin a regular activity with his wife. It's his responsibility to know what kind of people are in his home. So when Vanessa first visits an Arab woman, she often finds herself cross-examined by the husband.

How many times in my twenty years of ministry have I heard that question? Vanessa says to herself. As always, she answers, "I want to study with your wife so that she will be a better woman." When he sees that Vanessa is decent and her goals are beneficial, often a husband will give permission.

In the beginning God said it was not good for people to be alone. People are meant to live together in communities of meaning, particularly the community of marriage. Muslims recognize this. They don't leave singles to flounder on their own. If needed, the family stands ready to help a young person find a life partner.

Most Muslim women want to marry. Marriage shows that a woman is feminine and desirable. It gives her status. It usually produces children. If all goes well, it gives her a power base that will increase as she grows older. Maybe she will even find love.

But love is not essential. "Love is not important for marriage," says a young Saudi wife. What *is* important? "When a woman gets married, she can have her own home. . . . She can be controlled by one person only instead of many." Because Saudi society makes a woman feel she cannot survive without a man, "many Saudi women look upon marriage as their only way of freedom. Marriage is an identity card for a Saudi woman to enjoy her rights as a human being."[28]

Beauty and sex. Holding a man's attention is a major route to security and benefits. So beauty and sex matter. Yet a woman's body is shamefully polluting, not only physically but also spiritually, from a Muslim perspective. Pollutions at the core of her femininity bar her from prayer and have the potential to distract men from prayer.

Jesus didn't view a woman's body as polluted though. He reached out his hand to a woman who had been bleeding steadily for twelve years (Luke 8). How liberating it is for a Muslim woman to hear that the God who created her body saw that it was good, with all its functions.

A Christian can discuss beauty and sex in this context. Arlene, for example, drops in for an afternoon visit with Arab friends. She finds them blackening their eyelids with kohl and sampling perfumes. Maybe they are preparing to perform erotic dances for all-women audiences at a festival. All the while, they tease each other about sex, gossiping freely.

"Why must they view themselves as sex objects?" Arlene groans. Yet these topics are not a waste of time. They touch women's hearts. They can lead to the Lord Jesus.

"What is true beauty?" Arlene may ask. "Where does it come from? What is maidenly beauty? matronly beauty? aged beauty? What is a woman's worth?" The theme of beauty is rich in Scripture. Many texts may be a basis for meditation and discussion.

And the conversation may turn to the topic of love. What is love? Muslim women watch romantic TV and video dramas. They may read romantic novels, listen to radio dramas and pore over lurid comics. Their heartstrings are tugged when they hear traditional love songs and tales. What a context for teaching about biblical love!

Family planning also is a felt need. One American man working in Saudi Arabia enjoyed a Bible study with four Saudi military officers for several months. The group began when one officer learned that the American had had a vasectomy, and he wanted to know more.

Beauty and sex matter. If a wife becomes more beautiful and more loving as she follows the Lord, surely this will bless her husband. Xahima is an Uzbek believer who anchors her witness in the topic of marriage. A slave to her in-laws, she was deeply unhappy in her own marriage. She cried out to God, "If I was born only for slavery, why am I living on this earth?" *Allah is truth*, she thought. *But where is his truth?*

In her job in the civil service Xahima was promoted repeatedly. Since her home life was so miserable, she hoped to find meaning in her work. But the higher she rose, the dirtier the corruption she uncovered. "In the family I was a slave, but work was no better," she says.

After three children, her husband divorced her. She felt that she was nobody when she was transferred to a new city. Her neighbors, Russian Baptists, helped her. They listened to her story. Then they counseled her from a Christian perspective. For example, to build a strong family, a husband should leave his parents and cleave to his wife.

"Listening is important, but unbelievers do that too," Xahima says. "Believers do more. They explain how to live in this life according to God's laws."

How can I live by God's laws? Impossible! she thought. Her neighbors gave Xahima a Russian-language Bible. When she read it, it didn't make sense. They prayed, and then, she says, "God opened my eyes." Through the local Russian Baptist church, the *Jesus* film, a chance to dialogue with a visiting preacher and a book on the life of Christ in the Uzbek language, Xahima's life changed completely. "I understood that my life was wrong. I saw the right life in Christ."

Now she focuses on her fellow Uzbeks. Her daughter has come to Christ and is a strong witness on her university campus. Xahima shares the gospel by talking about marriage. Righteousness is not only praying and keeping laws, she counsels. It's also building a good family. That's hard to do, but Christ can show us how and empower us to do it.

Children. How do we raise godly children? This is the heart cry of many Muslim parents, just as it is for Christians. An imam in a mosque in Vancouver, Canada, addressed this problem in a sermon. While it's a special dilemma for immigrants to Western countries, he said, families in Muslim countries wrestle with it too. Here is what the imam advised.

> Remember, your children have been entrusted to you by Allah for only a short time, and you will answer to Him for your success or failure to raise them.
>
> Be an example to your children. . . . Remember, your children are watching you.
>
> Don't be so materialistic. Spend less money on material things and spend more money on the Islamic upbringing of your children. . . . If material things, fun times, and the successes of this world are all that parents are seen to value, then naturally these are what the children will come to value. So grow up and recognize what these things are: temporary diversions which are really not very important.
>
> Fathers, your children's upbringing is as much your responsibility as it is their mother's. Don't become so involved with your career or job that you rarely see your children.
>
> Too many parents come home from demanding jobs and then spend their time "relaxing" in front of the TV. . . . Parents, you don't have time to waste in such "relaxation." Spend your time with your children.
>
> Treat your sons and daughters equally and expect high standards of Islamic behavior from both. . . . Parents, sin and its punishment is the same for both males and females. Expect from your sons the same concern for modesty and chastity as you do from your daughters. . . . Be ready to provide

alternative social activities that are Islamically acceptable, even if it is incon-
venient for you. After all, they are your children.

We may die at any time, and then we'll have to face Allah on the Day of
Judgment. Are you prepared?

Raising godly children in today's world is a bewildering challenge.
Muslim teenagers log on to the Internet. Muslim families travel to societies with permissive values. Rock music, individualistic lack of respect for
parents, consumerism and sexual looseness tear at the fabric of traditional
morality. In countries like the United States, Muslim parents are no more
happy about the distribution of condoms in schools or graphic homosex-
ual films in sex education classes than Christian parents are.

This is common ground. A Muslim father wants ethical, respectful,
responsible children. His wife, even if she follows Jesus, wants this too.
She can teach her children truths from the Bible in a way that emphasizes
their character development. Many a father will value this. One Muslim
father in a restricted-access country encourages his children to sing Christian songs. Another is so impressed with his wife's conscientious lifestyle
that he comments, "I've never met another woman like my wife. I'd trust
her anywhere." When the results are beneficial, a man may well say, "Why
rock the boat?"

Relatives. In many countries, the challenges of singleness, husbands
and children are small compared to the challenge of relatives. Gada was
thrown out of her marriage after bearing six children, and her husband
kept the children. It was not her Christian faith that broke up the marriage. It was friction with relatives.

Gada's marriage had been happy. She was her husband's fourth wife.
He had divorced three, one after the other, because none of them had a
baby. But glory be to God, Gada produced one, two, three, four, five, six
children. Without question her husband appreciated her. She had filled
his house and rescued his reputation.

Gada was also blessed by friendship with a foreign teacher. Because of
Liz, Gada had come into personal relationship with God through Christ.

But Gada was plagued by relatives. Not only her husband and six children lived in their small apartment but also her parents. Then one night
her niece showed up at the door after a fight with her husband. What

could they do but take her in? Still, the personalities grated, and Gada scrambled for a solution.

Would her niece's husband take her back? In desperation, Gada made a day trip to consult a fortuneteller. Then she miscalculated. She missed the bus home and had to stay out all night.

This looked immoral. Her husband was so ashamed that he threw her out. After all, he had a lot of experience in casting off wives who displeased him.

Sobs echoed and tears fell in Liz's living room. Gada repented consulting the fortune teller. She ached for her children. What to do? One day she sneaked onto her preschool son's playground and snatched him away. Now at least she had one child.

Meanwhile, as the days passed, Gada grew to be a woman of prayer, whether in Liz's living room or in her own tiny apartment.

Knock! Knock! One morning banging shook Liz's front door. She opened it to Gamal, Gada's husband.

"Come in, come in!" she welcomed him. Had he come to take Gada back?

Not at all. He had come to ask if he could use Liz's phone to call Gada—to ask if she had received the order from the divorce court yet. Apparently he did not have access to a phone that was private enough in his own home.

"Take your time," Liz encouraged him. She left the room, shut the door and fell on her knees, hands wringing.

Gamal took Liz at her word. While she prayed in the next room, Gamal and Gada talked for an hour and a half. The result was a sweet reunion. Gamal tore up the divorce decree, and Gada moved back home.

Like all of us at times, Gada had made a very poor decision. Hers erupted out of stresses with relatives. For better or for worse, relatives play a big role in Muslim women's worlds. On one hand, an extended family can bring richness. In traditional contexts a wife may be closer to other women in the household than to her husband. The women work together. They relax together. In a segregated milieu, they even party together. They share confidences. They help each other in trouble.

Yet these relatives may cause problems for a Christian mother. Take child raising. In some traditional extended families, a mother-in-law may get most of her son's wages. With this money the older woman may buy occult amulets to pin on the children's clothes. She may spoil the children, laughing when they disobey. Even when a little monster throws rocks at the chandelier and pieces tinkle down, the grandmother may hold the mother back with the words, "You can't correct him, because he's small. Besides, he's a little man."

Meanwhile the mother may be kept busy as a drudge of all work, while the grandmother has leisure to spend with the children. It was this treatment, and her resulting hatred of her mother-in-law, that propelled one North African woman to the Lord Jesus. She realized that her hatred was poisoning her.

Yet even in such circumstances, Christian mothers can raise their sons and daughters by a different code. When as newlyweds they find charms placed under their pillows, or, later, in their babies' cribs, they can remove the charms. When illness or disorder accompanies the amulets, they can ask the church elders to pray. Healings have resulted in situations like these.

Although Umm Farouk lives in a restricted-access country and has a Muslim husband, she has raised all her children in the Lord and seen them married to believers. Beyond her family, Umm Farouk has spread her wings over many believing teens and young adults, guiding them with wise counsel. From time to time, she and other believers have been able to set up week-long camps for teens and children. She also has arranged Christian marriages for several pairs of young adults.

Umm Farouk shows us that being an older woman is not all bad. No longer a sex object, an older woman has freedom to be a person. She can interact in society across the spectrum. This is such a positive experience that the two outstanding female Muslim religious leaders in the Sufi order in Kano, Nigeria, both "negotiated early post-menopausal status" in order to minister more freely.[29]

Older Christian women even have opportunities to witness to young men. A proxy mother-son relationship can develop, and this in a milieu where the mother-son relationship is strong. One missionary woman in her forties says, "I learn things a missionary man never would, because these young men would never admit such needs, such weaknesses, to another man."

Relatives can cause problems. Yet in the end, relatives are gifts of God. When extended family members care genuinely for each other, the result is an ambiance of strength and warmth. Its power and beauty hardly can be comprehended by someone who knows only the nuclear family. And many a Muslim comes to Christ because a sister, a brother, a parent or a cousin believes. This is the ideal pattern.

Vahida was an Indian university student when she came to Christ simply through reading the New Testament. She had never met a genuine Christian. Although she was a lone believer, God's Word was fire in her bones. "As soon as I accepted Christ, God put it in my heart to share him," she recalls. Her brother came to mind. There were only the two siblings in the family. She began to pray for Aziz every day. "But I didn't have the guts to share about Christ," she admits.

Within three months, Aziz came to her. "Vahida, I have something to tell you. Do you remember the people who stand at the edge of campus distributing Christian Scriptures? I'm sure you do, because I think I've seen you reading that Scripture now and then. Well, I've been reading it too. And the strangest things have been happening to me . . ." Aziz too had come to Christ.

From that moment Vahida and Aziz began encouraging each other, praying together and sharing what they learned as they read the Bible. When Vahida was about to graduate, their dad began to entertain marriage proposals from suitors' families. Only one proposal pleased Vahida. And that one was unthinkable to their dad. Vahida's and Viju's families had done business together for years. Viju's family was Christian, but that had not bothered anybody—until he asked for her hand in marriage!

By word of mouth and by observation from afar, Viju had learned of Vahida's faith. In the same way she had learned of his commitment to ministry. When his proposal came, she wanted to accept. She tried to explain to her dad. "I'm not marrying Viju because I love him. But if I can't marry a Christian, I'll remain alone."

"Some Christian has brainwashed you," her dad stormed. "What do you know about the world? You're only a young girl. Your mom hasn't been strict enough with you—"

He confiscated her Bible and shipped her off to be confined in a distant relative's home. There she stayed for the next eight months, not going out at all. But in the end Vahida and Viju were allowed to marry. Her brother's support and advocacy played a big part.

Ideally, kin come to Christ together. When I asked an African about Muslim-background women in his country, he said, "Nobody stands out. I can't tell you of any specific cases. We are seeing hundreds believe. But nobody stands out, man or woman. They come as members of their families. Whole families decide together."

How beautiful it is when nobody's conversion stands out. In cultures where important decisions are made corporately, it is natural and appropriate for a household to follow Jesus Christ together. The apostle Paul appealed to this tendency when he challenged the Philippian jailer, "Believe in the Lord Jesus Christ, and you will be saved—you and your household" (Acts 16:31). Centuries earlier, Joshua had called to the Israelites, "Choose for yourselves this day whom you will serve. . . . But as for me and my household, we will serve the LORD" (Joshua 24:15).

Loss of Husband and Children
Sadly, however, Islam so resists the lordship of Jesus that even if relatives first hear the gospel together, they often hold each other back. Individuals must push on privately. When a husband or wife comes to Christ alone, divorce may follow. The believing wife may lose her children, like Maryam in West Africa, whom we'll meet in chapter eight. It is a husband's right to keep the children, especially after they reach the age of seven. Boys may go to their fathers at a younger age, girls at an older. From a Muslim husband's perspective, it is his very concern for the welfare of the family that makes him feel this cut is necessary.

Divorce works both ways. It is not enough to bring a man to Jesus and assume that his wife will follow, as some Western missiologists teach. If the husband becomes a Christian, the wife's family may force a divorce. Even if they don't, she may not necessarily come to Christ. Just as in some countries the believers are mostly women, single or married to Muslim husbands, so in other countries the believers are mostly men, single or married to Muslim wives. Both situations point to an unbalanced evangelism strategy. Given the shortage of Christian witnesses, balance is not always possible. But how beautiful it is when husband and wife come to faith together.

The Family of God

God is not limited to the natural family. When there are no believers in that network, God provides other sisters and brothers. Take Zaynab and Laila. Both are young mothers who live in a country closed to formal Christian witness. Immediately after her conversion, Zaynab started participating in a women's Bible study led by a local woman. Here she met Laila, a recently baptized believer.

One day Zaynab announced her regrets because she was going to have to miss the next study. "Sorry I won't be able to attend the meeting next month," she apologized to the leader. "I have to take Hamid over to France for an appointment at a hospital."

"Is that so?" Laila exclaimed. "As a matter of fact, I too am going to France next month, because my son also has a doctor's appointment."

"What a coincidence!" Zaynab said. "What hospital do you use?"

Zaynab and Laila discovered that they had appointments on the same day, at the same hour, at the same hospital in France, for sons who shared the same medical problem! So these new sisters in Christ, often restricted at home, were able to travel into the larger world together along with their little boys, fellowshiping, questioning, learning and encouraging each other. "God sets the lonely in families" (Psalm 68:6).

"Get a Ouija Board."

Fatma and Mehmed, wife and husband, came to Christ together. They were students from Turkey, studying in the United States. Competent and cosmopolitan, they made friends easily. But when Fatma's mother died, she fell into a pit of grief. "If only I could have been there. If only I could talk to her one more time. Oh my mother—"

Mehmed wondered how to comfort his wife. One day in the Seattle Public Library he found a book titled *How to Contact Dead Souls*. He wondered, *Could this help Fatma?* Could she communicate with her mother, even though her mother had passed on? Mehmed settled into a chair by a window and began to read.

The book told him how to use a ouija board, an occult device for contacting spirits. Mehmed looked up from the book. "Right. That I understand." Ouija boards were known in Turkey. When he left the library, he set off to buy one.

No doubt about it, the ouija board made a difference. Fatma and Mehmed asked questions, and they got answers. A spirit guide named Ali became their personal consultant. Fatma felt she made contact with her mother. The esoteric insights were exhilarating. Yet as time passed, something happened. They lost their appetites. They couldn't sleep. And Fatma began to get strange messages, like one telling her to hit Mehmed over the head with a tennis racquet.

Time to draw the line, Mehmed decided. But how? Now that they had opened Pandora's box, how could they close it? Mehmed was not trained in research for nothing. He located the author of the book, called him up and described their experience. "We bought your book, followed your advice, and look what's happened. Now what do we do?"

"Contact your religious leader," said the author, and hung up the phone.

"Well, *that* was a lot of help. Our religious leader is half a world away," Mehmed muttered. Still, something had to be done. A religious leader. Where could they find one? Hmmm. Wait. Occasionally Fatma attended a Transcendental Meditation group. They had never thought of this as religious. They considered it exercise and relaxation. Now, however, Mehmed wondered if the TM leader could help.

When Mehmed approached him, the TM group leader shook his head. "Frankly, it sounds like a demon has entered Fatma's body. And when that happens, there's nothing you can do," he said.

"That's not true!" Mehmed retorted. "I've seen *The Exorcist* movie, and I know that Christians can get demons out of bodies!"

Nettled, the TM leader agreed to try. He took the pair to the main Unity church downtown. From there they were directed to a local Hindu temple. Here they got some relief. They paid their money and received mantras and ritual instructions. Back home, as they recited the mantras and performed the rituals, the weird messages decreased, but they still were not able to sleep and eat normally.

After a few weeks Mehmed had had enough. "This was all right in a crisis," he told Fatma. "But as a way of life, it's wrong. We know that God is not an idol. God is the holy Creator. God is One. We can't go on like this. It's not the right way for civilized people to live." Finally he came to a conclusion. "Fatma, we've got to go to the Christians. We've tried everything else. There's no other alternative."

Mehmed and Fatma had been friends with Christians for years. In particular, they had enjoyed the company of a some friends who ministered to international students. Through these friends Mehmed and Fatma had heard the gospel. They had no interest in it. But they understood that Christians felt a duty to witness to their faith. So they were willing to listen politely before enjoying a ski weekend or holiday party with these good people. Now, however, as they approached their Christian friends with their dilemma, they knew what they would hear: "First of all, you must open yourselves to Jesus as Lord."

Whether or not the international ministers were in fact this abrupt in their presentation, that was what Mehmed heard. And he was desperate for action.

"Right. We're ready," he nodded.

So the couple prayed to receive Christ as personal Lord and Savior.

Raising his head, Mehmed said briskly, "Fine. Now what about the exorcism?"

This posed a problem. The international ministry team were Presbyterians. Exorcisms were not their forte. Still, they believed in the Holy Spirit. So they pulled themselves together and began to pray. It took some months and help from some Pentecostals, but in the end Mehmed and Fatma were delivered from all oppression. They learned to rebuke in each other any openness to powers other than the Lord Jesus.

Since then Mehmed has graduated from seminary. Today he is the pastor of a Presbyterian church. Together Mehmed and Fatma are the parents of three beautiful children, the first born the year after they came to Christ.

What about Fatma's side of the story? One day I asked her.

"I prayed to receive Christ because my husband told me to," this elegant, college-educated woman answered. "But after that, I decided I must study what we had gotten ourselves into. So I began to read the Bible seriously. Actually, I had read part of it a few years earlier when Mehmed was enrolled in the university in Madison, Wisconsin. A friend gave me a Bible, and I read it to improve my English. Now I began to *study* the Bible. I had the time. I wasn't enrolled in classes just then. So for several hours every day I read the Bible and meditated on it."

"What happened?" I asked.

"One night , almost a year after our conversions, I had a dream," Fatma remembered. "I was in a fast-flowing sewer. I scrambled to get out. But the more I clawed for a hand-hold, the more I was sucked down. Suddenly a great, strong hand came out of nowhere, lifted me up and set me on solid ground. I stood in front of a glorious high throne.

"On the throne was the Lord Jesus. He spoke to me. 'I've taken you out of a filthy place. Now what are you going to do?'

" 'I will read the Bible, and I will teach the Bible,' " I answered him.

And that is what she has been doing—in mother's groups, in church classes, with international students and with her own children.

Fatma came to Christ as a married woman, together with her husband. Others come differently. In God's economy there is a place for singleness, for marriage, for sex, for beauty, for children, for kin. In all cases, however, women are not "ropes of Satan," but people learning to grow in relationships and community.

7
Southeast Asian Sisters

Nona, what's happened to your maid? She sings all the time."

Geared for shopping in the early morning market, plastic bags draped over their arms, Nona and her neighbor had stepped out of their front doors simultaneously.

"That maid of yours"—the neighbor persisted—"she used to look dull, even stupid. Now we hear her singing from morning to night. What's happened to her?"

No question about it, something was different about Bibi.

Bibi: New Stories, New Songs

Nona and her husband, Sartono, ministered to Indonesian university students. The world's fourth-largest nation, Indonesia is the biggest Muslim-majority country. Combined with Malaysia and the southern Philippines, this makes Southeast Asia a major Muslim region.

Nona and Sartono's apartment pulsated with bodies, ideas, questions, appetites. To help serve the steady stream of visitors, Nona employed a couple of servant girls, as did many other educated Indonesians. All the girls were Muslims. Over the years all the girls became Christians. They in turn became channels of God's grace to others.

Bibi was lucky to get a job as Nona's maid. Twenty years old when she came to the city and discovered that her factory job had fallen through, she could have ended up living off garbage. Or she could have been squeezed into prostitution. Tourism, transnational companies, foreign military bases and the desperate lack of jobs all pull women to sell their bodies throughout Southeast Asia. Some of Bibi's friends had ended up on the streets. But thanks be to God, Bibi had a connection that had brought her to Nona's attention just when a maid was needed.

How strange Nona and Sartono's home was, Bibi thought. For one thing, the husband and wife cared for each other. And this love spiraled out to those around them, even to Bibi. Then there was the music. And the stories about God. And the actual experience of union with God that Nona and Sartono seemed to enjoy.

Chop!

Sitting on the woven floor mat, holding the sharp metal adze between her feet, Bibi raised the green coconut to shoulder level and brought it crashing down onto the adze. Then she switched to a smaller implement to scrape out the coconut meat.

Chop!

A slice of slippery white coconut meat slivered off.

Chop!

Hunks of goat meat rose in a mound on the other side of the room, where Sartono wielded the cleaver. Above the neck of his T-shirt, sweat beaded his skin. Small hills of vegetables piled up where Nona and her friends shredded carrots and greens. Smells of shrimp and fish rose from baskets nearby. Here lay bunches of tiny bananas, each bunch shaped like a baseball glove. Over there were hot chili peppers and spices.

Rain drummed on the tin roof, but rain never stopped a party. Wading through flooded streets, the dripping guests would tumble in laughing, rivulets cascading in torrents off their umbrellas and plastic sheets. Voices would rise in anticipation above the noise of the rain's throbbing, amid the piles of goat meat and carrots, around the odors of seafood and spices. It seemed that everybody talked at once, trying to cap each other's jokes.

Under her breath Bibi sang. Getting ready was half the fun.

Chop!

Bibi's rhythmic thunks took her back to the *slametans*, the feasts, of her childhood—to her mother, to her aunts, to her neighbors chopping, chopping. For the really big feasts there had been music and dramas too. In the mysterious dark everyone would gather in rows before the flickering stage, mesmerized by the hypnotic great round tones of the *gamelan* orchestra gongs. Long past midnight the puppets or actors would float in and out of the shadows, now wheedling, now teasing, now thundering. Bibi would fall asleep on her sister's shoulder during the love scenes, sticky peanut candy melting in her hand, and then wake with a start during the crash of the battle scenes.

"Bibi," Nona called out. "You start the rice. I'll finish chopping."

"Yes, ma'am." Bibi hunkered to her feet, located the rice scoop and dipped into the rice bin, humming all the while.

Food. Music. Stories. People milling everywhere, bursting the seams of the house. The parties of her childhood. And that's the way it would be at Nona and Sartono's party tonight. Yet subtly, the stories would be different. The music would be different. The people would be different.

Take the battle between the five Pendawa brothers and the hundred Kurawas from the *Mahabharata* epic. How many times had Bibi watched that? From nine to midnight, the puppet nobles argued their points. Up and down the puppeteer's log in front of his lantern they strutted.

Clowns would pop up to poke fun at pretensions, to raise questions, to ask the unmentionable, to critique the sacred, to mock stuffy local leaders—to force the audience to take a broader view, to "see the forest rather than the trees."

"Inshallah, inshallah, inshallah," the clowns would intone nasally, mocking pious Muslims. Such fundamentalists were too rigid. They saw everything in black and white. They always wanted to argue. Inevitably they were a butt for jokes.

Crash! Inevitably, just as Bibi had snuggled down for the night, the battle would erupt. Puppets would crash together. A gong would clang on and on, powered by the puppeteer's foot pump. The five Pendawa brother puppets, symbolizing the five senses, would hack away at the hundred Kurawas, symbols of our undisciplined impulses. Eventually the five Pendawas would learn to work together. Then they would conquer the hundred Kurawas. Power through self-control: that was the moral of the story.

Was this Muslim? Bibi and all her friends were Muslims. Nearly the whole audience was. The story, however, represented a Hindu-Buddhist worldview. Indonesia's beloved epic dramas are based on stories from the Hindu *Ramayana* and *Mahabharata*. Introduced in the fifth century A.D., Hinduism and Buddhism both preceded Islam in these islands.

In other countries, many Muslims have combined Islam and spiritism. Southeast Asians have gone further, mixing religions with abandon. Indonesia's President Sukarno once announced proudly, "I am a Muslim and a Buddhist and a Hindu and a Christian." Whatever their registered religion, many Indonesians are syncretistic like Sukarno. Bibi's family, for example, considered themselves as Muslim as any Muslims on earth. Yet they didn't fast, pray, pay religious tax or go on pilgrimage. They loved to eat pork.

And much of their worldview was Hindu-Buddhist. Like most Indonesians, they aspired to empty themselves of feelings in order to get close to God and get spiritual power. They aimed for pure peace, untouched by emotion. Feelings are like the Kurawas, distracting. So at an important moment, at a wedding, for example, the bride and groom will sit immobile. "To sit absolutely quiet, without food or sleep, and with your whole mind concentrated on a single imaginary point until it is empty of all thought and sensation—to *tapa*—is the major road to inward strength and outward power," says anthropologist Clifford Geertz.[1] At a funeral the bereaved will apologize if he seems upset. To struggle is crude. To conform gracefully, to be resigned, to be tranquil, to fit harmoniously into the pattern of life and death without passion: this is the true path. Many mystical associations practice mind-emptying spiritual disciplines. The members hope that as they surrender themselves they will flow into union with God.

Getting power by learning to let go, learning not to feel passion: that was the recurring theme of the stories of Bibi's childhood.

How diametrically different were the stories in Nona's house. Take the tale of the ninety-nine sheep. Rinsing the rice, Bibi pondered it again. Ninety-nine sheep were penned safely in a fold. The total flock numbered one hundred. One sheep was lost, wandering somewhere on the mountain. That was no tragedy, surely. There's always some loss in life. Ninety-nine out of a hundred is a fine statistical proportion.

But the shepherd was not tranquil. He was not resigned. He *cared* for the one sheep that was lost. So in the darkness he fumbled his way over the rocky foothills, braving wolves and snakes and pits, searching.

"This is like God searching passionately for us," Nona had explained. "God has not waited for us to flow into union with him. He has visited us in our human situation. He has even gone down to death in order to bring us fresh life. He is active. And he suffers, not just for social leaders, but for those in the lowest jobs. For you, Bibi. Every one of us is valuable to him."

A God who got involved. This touched something in Bibi. From time to time she had wondered how practical it was to aim for emptiness. "Men may aim for tranquility. But servant girls can't," she had decided. "In fact, most hard-working women can't. For sure the pot will boil over, the hungry baby will scream, the laundry will stink and mildew, the trader in the market will cheat if the woman of the house goes around blissfully oblivious."

Aware of gender differences, Nona and Sartono used different Scripture passages in women's Bible studies than they used in men's studies. With men Sartono often read John 1, which tells about the mystical relationship between people and God, the *logos*, the ground of all being. Mysticism is a part of life for many Indonesian men. But with women, including her maids, Nona used Jesus' parables and the stories of his life. His miraculous power and his love touched them. The practical farming and fishing metaphors grabbed their attention too.

If there were stories about the Muslim faith, Bibi had never been privileged to hear them, except for a few vague episodes from the life of the prophet Muhammad. There was no music in the mosque, either. But here somebody was singing every day. And it was not the trance-inducing gong music of the epic dramas. It was music that tickled you into wakefulness, that pulled you into life.

Selamat, peaceful well-being: that had been the core of Bibi's religion. The feasts of her childhood were called *slametan*, and were intended to bring harmony in the community, in the person and in the cosmos. But that harmony comes to us through Jesus, Nona explained: the word for God's salvation in Christ is *keslametan*.

Most riveting was the love Bibi saw in this home. As a Muslim, you worried that your husband might take another wife. If you were an Indonesian woman, that didn't make sense, since Southeast Asian women have been active partners with men for centuries, running businesses and families. Yet even if you stayed monogamous, what did marriage amount to? Husbands and wives often were cool to each other. Why shouldn't they be, if it's bad to have feelings and passions? But Sartono and Nona weren't cool. The way Sartono treated Nona—that's what Bibi hungered for if she ever got married. *That's what marriage should be*, she whispered to herself.

The family's love encompassed Bibi too. She was unusual in that she could read Arabic, having had six years of religious school. Yet she couldn't read Indonesian. Sartono noticed this. So he taught her to read her own language, using Sunday school materials as curriculum.

Bibi couldn't resist. As a child, she had learned a proverb:

A person without a sense of worship
is like a water buffalo listening to an orchestra.

Now, surrounded by the surprising grace of God in stories, music, love and people, could she continue to respond like an animal? No. Bibi came to follow the Lord Jesus Christ. Soon the neighbors were wondering, "Why is that dull servant girl singing all day while she scrubs?"

Gathering banana tree leaves big as elephant ears to use as dinner plates, Bibi smiled and shook her head, amazed. So much had happened. Before she was a Christian she often felt stupid, and people often saw her that way. But in Christ she became more confident. People discovered she was more capable than they had thought. Now if students dropped by when Sartono and Nona weren't home, Bibi welcomed them.

"Please come in," she would smile. "I'm not sure when Nona will be home, but you're welcome to wait awhile. Let me bring you something to drink." And she would sing as she slipped away to the kitchen alcove.

While students relaxed and rested, they unloaded their worries on Bibi.

"I can't do much, but at least I can pray," she would say. Soon she found herself in a counseling ministry.

Since she spent her days in and around the house, Bibi had always joked with the children of the neighborhood. Now she ached to tell them about Jesus. But what did she know? Could she teach? Cleverly, she called in some of her debts. Christian university students had talked her ear off, wrestling with their problems. She had listened, prayed and encouraged. Now she told them, "I'm starting a Bible class in this house for the children of the neighborhood, like the Bible classes that Nona has with students. I need you to teach!"

Stressing mutual obligations, she got her teachers and ran her class.

Nona comments, "As a maidservant enters the kingdom, she becomes a part of the team." Sadly, Nona observes, some Christians don't witness to their servants because they don't want their servants to become equal. In Nona's case, the mistress and servant are seen to have different roles and responsibilities, but the relationship is beneficial for both.

Nona's servants don't usually go to her church. They prefer a church of their peers, where they feel more comfortable. In Indonesia status differences are marked. Bosses and subordinates even use different language expressions. It is easy to exploit servants when such status differences exist. But it is also possible to respect a person's rights within a hierarchy. To figure out how to do so, employers may be driven back to the Scriptures to read about masters and servants. Some have found this an extremely useful exercise.

What will happen when Bibi retires to her village a few years from now? Will she be like Rendra, Nona's former maid? When Rendra went home, it was to a completely Muslim village. She began to tell stories about Jesus to the children. They excitedly told the stories to their parents. Some were drawn to Christ, while others were furious about the non-Muslim teaching.

The local Muslim religious leader reproved Rendra. But it happened that Rendra's uncle was the headman. Family loyalty took precedence. He backed Rendra's right to witness graciously about the prophet Jesus. Today there is a 1000-square-meter church in that village bursting its seams as a result of the witness of this Muslim-background maidservant.

Most Muslim women who come to Christ in Indonesia do not come as lone individuals like Bibi. They come as members of a group like those in Rendra's village. They come with their husbands and children and brothers and sisters. Village Indonesians often make important decisions as groups—households or neighborhoods or communities.

But in the city, where Sartono, Nona and Bibi live, "decisions among urban groups are primarily of a different type; they consist of chain reactions centered around vocations, neighborhoods, classes, and age groups."[2] In either case, whether in the village or the city, witness is not simply one-on-one, oblivious of a friend's social context. A witness is a conscious link in a chain—and sometimes a catalyst for a whole group's turning to Christ.

Rain sloshed down in great vertical sheets, bouncing up again six inches from its impact with the pavement. Inside, mold spread spotty tentacles across clammy walls. Insects wriggled in, searching for some dry place. Outside, gutters overflowed in torrents. Green fronds clutched at the windows. Tendrils poked through cracks. Wherever there was soil, green vegetation lengthened and thickened daily in this land where a papaya tree could grow twelve feet in a season. Everything grew: mosquitos, spirochetes, bacilli, malaria, yaws, hookworm, snakes, but also fruits, rice and vegetables. The rain pounded and pulsed in Bibi's blood. "O joy!" she vibrated to the drumming, "However clammy, however sodden we may be, food bursts out of the ground again, coming from God who is not only our Creator but also our Friend."

Up the stairs feet pounded. *Knock! Knock!*

Rising, Bibi surveyed the scene. All was ready. Song bubbled up inside her. She glided to the door. "Please come in," she smiled.

Irin: Serving the Community from a Position of Strength

"In the name of God, the Merciful, the Compassionate," Irin murmured, as she always did when entering a polluted area. She stepped across the bathroom threshold, poured out water and picked up her washcloth.

Morning mist scarved the hills. Roosters competed in a crowing contest. Hens toddled out to scratch the ground. Then, unbidden, as Irin wiped her face, lines from yesterday's Indonesian literature class drifted into her mind. She threw down her face cloth, disgusted. *Why do my countrymen write poems about merger with God? Why do they fail to keep God separate? Allahu Akbar, God is most great.*

"Irin!"

"Coming, Mother—"

"Please take your grandfather his morning tea."

Not only her grandfather but two of his former students lounged on the front porch surrounded by red hibiscus. Thank God Grandfather kept the true faith in this forest of ignorance that was Indonesia. Through all his years of Qur'anic teaching, he had protected the Divine Law against the pagan crudities of traditional custom. Respect surrounded him now.

Irin's grandfather was a part of the Indonesian minority who are fierce fundamentalists. They cluster in certain ethnic groups. In those places, church growth is very slow. Yet even there, Muslim women can come to Christ. Irin is such a woman.

Her grandfather was her model. She was determined to follow in his steps. Playful though she might look in her tight wraparound sarong skirt with colorful headscarf framing a pretty face, Irin was serious and focused. She intended to serve God and her country through some position of leadership.

Southeast Asian women always have taken a lot of responsibility in their communities. Widespread bilateral kinship structures make women's connections and inheritances as important as men's. Women are active producers in the tropical farming and fishing economies. Women sell garden produce and crafts, and keep the income they earn. Naturally, then, women take it as their right to help shape society. In the twentieth century, local, regional and national women's organizations have networked the country. While it is true that outside powers—European colonists and Islam—have curtailed women's sphere, Indonesian women still exhibit great competency.

As a high school senior, Irin was chosen regional secretary of the Muslim Students Movement. After graduation she entered law school. In due time she took a course in Islamic law.

"What other kinds of ethical bases for law could there be?" she wondered aloud one day.

"Christian law?" her friend Sita suggested. "Marxist law—"

"It would be fun to compare them, to prove what a superior ethical code Islam is for modern people," Irin mused. "Remember our speaker at the prayer meeting last week? Remember how he said the Qur'an contains the core of all modern thought?"

"Right. Hygiene, medicine, chemistry, physics, astronomy—all the necessary rules are in the Qur'an."

"So, without the Qur'an, how can Christian or Marxist law work?" Irin wondered.

"Well, if you want to compare them, I have a Bible, as it happens, " Sita shrugged.

"Can I borrow it?" Irin asked.

With a Bible on loan, Irin began a formidable task. Struggling through the complexities of Leviticus and Romans, she jotted down comparisons between Muslim and Christian law.

This was not her first brush with Christianity. In high school she had had a friend named Mary.

"Why don't you fast?" Irin had asked with great surprise when she found that Mary was eating right through the fast of Ramadan.

"My family is Catholic," Mary explained.

What was Catholic? Not the true faith, Irin soon learned. But Mary remained a friend. One week Irin asked, "Your day of worship is what—Sunday? Could I . . . do you think it would be possible for me to visit your place of worship one time?"

They did go to church together. But Irin's aim was not reverence. Already a budding lawyer, she was determined to find weaknesses in Christianity so she could prove how false it was, so she could poke holes in it.

Now, with the Bible in her lap, her aim was the same. Imagine her surprise, then, as the chapters unrolled. "Abraham is a great man of faith and our spiritual father," she read. *Yes. Ishmael is the "seed of Abraham" in which the world is to be blessed, and the forerunner of the prophets Jacob, Joseph, David, Jesus—wait. What's this?* Isaac? *Isaac is the ancestor of all our Qur'anic prophets? No. It couldn't be.*

And yet, with Irin's honest respect for evidence, she couldn't alter the record to suit her preferences.

How about the genealogy of the prophet Muhammad? He was descended from Ishmael, she had been taught. Sadly, her Bible study didn't show this. Ishmael's descendants simply didn't count for much in the prophetic line.

As she continued reading, she was struck by the prayers. Miriam's prayer. Hannah's prayer. David's prayers. Daniel's. Paul's. Irin was a woman of prayer She knelt down five times a day. But how different from her rote prayers were these biblical conversations with God.

Our Muslim prayer words are all the same, she mused. *But human needs and problems vary from time to time and from person to person. And why—* she cried out in her heart—*why must I pray in Arabic, which I don't really understand, which I've learned by rote?—and which most Indonesians comprehend even less? Why can't we pour out our hearts fully, like these holy people in the Bible?*

Then she shook herself. *Well, never mind.* She returned the Bible to Sita and shelved her interest in comparative law. *Even though Christianity may be more attractive than I'd expected, it would be impossible for me to leave the Islamic faith. As if I would ever want to!* she muttered to herself.

Rijaja burst upon Irin's community, that great festival at the end of the Fast, a holiday as crucial as Christmas in the West. There were colorful new sarongs for everybody in the family. Coconut-and-rice candies. Six kinds of curry. Mass prayers at dawn in the town square. Gifts handed out to the poor. Parties. Visits from long-absent relatives.

At the heart of the activities, everybody asks forgiveness from his superiors. The worker begs pardon from his boss, going to the boss's home and being received with tea and snacks. The student begs pardon from his former teacher, the cured patient from the traditional healer. Children beg pardon from their parents.

Bowing to her parents and grandparents, Irin told herself, *You received the faith of Islam from your ancestors. There is no one among your folks who is not Muslim. You can never leave.*

Four years passed. Irin was striding toward graduation and a job with the government. Then she met Subadjo, a fellow law student who loved Jesus.

Subadjo could argue apologetics. Sometimes mystically inclined students criticized Irin's conservative Islam. "Pilgrimage to Mecca! How misguided! What a waste!" one of them mocked. "The real holy place is within a person, in his inner spirit. I make my pilgrimage to that."

Subadjo cut the foundations from the mystic's argument. "How can inner mysticism provide a demonstrable basis for social ethics? If people just do what feels good—if they believe whatever feels harmonious—with reason thrown out the window, we're prey to clever manipulators!"

Subadjo's realism and care for society attracted Irin. But Subadjo did more than talk. His denomination had an arm that pioneered economic self-help in poor communities. They had small outreaches to the handicapped and even to prostitutes. Quite a remarkable percentage of Indonesia's founding government and professional people had been Christians, Irin learned. Christian doctors and nurses had lived compassion throughout the islands. So had Christian teachers. Christians edited newspapers, wrote poetry, painted. Christian lawyers had helped shape the Constitution. Subadjo was one of these socially concerned citizens. Yet he didn't treat people merely as projects, as many humanitarian lawyers did. In his everyday encounters, Subadjo served society with love.

For quite a while, Irin watched Subadjo's life. Finally she went out, bought a Bible for herself and started to read once more. Jesus' teachings, so full of love, drew her.

Often Irin had prayed the Qur'anic verse, "Oh God, show me your straight and true way."

One afternoon she read the words of Jesus in John 14:6, "I am the way and the truth and the life."

That was it.

Grandfather, heritage—all were superseded. When God points the way, you go: Irin became a Christian. She entered government service, where she worked for eight years. Then she became an administrator and editor for a large and lively church denomination. As a young girl and as a law student, Irin had hoped to serve her society, to work for a set of values that would revitalize her culture. Today, through her writing, speaking and directing, she does just that. The virtues of thrift, hard work, efficient use of time, individual effort and sound business methods, which Irin learned in her serious Muslim family, now are put to use in the service of the Lord Jesus Christ.

Unfortunately Irin isn't as typical as she should be. "The church is more regressed than the rest of the society when it comes to women's leadership. A leading Indonesian evangelical confesses, "We haven't thought about how Christian women can be used fully to the glory of God."

Irin, in the tradition of Indonesian women leaders through the centuries, serves God and her country from a position of strength.

Sitting in the pews are many more potential Irins.

Zaide: Finding Forgiveness

Zaide was a Muslim who heard God through a metaphor—one of the strangest in Scripture.

Graduating with honors from the university, Zaide landed a job in national radio. She went on to do TV advertising, and eventually she became national marketing director for some large companies, making a great deal of money. In her leisure hours she was immersed in music, art, drama, books, clothes, dancing and entertainment. Active in the performing arts, she was a popular amateur singer.

A young man returned from the United States with an M.A. in theater. Soon he was head of a major theater group. Jorum was handsome; he was a good dancer; he knew all about music. He was radical, he tasted everything, he strutted around, and he flirted outrageously. Zaide was hungry for knowledge and experience. She wanted to grow and learn and broaden. They began to date.

Before long Jorum was pressuring her. "Why won't you go all the way with me?" he urged.

"Let's wait for marriage," she said.

"Ha! You put on a facade that you're so sophisticated, but really you're not," he taunted her.

So they had sex. Then she got pregnant. He sent her to a doctor to get an abortion. The doctor deliberately was incompetent. He gave her injection after injection, but nothing happened. Eventually Jorum married Zaide, but he did so reluctantly.

The marriage was not happy. Abuse began to rear its ugly head. And in the evenings Jorum would dress up and go out to night clubs.

"Can't we spend some time together, Jorum?" Zaide would ask.

"I'm going out, and you're not coming with me," he would sneer. "If you want to go out and find your own fun, do it. But not with me."

One night Zaide sat on the steps in the backyard, looked at the stars, and clenched her fists. "I will avenge myself," she swore.

Meanwhile, in spite of her domestic disaster, Zaide's career soared. Moving from one high-paying job to another, she had power over huge budgets. She wrote a nationally recognized magazine column. She appeared on the radio and TV. She drove the latest cars. Many people jumped to do her bidding. And she was proud of all this.

Then she fell in love. Her beloved was a man named Sharif, a very public figure. Zaide abandoned her husband and two children and moved in with Sharif.

She loved Sharif, and she believed he loved her. They had a daughter. Still, Sharif also had a wife, and they continued to have children. In time Zaide began to realize how much she had lost—her good name as well as her children.

Stresses spiraled. Zaide was robbed twice at knife-point. Her car was demolished in a wreck, though she escaped unscathed. At several points she teetered on the brink of bankruptcy. Evil seemed to be stalking her.

More troubling than these external problems, however, was her sense of personal sin. How she longed to be clean before God once again. Turning to religion, she started wearing the veil, praying five times a day and fasting. But her greatest desire was to experience forgiveness from God. She searched the Qur'an for a verse that would wash her clean from her life of sin, but the verses she read condemned her to hell.

One day she encountered a fellow journalist whom she had known for years. As they talked, his peace impressed her. "Bob, what's happening in your life these days?" Zaide asked. "You look so relaxed."

"Well, to be honest, I'm involved in a Bible study group. And on weekends I go to prisons. I talk to drug addicts and other prisoners. I get a lot of fulfillment out of that." Bob's background was not Muslim.

"A Bible study!" she exclaimed. "I haven't seen a Bible in thirty years. Not since school." Zaide had attended an Anglican school for a few years as a young girl.

"I'll find you a Bible," Bob said.

The next day, when she came into her office as usual, all her secretaries looked at her strangely. "Ma'am, a gentleman has left something on your desk," one said.

There was a Bible. Of course the secretaries were thinking, "What's this Muslim woman doing with a Bible?"

But Zaide was touched by Bob's thoughtfulness. *How kind of him to remember our casual conversation and go to the trouble to bring me this book,* she thought.

As it happened, it was the hour for prayer. Usually Zaide retired into her prayer room at this time. Today she picked up the Bible and took it with her so the secretaries wouldn't continue to be distracted. Placing the Bible on a side table, she prepared herself for ritualistic worship. She slipped on the white *telekung* that covered her entire body, leaving bare only her face, which she had wiped clean of any make-up. Then she rolled out the prayer mat.

But she could not focus on her recitations. The nearby Bible broke into her concentration.

In a burst of impatience, she grabbed it, muttering, *If there is a God, let him speak now!* At random she opened the book and read:

Rebuke your mother, rebuke her,
    for she is not my wife
    and I am not her husband.
Let her remove the adulterous look from her face
    and the unfaithfulness from between her breasts.
Otherwise I will strip her naked
    and make her as bare as on the day she was born;
I will make her like a desert,
    turn her into a parched land,
    and slay her with thirst.
I will not show my love to her children,
    because they are the children of adultery.
Their mother has been unfaithful
    and has conceived them in disgrace.
She said, "I will go after my lovers,
    who give me my food and my water,
    my wool and my linen, my oil and my drink." (Hosea 2:2-5)

Zaide's heart was pounding. "This is about *me*," she said, trembling. "*My* child was conceived like this. I abandoned my other children. I chased after a man. And I am a desert."

Hosea is the strange story of a godly man whose wife became a prostitute. He pursued her, at God's direction, and loved her back. They lived a metaphor of God and his people. God's people were faithless, but God went after them and loved them back. God's loving, forgiving faithfulness is what Zaide discovered when she read on. So many promises:

> I will lead her into the desert
> and speak tenderly to her.
> There I will give her back her vineyards,
> and will make the Valley of Achor [trouble] a door of hope.
> There she will sing as in the days of her youth. . . .

> I will betroth you to me forever;
> I will betroth you in righteousness and justice,
> in love and compassion.
> I will betroth you in faithfulness,
> and you will acknowledge the LORD.

> "In that day I will respond,"
> declares the LORD—
> "I will respond to the skies,
> and they will respond to the earth;
> and the earth will respond to the grain,
> the new wine and oil. . . .
> "I will plant her for myself in the land;
> I will show my love to the one I called 'Not my loved one.'
> "I will say to those called 'Not my people,' 'You are my people';
> and they will say, 'You are my God.'" (Hosea 2:14-15, 19-23)

Kneeling, Zaide sobbed for a long time, touched especially by the "door of hope" given to her in verse 15. And such promises of love, compassion, justice and faithfulness. "No man ever gave me an oath like this," she said. And she came to the Lord Jesus Christ then and there.

That was ten years ago. Since then Zaide has taken formal Bible courses. She lives a simple, godfearing life. Two of her children have believed and been baptized, although one has recanted because of political and social pressure.

For the past several years Zaide has been teaching English as a Second Language to atheist Russian Jewish immigrants. Using the Bible as one of her texts, she joyfully introduces them to their father Abraham and to his descendants by faith.

8

Singing Our Theology

My daddy and I were raking the lawn. I was thinking about my grandpa, who had been an Irish immigrant pastor.

"Daddy, did you become a Christian because of your dad's preaching?" I asked.

He leaned on his rake handle and looked off into the distance. "No," he said softly. "I think it was because of my mother's singing."

Sermons and talks are not always the best way to share the good news of the Lord Jesus Christ. Nonlinear approaches—songs, stories, analogies, proverbs—may work better. Symbols often impact us more than syllogisms.

God's revelation of himself is story. The Bible is not primarily doctrines. It is mostly the stories of people who have known God. Jesus used stories a lot of the time.

How do Muslim women learn God's message? Many learn more through imaginative forms than through sermons or systematic Bible studies. Nor is this merely surface-level communication. Balanced teaching, meaty teaching, can be understood and retained when imaginative media are used well.

The Power of Stories

King David once saw another man's wife, took her, had sex with her and eventually had her husband killed. Because he did it so cleverly, no one knew exactly what was going on.

Then God revealed it to Nathan the prophet and sent him to confront the king.

How did Nathan go about this? With theology? With moral arguments? Did he thunder at David, "Thus saith the Lord . . ."?

Not at all. He simply told the king a story.

"There were two neighbors," Nathan began. "A rich man, with great flocks, and a poor man, with one pet lamb. But one day, when the rich man had dinner guests, he took the poor man's pet lamb and served it up as mutton stew."

Perhaps Nathan intended to ask, "What is your judgment? What punishment should be meted out?" But before he could do so, King David roared angrily, "The person who did such a thing must die!"

"Sire, you are the man," Nathan answered. (See 2 Samuel 12:1-7.)

Immediately David was pierced to the heart. He understood at last the ugliness of what he had done. David broke down, repented and, according to tradition, wrote the great Psalm 51. A story had brought the truth home.

Stories have power. They touch us at many levels. Not only our cognitions, but also our sensations and emotions are kindled. Stories are specific. We smell scents, we hear sounds, we feel textures. We are drawn to characters or repulsed by them.

Stories meet our need to be actively involved in learning through discovery. Stories poke us with surprises. "Important truths *must* be expressed through symbols," says Justin Oforo of Tanzania. "If an idea is stated plainly, we don't take it seriously." If a speaker doesn't care enough to package his or her idea attractively, it must not be important, people feel. But when a speaker draws on the resource bank of a people's own symbols, it shows that he or she cares.

Stories show that a speaker respects the audience enough to give them the very best. "Only an uncouth person needs a complete, frank verbal statement," says anthropologist Takie Sugiyama Lebra about Japan. In that country, if you are a person of any refinement, you will find a more indirect, metaphorical, nuanced way to get your point across.

Jean Baird discovered the power of symbolic narrative while swaying on a bridge in the Himalayas.

She met an old man in the middle of a rope bridge high above a river. After they introduced themselves, the old man asked her, "Are you married? Do you have sons?"

"No," Jean answered.

"How terrible!" the old man exclaimed. "Without sons, who will perform your death ritual? Your spirit will wander unappeased. Child, you are no longer young. You will soon be dried up and unable to conceive. This is awful. I wonder—perhaps there is some man in my own village who would be available?"

Stifling laughter and exasperation simultaneously, Jean looked at the old man as they swayed above the river. Suddenly she had an inspiration.

"Tell me, old father, which would be more powerful in performing my death ritual—a son of mine, or a son of God?"

"Well . . . well . . ." he sputtered. "I suppose a son of God would be more powerful."

"Then you don't need to worry about me any more, because the Son of God *has* come and *has* performed my death ritual, and I will not be a wandering spirit."

"But that can't be! You're not dead yet!" he burst out.

"My body isn't dead yet, true," she conceded. "But my spirit has died and been brought to life again through the power of the Son of God who performed my death ritual."

"Then you're all right!" His face broke into a big smile. "You don't need human sons."

Sometimes we can make a point powerfully when we use symbolic language.

Some of our best learning is by analogy. Even if a story's locale is strange, we tend to identify it with our own context by analogy. Since we live in specific circumstances ourselves, we can connect with specific story situations more than with abstractions.

For all of these reasons, stories make excellent teachers. Jesus used stories. In communicating to Muslim women, veteran Pakistan worker

Vivienne Stacey recommends these stories of Jesus:

On sin

- ☐ The Pharisees and the publican: Luke 18:9-14
- ☐ The rich fool (covetousness): Luke 12:16-21
- ☐ Ceremonial and real defilement: Matthew 15:1-20

On God's love and our need to repent

- ☐ The lost sheep: Luke 15:3-7
- ☐ The lost coin: Luke 15: 8-10
- ☐ The lost son: Luke 15:11-32

On the judgment of God

- ☐ The draw-net: Matthew 13:47-50
- ☐ The wheat and the tares: Matthew 13:24-30

On God's way for the salvation of humans

- ☐ The great supper, the garment of righteousness: Luke 14:16-24
- ☐ The wicked tenants: Luke 20:9-18

On the cost of following Christ

- ☐ The hidden treasure: Matthew 13:44
- ☐ The precious pearl: Matthew 13:45-46
- ☐ The house on the sand: Luke 6:48-49

On Christian living and stewardship

- ☐ The two debtors (forgiveness): Luke 7:41-43
- ☐ The unmerciful servant: Matthew 18:23-35
- ☐ The wise steward: Luke 12:42-48
- ☐ The talents: Luke 19:11-27
- ☐ The good Samaritan: Luke 10:30-37
- ☐ The new cloth and the new wine: Luke 5:36-391

In Southeast Asia, Aisha has brought two maids, her nephew and her mother to Christ, using such Bible stories. Aisha is a professional woman.

In the United States Judy shares Bible stories with her Arab housemate and friends. Last Christmas they read together in the Qur'an about Maryam, the mother of Jesus. Then they read in the Bible about the birth of Jesus. Judy finds that her Arab women friends, who are graduate students, aren't very interested in discussing doctrines. But they sometimes like to reflect on Bible stories. And they love to hear stories from Judy's own life, stories about how God has met her at point after point of need.

In North Africa Heather was telling the story of Lazarus to the women sitting around in her neighbor's yard one afternoon. They were enthralled. The daughter of the house, running in and out of the kitchen to check the couscous, kept calling out, "Don't forget, I haven't heard this part! Make sure to tell me tomorrow!"

A. H. has been ministering among Arab women for twenty-five years. Out of her successes and failures, she has crafted a Bible story series for Muslim women. Now resident in Europe, A. H. teaches each group of women for nine months, the length of a school year. This seems to be the extent of time that she can count on her urban friends to stay in one place.

Beginning in the Old Testament, the stories have been chosen to reveal central doctrines and confront major stumblingblocks, but they do this narratively rather than didactically. After telling a story, A. H. does not spell out the implications. She just raises questions. Her friends learn through discovery. Difficult themes are addressed more than once, through multiple stories. A. H.'s curriculum guide, complete with discussion questions, is available.[2]

The beautiful, powerful *Jesus* video—portraying the Gospel of Luke—is available at low cost in 638 languages, including 73 Indian languages, 36 Nigerian languages and 10 varieties of Arabic, such as Sudanese, Chadian, Mauritanian, Moroccan and Algerian.[3]

How do Muslim-background women learn God's message? Many will learn through stories. In time, they will realize that the biblical people can be *their* people, and they can be part of the story too. What an empowering message. Here is a great cloud of witnesses. Here are role models, both positive and negative. Certainly these biblical characters sinned. Yet they found God real and relevant not just in their holy moods but also in their failures. How this comforts a woman. Like David in the Psalms, she may doubt. Like Jeremiah, she may despair. Like Esther, she may be confronted with overwhelming odds. Like Hagar, she may be rejected. Remembering these spiritual foremothers and fathers when she is surrounded by troubles outside and sins inside, she is reminded that nothing can separate her from the love of God. Amid the variety of personalities in the Bible—farmers, soldiers, scholars, religious workers, mothers, childless women, prostitutes, eunuchs—there is a place for her. Although diverse, all are measured by how well they responded to the grace of God in their generation. That's her call too.

When the various Bible characters died, they had not yet received fulfillment of all the promises, according to the book of Hebrews. They were waiting for others. The community was not complete. Today they wait for Muslim-background women to help complete the circle.

What a high call for a daughter of Hagar.

Balanced Teaching

Can we provide balanced teaching if we rely on stories? Which stories matter? How complete does our repertoire of stories need to be? How much should we interpret a story?

Doctrines. Selecting snippets of Scripture that catch our interest is not enough. God has given us minds. He expects us to use them to understand his Word. Believers are to grow up, to mature in their judgment.

One helpful strategy is to consider our stories/lessons in relation to a list of key *doctrines*. These might include the following:

☐ God (theology)
☐ Human nature and the created universe (anthropology)
☐ Jesus and salvation (Christology and soteriology)
☐ Holy Spirit (pneumatology)
☐ Church (ecclesiology)
☐ Completion of God's plan for creation (eschatology)

Each of these doctrines has several crucial dimensions. God, for example, is Creator of the cosmos, its Sustainer, and the Culminator of history at the end of time. God is all-powerful and all-knowing, holy, just, loving and personal. Of course, God is one, as Muslims affirm, and as Jesus himself professed all his life. At the same time God demonstrates in his own being the primacy of personal relationships, in that God is three persons in one.

A skillful storyteller can layer in these themes subtly and unobtrusively. In discussion she can highlight them. Similar themes can be teased out in relation to all the other doctrines. To prepare, the teacher will need a doctrine reference book or Bible dictionary. An excellent model of how to do this is provided by A. H., based on her work with Arab women in Paris.[4]

Disciplines. Another way to balance our teaching is to relate it to a list of Christian *disciplines*, such as worship, prayer, Bible study, fellowship, resisting temptation, repentance and reconciliation, witness and service.

Sometimes a gifted storyteller and a systematic teacher can work together, interweaving their material. This kind of teaching team maximizes everybody's strengths.

Neither doctrines nor disciplines can be pulled out of a Western theology book for universal application. Instead, as we prepare to teach, we must think carefully about how to discuss doctrines, disciplines and stories in the context of common themes: *Muslim themes, cultural themes* and *women's themes.*

Muslim themes. In chapter four we explored a number of Muslim themes.

Cultural themes. To some extent, prevalent themes differ from culture to culture and from group to group within a culture, like fundamentalists or folk religionists. There are nonreligious themes that shape Muslims' lives too. Consider Tim Matheny's list of felt needs among "transitional" Arab men in Lebanon:[5]

☐ Need to solve basic human problems
☐ Need to solve urgent social and communal problems
☐ Need to reconcile modern thought with religion
☐ Need for community
☐ Need for honor
☐ Need to show hospitality
☐ Need for an all-encompassing religion
☐ Need for protection from the evil eye and spirits
☐ Need for blessings
☐ Need for freedom from sickness
☐ Need for freedom from guilt

☐ Need to surrender to God's will
☐ Need to be thankful
☐ Need for inward spiritual vitality
☐ Need to overcome the fear of death
☐ Need for a mediator between God and man
☐ Need for individual freedom
☐ Need for an education

Christian teachers must start from the themes and patterns that matter to people. Consider the first two points in Matheny's list:

☐ Need to solve basic human problems
☐ Need to solve urgent social and communal problems

This strong social concern gives an opening for the gospel quite different from an individualistic Western approach. Of course Christ came to save individuals, not societies. There will be redeemed individuals in heaven, not redeemed societies. Nevertheless, Christ's people bless the societies where they live.

"We [Westerners] usually stress the benefits of salvation for the individual," says Matheny, "but Muslims may be more aware of the needs of society. Goldsmith tells of a Muslim convert who became convicted of the truth of the claims of Christ not because of personal need but because he was deeply conscious of the needs of his people. . . . Might it therefore be right to start our Christian witness in such societies with a message of what Christ can do for a whole society rather than just for the individual believer?"

To find culture themes, we should look for family patterns, economic patterns, communication patterns and value patterns. Among the Kalimantan Kenyah people of Borneo, for example, William Conley finds these key cultural themes:[6]

☐ supernaturalism
☐ communalism
☐ status and rank
☐ children
☐ rice agriculture
☐ riverine orientation

How can Christian teachers tap into such themes? They can use metaphors of rice and rivers, just as Jesus used sheep and bread. Details from these important physical domains can illustrate teaching on economic justice, generosity, service and tithing. When teaching on relationships, they can begin with the Kenyah people's complex patterns regarding communalism, status and rank, and children. Teachings on God, Christ, sin and salvation must be compared and contrasted with the Kenyahs' traditional supernatural beliefs. In fact, Kenyah churches do make use of these themes extensively, as Conley describes in his book *The Kalimantan Kenyah: A Study of Tribal Conversion in Terms of Dynamic Cultural Themes*.

Women's themes. Christian teaching for women must speak to female questions. Are there any universal "women's themes"? Women's experience in most societies is similar in certain ways:

☐ Women nurture.

☐ Women are vulnerable.

☐ Women are interdependent.

☐ Women tell stories.

☐ Women multitask holistically.

Of course these "women's themes" are not absolutes. Some men are more nurturant than some women, for example. We suggest these themes merely to remind ourselves that those who teach women must consider women's needs and hopes.

Take the low-caste Dalit women of India. Long-term missionary John Webster has pondered how well the Church of South India liturgy serves these women. Not too well, he concludes. He comments:

> The opening section of the service, entitled "The Preparation," while quite good at putting autonomous, confident, male professionals "in their place," does three serious things to the Dalit Christian woman. It reinforces both her own sense of distance from an awesome God and the pervasive cultural stereotype of her as an impure, unworthy and sinning person. She is then called a brother, and her presence at worship is explained in very narrow and purely passive terms which completely ignore all that she brings to worship. The prayer of confession misrepresents her situation before God as an autonomous and free person, rather than as a person in bondage to institutionalized sin. . . .
>
> The section entitled "The Ministry of the Word" . . . refers to the poor and

hungry as though they were "others," outside the worshipping congregation rather than as part of "us." . . .

The final section, "The Breaking of the Bread" . . . stresses the unworthiness and uncleanness of the worshipper in the Prayer of Humble Access, and in the concluding thanksgiving assumes that the worshipper indeed has a self to present to God, something which in fact the Dalit Christian woman is struggling constantly to attain and to define. Finally, throughout the entire service a very masculine image of God is presented not only in the specific referents to God (Father, King, He, etc.) but also in its emphasis upon God's majesty, power, will. . . . There is a reference to God's "tender love towards mankind," but otherwise the love (usually in "giving His Son") is that of a distant authoritarian father rather than of a warm, close, empathetic, nurturing and empowering mother.

Webster sums up his findings:

This is quite an ordeal to put a Dalit Christian woman through week after week! Her situation before God is misrepresented, demeaning cultural stereotypes of her are reinforced, and her own person, presence, needs and struggles are ignored rather than affirmed. If this liturgy gets into her subconscious and helps shape her self-image, it is not a means of grace to her but just the opposite. This need not be the case. Liturgy can be changed: alternative words can be substituted so that the value of liturgy is retained and its content made more grace-filled to the Dalit Christian woman.

As alternatives, Webster has written several new prayers. Here is one:

Wonderful God, you have invited us to a life far better than we can imagine. Yet we seem trapped in our present difficulties, overwhelmed by so much that is opposed to you. We are hungry and we are thirsty, but spend our substance and labor on that which does not satisfy. We are easily hurt. We often feel helpless and discouraged. Our hearts are too full of fear, or shame, or anger, false pride and misguided ambition. Forgive us, we pray. We want to return to you; we want your mercy and your pardon, your joy and your peace. May your promised Holy Spirit come to us and so fill our minds and hearts with faith and hope and love that we may walk out of our present bondage in the way which you open up before us, and may give thanks to you in loving service all our days. Make it so, through Jesus Christ we pray. Amen.[7]

Whatever medium we use—stories or sermons, Internet or memorized chants—balanced teaching is essential. Finding the balance is hard but not impossible. In fact, it is not only possible but powerful when we weave doctrines and disciplines together with Muslim, cultural and women's concerns.

Memorizing

"But of course we must disciple them through inductive Bible studies," said the American missionary, after several single Muslim women had opened their hearts to the Lord Jesus.

For the German missionaries on the team, discipling meant a teacher speaking and the new converts listening. They were not familiar with "inductive Bible studies." However, since the Americans had more mission experience, the Germans deferred to their teaching style.

Two months later, all the new believers were jailed, and their Bibles were confiscated. As I write this, they are still in jail.

"Neither of us was right," a German missionary woman sighs now. "We should have helped the women memorize Scripture."

This chapter began with a focus on form—story—and a focus on content—balanced teaching. In the rest of the chapter, we will explore several more forms that impact Muslims powerfully. Memorizing is one form with surprising effectiveness.

In Pakistan a woman medic has seen 640 Muslims come to faith over a thirty-year period. Each new believer immediately is set to memorizing forty-two verses on salvation from the Gospel of John. With this limited resource, an illiterate Baluchi woman, a field laborer, became an effective flaming evangelist all her life long. Others have stretched far beyond the forty-two verses. Motivated partly by contests and prizes, many young Pakistanis in this community have memorized whole books of the Bible, especially Ephesians, Colossians and Philippians. The crowning blessing is that out of this mostly female body of believers, eleven boys have grown up to become pastors in the Pakistani church.

The Lord Jesus came to manhood in a tradition in which memorizing Scripture was "sweeter than honey, more precious than gold." He himself learned a lot of his Scripture in the synagogue as he read it aloud, chanted it and memorized it.

For Muslims, too, silent reading is not the right way to use God's Word.

Scripture must be memorized. Then "the speech of God comes into the storehouse of memory and the currency of our lips," says Kenneth Cragg.[8]

In chapter three we met Susan, who was challenged at a wedding, "Give me your daughter Mary for my son Fazlur!" With her memory full of Scripture, Susan turned the conversation to the "circumcision of the heart." She won everyone's respect as she chanted Scripture aloud.

"But rote memory is mindless!" many Westerners protest. "And people in a fast-changing society don't need outdated facts. We need problem-solving competencies. We don't need information per se. We need skills to find information when we need it."

Yet who can deny the power in the spoken, memorized word? Around the world, where memorization is valued, schoolchildren chant their lessons. Religious adepts murmur their Scriptures aloud. Later, when needed for law or ethics or pleasure, the poetry and the doctrines and the narratives are ready to pull out of the mind.

"Give tongue!" How often the psalmist says that. "I will speak." "Sing aloud." "Make a joyful noise." "Make a loud noise." Tongue, larynx, uvula, lungs and voice box resonate. Eardrums catch the waves of sound. Body energy pours toward God. Mouth and mind together give him glory. Recited in a group, the words nourish the community.

In Muslim countries, the call from the minaret sounds throughout the neighborhood five times a day. It crashes into early morning sleep. Sometimes it jangles in the ears like sounding brass or a clanging cymbal. Yet there is a wrenching poignancy as the cry floats over the city, calling the community together to honor their Creator, hallowing the rhythms of morning, noon and evening.

Allahu Akbar!
Come to prayer.
God is great.
Prayer is better than sleep.

"The chanting of the Quran was so beautiful. Sometimes I'd hear it on the radio and my whole being would go into turmoil," remembers Latifa even after twenty-five years as a Christian.

Muslim women come from a tradition where their sacred scripture is chanted and memorized as a matter of course. They feel honored when they are directed to memorize God's Word, and when their memorization is checked. This is a learning style that should not be devalued.

Songs

Ghinnawa are a popular type of song composed by the Bedouin of Western Egypt and Libya. For at least a hundred years these desert people have been composing in this folk art form. According to anthropologist Lila Abu-Lughod in her book *Veiled Sentiments: Honor and Poetry in a Bedouin Society*, *ghinnawa* songs play a pivotal role in local culture. Specifically, the songs bring balance to the people's worldview.[9]

In daily life these people admire toughness, self-control and honor. But the *ghinnawa* songs ring with markedly different motifs—themes of vulnerability, feeling and caring. The Bedouin don't discuss these sentiments. They simply sing about them. Without these songs Bedouin life would be off kilter, Abu-Lughod argues. It would be an unbalanced and impoverished worldview.

What a rich balance Christian songs can provide for Muslim-background women. Many of these women may not be free to attend church regularly. Christian music tapes in Arabic, Berber, Farsi, Turkish, Swahili, Uzbek, Malay and Hui can help them enormously. A new believer can learn twenty hymns in a week using a cassette tape, according to Viggo Sogaard, author of *Everything You Need to Know for a Cassette Ministry*.[10]

Songs can teach the basic themes of the faith and make them easy to remember. Songs can give a woman words in her own language for Christian doctrines. Songs can provide her with an outlet for celebrating—and an outlet for lament. Songs can connect her with the singing church throughout her ethnic group, and indeed throughout history. When a woman feels alone, when she wants to cry, or when she wants to praise God, what is better than music?[11]

Systematic teaching can be woven through songs. A long-term effort involving both local Bible teachers and local composers is ideal. For example, if ballads are a popular medium, why not sponsor a two-week ballad-writing workshop? Bring together the imaginative specialists and the doctrinal specialists. The result might be, for example, (1) a series of biographical ballads, moving all the way from Adam to the apostle John on the Isle of Patmos, and (2) a series of topical ballads including doctrines *and* local Christian-life issues like

- ☐ happy families
- ☐ protection from spirits
- ☐ peacemaking instead of feuding
- ☐ business ethics
- ☐ dreams and guidance
- ☐ agriculture on God's earth
- ☐ local values—affirming and confronting them

Armed with this body of songs, a mother in her courtyard or a professional woman striding to her bus could sing systematically through the major themes of Scripture, juxtaposed against the cutting issues of the day. She could go through the hours of her day accompanied by Abraham and Hannah, Esther and Jeremiah, Barnabas and Priscilla. And her songs would resonate in the memories of those who heard her sing.

Body Language

People remember more of what they do than what they hear or see. Directed action can be a wonderful teacher, whether through dramas, liturgies or apprenticeships. Even the simplest bodily involvement in coffee shops or sewing clubs has enhanced Christian teaching.

"Give us good theatre, and we'll give you a great people!" is a Moroccan saying. Even in their fledgling churches, various local Christians write plays for Christmas or Easter. Then the church performs the best one. A recent plot featured Abraham and his two wives, for example, and the long purposes of God in preparing the way for the son of Abraham who was also the Son of God.

At short-term Bible schools, North African believers make up skits. One cosmopolitan presentation involved hand puppets. Another pantomimed a telephone call between North Africa and France, playing on double meanings, giving Christians a chance to laugh at their oppression.

"How are the little ones?"

"They're growing. Oh, and you know the two that were lost?"

"Right."

"We found one, and he came back so dirty that we threw him in the water!" This was a reference to baptism.

In South and Southeast Asia, where drama sometimes is more important than food, Christians have dramatized Old Testament and New Testament narratives. In India, for example, a Christian troupe developed a series of episodes spanning from Abraham to Nehemiah. Forty-eight songs were composed. Dozens of dances were choreographed. The performances lasted for several nights, five hours a night.

Later this troupe dramatized the life of Christ in a similar series. As with Hindu actors, the actors were dedicated to God on stage. Unlike the Hindus, they were dedicated to the Lord Jesus Christ. During the performances, volunteer prayer intercessors from local congregations mingled throughout the audience. Afterward, the troupe sometimes was able to team up with Bible sellers who walked through the community asking, "Did you understand what you saw?" Around five thousand people watched the plays each night.

A Christian youth group in Pakistan performed a play about the prodigal son a few years ago. During their practices, several Muslim friends asked, "May we join you? May we be part of the cast too?" The Christians welcomed them. As the Muslims discussed what the play meant, and as they themselves took on parts, the gospel truths of this parable became clear.

Debate

"Susan! Give me your daughter Mary for my son Fazlur!" Farza challenged Susan in chapter three.

Susan roared back, "Great! We would be honored. And—to sweeten the tie—you give me your daughter Fatimah for my son John!"

The women attending the wedding pounded the floor with approval at this repartee, and the informal battle of words and wits was on. Eventually Susan led the talk around to the subject of circumcision of the heart. "You must build up to a rhetorical point," Susan commented later.

Overstatement seems to be part of Arabic conversational style. "Arabs are forced to overassert and exaggerate in almost all types of communication if they do not wish to be misunderstood," says Eli Shouby in an article on the effect of the Arabic language on thought.[12]

Elizabeth Fernea found this out when she went to Iraq with her anthropologist husband. She spent her days with the women in the local sheikh's harem. They dried dates together, embroidered, scurried under veils on special outings and relaxed over unending cups of tea and coffee. To these women she sent her servant with a cry for help whenever a household disaster threatened. They became her friends.

Several months after her arrival, something irritated Elizabeth. She flared up and turned on another woman with a sharp retort.

Immediately she was ashamed. Had she torn her rapport with her friends?

By no means. They sat up, took a second look and nudged each other. "She's got guts after all!" they chuckled.

In the days that followed, Elizabeth was included in more serious conversations. She discovered that, while these women liked satire, sarcasm, jokes and vigorous repartee, they had found her sweet, gentle, adaptive, gracious—and boring! Like Susan, Elizabeth learned to adopt a more vigorous Arab speaking style.[13]

At a more formal level, debates can be classified into various types. One genre that pops up in cultures from Kazakhstan to the Amazon rain forest is the stylized song debate. In several places where Christians have been invited into such song jousts, large groups of people have come to Christ following the event, and enduring churches have taken root.

One of the biggest groups of Filipino Muslims, the Maguindanao, enjoy all-night song debates called *dayang-dayangs*. The performers are two women and a man, or two men and a woman. The story line is a romantic narrative.

Several years ago a group of Maguindanao returned from Egypt where they had been studying on Egyptian scholarships. They came home charged with zeal to reform Filipino Islam. One of their targets was the *dayang-dayangs*. "These are abominations!" they thundered. "Men and women performing together? Romantic content? This is worse than pornographic movies," they said. "Foreigners make those movies. That's not our fault. But we Maguindanao make the *dayang-dayangs*."

Did they persuade the Maguindanao Muslims to abandon their song debates? Not at all. Even when an imam was called in to mediate, he supported the song debates. He made the withering remark, "Allah revealed himself to the Arabs precisely because the Arabs were so wicked. Islamization is not Arabization."

Groups of Filipinos have come to Christ through song debates. As far as I know, this has not happened among the Maguindanao. But it may.

Finally, a very different kind of debate is available in Internet chat rooms. Most Muslim women don't have access to these. A computer costs more than eight years' income in Bangladesh, for example. On the other hand, student and professional Muslim women use the Internet a lot. Christians need to meet them here. Indonesian students have done this. Over the Internet, Muslim and Christian Indonesians have been able to discuss their faiths with a frankness that would not have been tolerated in public face-to-face encounters.

In debates, as in life, we must speak with respect. Sensitive subjects include a person's own honor, the honor of her family, the honor of the prophet Muhammad, Palestine and America on the world scene. It is never profitable to say anything critical about the prophet Muhammad. Instead you can say, "I am no authority on the prophet Muhammad. What I *can* talk about is the Lord Jesus."

Within such limits, lively exchanges usually are welcome. "Arab Muslims don't appreciate 'apologetics' as much as they do 'aggressoletics'!" says an Egyptian believer.

Picture Language

"Bedouins are sensitive to the graces and evocative power of oral textual elements such as sound, alliteration, intonation, and rhythm . . . metaphors and new images . . . even familiar and ordinary images . . . derive great connotative richness from subliminal intertextual comparisons. Individuals know so many poems that each new one undoubtedly evokes image-traces and feeling-traces from others with shared words, phrases, or themes," says anthropologist Lila Abu-Lughod.[14]

Nothing important in such cultures should be communicated without attention to style. This need not be elaborate. Local proverbs may provide all that we need. In Pakistan, Vivienne Stacey has used these proverbs as springboards for conversations about God:

"One fish makes the whole pond dirty."

"The Quran under his arm and his eye on the bullock."

"Having eaten seven hundred mice, the cat goes to Mecca."

"No theft, friendship or service takes place without a go-between."

Even sermons—especially sermons—need picture language. The finest sermons in the Muslim world are full of pictures. Consider these from a sermon in rural India, based on Isaiah 12:3: "With joy you will draw water from the wells of salvation."

1. *The dry well.* Strongly built with stone and cement, equipped with pulley and rope—but without water. Represents the nominal Christian who has all the outward appearances of Christianity but has not received the water of salvation.

2. *The monsoon well.* Full of water during the rainy season but dry during the summer. Represents the unsteady Christian, who is full of zeal at times and indifferent at others.

3. *The closed well.* Once it was a good well, but later it was filled in and closed. Represents the backslider, who once knew the Lord but has allowed sin to come into his life and crowd out the water of salvation. What is needed is to clean out the well and allow the water of salvation to flow in again.

4. *The caste well.* Has plenty of water, but people of another caste are not permitted to draw from it. Represents the selfish Christian, who has received the water of salvation but does not share it with others.

5. *The artesian well.* Always full of fresh water, in season and out of season. Represents the Spirit-filled life, which draws on all the resources of God and brings rich blessing to the lives of others.[15]

In another sermon from rural India, preached against the backdrop of sheep and goats scratching around the village, these were the points made:

1. Note the head of the two animals. The sheep usually goes around with its head down, but the goat with its head high in the air. The sheep stands for humility, the goat for pride. God's people are humble and meek in spirit; the devil's followers strut with their heads in the air, proud, arrogant, self-conceited.

2. Note the horns. The horns of the sheep are usually curved and blunt;

those of the goat are straight and sharp. Sheep are generally harmless, while goats love to prance around butting one another. In the same way, God's people are peaceful and loving; Satan's followers are stubborn and quarrelsome.

3. *Note the grazing habits.* Sheep generally keep together in a huddle. Where one goes, all go. Thus it is easy for one shepherd to take care of a large flock of sheep. As for the goats, each one goes its own way. This makes it hard for the goatherd to look after them. And so among God's people there is found unity and fellowship. They will readily follow the Shepherd. As for the devil's crowd, each one is for himself. There are often confusion, division and strife. This makes things difficult for the pastor.

4. *Note the flesh of the animals.* The meat of the sheep is tender; that of the goat is tough. The believer is tenderhearted; he quickly responds to the gospel message. The sinner is hardened in mind and heart. He is rebellious and obstinate.

5. *Note the hair of the animals.* The sheep grows long, soft wool; goat hair is short and stiff. The sheep works for 365 days in the year, giving us beautiful wool to provide blankets and clothing. Goat hair is useless. Children of God are generous and bring blessing to others, while children of Satan are selfish and live only for themselves.[16]

In North Africa, sermons are treasured. "Every Easter we remember, through discussion, the good Easter sermons we've heard," says one rural Moroccan. "We struggle to see who can remember the most, and we egg each other on. We also vie to remember good apologetic arguments that we've heard." When one Moroccan leader died, his widow repeated his sermons for weeks afterward. In this outgoing way she worked through her grief and at the same time honored him with a vibrant memorial.

Where oral literary devices are used like this in order to help people remember points, we should choose picturesque words. Scripture ripples with picture language. The grapes of wrath. The whore of Babylon. Images of love in the Song of Solomon. Jesus' pithy aphorisms. It was the pictures in Hosea that awakened Zaide in chapter six. When she read about parched land, desert, nakedness, food and water, wool and linen, oil and drink, it was the picture language that pierced her veneer.

Not many of us are great poets. But all of us can pray for the Lord to raise up local poets and composers and performers just as specifically as we pray for evangelists and teachers and medics. We can memorize a stock of local proverbs. And we can try to hone the quality of our imaginations. The book of Proverbs and the parables of Jesus are good places to start.

The Way We Learn

How do women learn? How do *all* people learn? Aristotle identified three strategies for teaching and learning: propositions, poetry and practice.

Westerners have developed propositional arguments. Now we must learn to teach through picture language and directed action. Women — up to our elbows in earthy, everyday crises — need more than systematic theology. We need pictures and activities as well. All are crucial parts of the way we learn.

For me this is personal. Where would I be without my grandmother's singing?

9
African Sisters

F ifteen years old, Maryam lost her baby because of her faith in Christ.
   She was ten when she first heard about the Lord Jesus. She had poked
her friend Fatima: "What's the crowd?" They squinted at a cloud of dust
shrouding dim human shapes under a clump of *eedi* trees.

"Let's go see," Fatima nodded.

Maryam and Fatima were Fulanis. This population of twenty million
migrates across several West African countries where scrub trees poke
up out of dirt and sand to shade their herds. Fulanis trace their ancestry
to the great civilizations of West Africa which flourished before the
European slave trade. Outstanding Fulani leaders in the early 1800s
drew them into regional Islamic wars of conquest, remembered now
with pride. Because of this history, being Fulani generally means being
Muslim. Throughout the decades many have settled in towns. Some of
these town Fulani are strict fundamentalists, the women veiled and shut
in. But the women in Maryam's tribe traveled freely and worked
unveiled.

Maryam: Torn from Her Baby

"God is the herder who knows every cow by name," Maryam heard as they sidled up to the edge of the group under the trees. "God knows me. He knows you. He calls you by your personal name—"

What a startling thought! Maryam's father and brothers knew many cows by name. They knew every cow's ancestry for several generations. They could call a cow, and it might come to them out of their herd. But Allah didn't call her by name. She was a speck in his creation. If the spirits ever called her by name, she would dissolve in fright. Scorpion bites, madness, evil winds—those were what the spirits brought. Maryam shivered.

Under the elbows of her uncles, Maryam peered out. Ho! Here was a black man, round-faced, thick-chested. Not elegantly tall and slim like her willowy people. By his accent, a Hausa. But he was speaking Fulani, and the book he was reading from was in the Fulani language.

Every day when the evangelist showed up, Maryam slipped away to listen. That meant she had to get up extra early. Daily she had to scrounge the grassland for burnable wood. She walked miles. Sometimes the heat was 120 degrees. After gathering enough firewood, Maryam and her sister would go to wait their turn at the 130-foot-deep well where men used animal power to haul up 30-liter skins full of water. Together the girls would lug home a few precious gallons, delighting in the rare drops that splashed on their dusty feet. Then Maryam would milk the cows, the camels, the goats. As impatient baby animals bleated and butted around her feet, blocking her moves, she would hurry to pour out milk for them. Shearing and spinning and weaving and embroidery, cosmetic manufacture, calabash decorating and utensil manufacture, childcare, cooking and serving—these rounded out Maryam's days. Most of her hours were spent either grinding millet or packing and unpacking for their constant migrations.

Yet somehow Maryam would make time to stroll toward the *eedi* trees and eavesdrop on the strange words about God.

"Where's that girl?" Her mother would scan the horizon. "Is that her over there by the trees?" Then the woman would glance around the camp, and shrug. "Well, she's gathered the wood. She's hauled the water. She's pounded the millet flour. So let her listen. I wonder what she finds so interesting?"

What Maryam found interesting were the stories about the blessing of God. For Fulani, there is nothing more blessed than to have lots of children, lots of cattle and an honorable life. In the beginning, Maryam learned, God told people, "Have children. Take charge over animals." The prophet Adam named all the animals. The prophet Abel began animal sacrifices. The prophet Noah corralled the most amazing herd in history! The prophet Abraham migrated with enormous herds. The prophet David was brought in from herding to be anointed king. What a noble heritage Maryam's people followed.

More strange were the stories about the prophet Jesus. He sounded like an ideal Fulani. Maryam's people valued endurance and self-control, a trait called *munyal*. No matter what they suffered, they would put up a strong front. To toughen young men, they put them through a *soro* ceremony. Here the men whipped each other. Everyone would act like he enjoyed the whipping. Today nations like Nigeria have banned *soro* rites. Nevertheless, the roving Fulani could always find another location in which to perform the ceremonies. Without the *soro*, they believed, their young men wouldn't be tough enough.

Now Maryam heard that the prophet Jesus bore thirty-nine lashes without opening his mouth. What *munyal*.

Fulani also value *hakkiilo*—wise, hospitable, prudent forethought in interactions. *Hakkiilo* means knowing how to handle difficult situations between people. The prophet Jesus seemed to shine at *hakkiilo* too. Even at the age of twelve he argued skillfully with the wisest elders in his tribe. By the time he was a grown man, the most clever lawyers could not outsmart him.

One day the Hausa evangelist was confronted by a listener who had been lounging under the tree. "Jesus is God's prophet? What does Jesus have to do with the Fulani?" the listener scoffed. "If a man became a Christian, he would lose his Fulani heritage!"[1]

"Is that so?" retorted the evangelist. "May I ask you: In what language do you pray?"

"Arabic," answered the scoffer.

"Ho!" responded the evangelist. "But I as a Christian have prayed with you in the Fulani language. May I ask you further: What tribe was Moses who gave us the Torah?"

"Israelite," the startled scoffer answered.

"What tribe was David who gave us the Psalms?" pursued the evangelist.

"Israelite."

"What tribe was Jesus who gave us the gospel?"

"Israelite."

"What language do you read them in?"

"Arabic."

"But I as a Christian read them in the Fulani language," the evangelist pointed out. "Which of us has given up his heritage?"[2]

"True," Maryam murmured thoughtfully. She was an intelligent girl. And she was not afraid to think. In her own quiet way she had *hakkiilo* and *munyal* too, though she didn't know it. In time that would be tested. She would go through her own spiritual, social and physical *soro*.

Now and then Maryam traveled to town with other womenfolk to sell weavings, dairy products and desert herbs. Twice they passed a church in worship. Drums thudded, and the mellow tones of the *balafon*, the local marimba, vibrated alongside the crooning of the Christians. Slowing her pace, Maryam peered in the open church door. Women in colorful robes and headcloths—red, blue, yellow, green—clapped and swayed. Men raised their hands. How different from quiet Muslim prayer. Once in the dusk she came across a congregation heading for a baptism at the river. Again the drums, the singing, the clapping. This time the Christians wore white and carried candles against the dark. Out of the gloom their faces glowed. Maryam studied a girl her age. Did *she* hear God call her by name?

When she was scarcely out of her childhood, Maryam's wedding was celebrated. When dark clouds swell the sky at rainy season, then it is wedding time. When life-giving water smoothes out the cracks in the earth, when huge drops pound like jackhammers, bouncing up nearly a foot, when all the animal kingdom pulses with new energy—herds and flocks and insects and snakes—then people know that life will go on for another year. Herders who have searched for pasture in ever widening circles can come home. There will be water for all in the central wells. For a season the home pasture will support the whole group. Now it is time for weddings. It is time for new babies to be conceived. There is hope.

At birth Maryam had been betrothed to Noji. Now in her thirteenth year they were married. Maryam's hair was buttered and braided, the braids arranged in layers elaborately. A fuzzy topknot puffed out in front. Eight pairs of heavy gold earrings hung to her shoulders. Special talismans protected her from evil spirits. Her mother haggled with the herbalist for love charms to make her pleasing to Noji. Oh, it was fine—arrayed as she was in her new multicolored skirt and sleeveless blouse and turban, hand-woven and individually embroidered—it was fine to carry around a great calabash of milk from which the guests drank one by one. What a party. They sang. They danced. They sat spellbound before skilled storytellers. They gorged on fresh roast meat. They greeted long-lost cousins. They caught up on a year's gossip.

Was it the love charms? Was it the blessing of God? In any case, Maryam and Noji were happy together, and a year later at the rainy season celebrations, drums pounded and wrist castanets clicked for Woma, Maryam's new baby boy.

Now, with Woma bouncing on her back, Maryam would sway proudly through the market, past goats, jeeps, brightly dressed town matrons in flowing *boubous* and matching turbans, men more soberly garbed in ankle-length grey robes, and svelte young professionals wearing sunglasses and off-the-shoulder French fashions as they teetered around on motorcycles.

It was in the fullness of her joy that Maryam heard God call her name.

Was it a vision? Did the teachings and the stories fall together in such a way that they could not be denied? Was it the character of Christians, the evangelist, the townspeople? I do not have the details. What *is* clear is that Maryam, having heard the gospel from itinerant Hausa evangelists over a period of five years, decided at age fifteen that she must confess Jesus Christ as Lord.

The guillotine fell. Noji disowned her and threw her out. His family tore baby Woma from her arms.

They tried to reason with her first. Her husband tried, her family tried, the community elders tried. They beat her, mildly poisoned her and threatened worse. Finally they convened a *sharia* court. Here her marriage was dissolved, and her child was taken.

At age fifteen Maryam lost both husband and baby because of her faith in Christ. Who could have predicted, seeing her then in the depth of her loss, that a dozen years later she would have graduated from Bible school at the top of her class? That she would become the wife of an evangelist, and an evangelist in her own right? And that she would be the mother of eight healthy children? But that is what happened.

Maryam suffered her own *soro*, a *soro* of the spirit. She came through with *munyal*. Today Sister Maryam is a mature Fulani with a full life, working actively in her home and in her community for the Lord Jesus.

Saulati: "Should I Get Baptized?"

The question bounced around in Saulati's head as she pushed her plastic tray along metal rungs in the university cafeteria. *Should I get baptized?*

"Rice. And some of—" Saulati pointed with her chin at a Chinese meat and vegetable mix, the tastiest option for her "—some of that, please."

Now she would have to find a free table. Cautiously she would try the food. Then she would dress again in layers: coat, gloves, scarf, hat, boots. Trudging through the snow and whipping wind of Minnesota, she would plod to class, then to the library. What a place for a woman from the palm-lined shores of East Africa.

She had not been given a choice. Somehow Saulati had been gifted with brains. As a university lecturer in computer science, she had been selected by her government to study for the master's degree in America. You didn't refuse a government scholarship. First, the country's need was too great. Only half the population was literate. The national university itself was just twenty-five years old. Everybody who *could* teach had a moral obligation to do so. And if you got a chance to become a better teacher, how could you say no? Besides, neither the current one-party government nor the traditional society which had preceded it made much allowance for individuals to follow their own private paths.

So here she was, on a continent of snow.

Yet here such surprising things had happened that now she faced the question "Should I get baptized?"

Wood smoke from cooking fires mingled with the pungent aroma of roasting plantains, tropical flowers, and chicken and goat dung in the community where Saulati grew up. Usually she stayed in her father's home. Sometimes she visited her grandmother's home, where her mother lived, since Saulati's father—like her grandfather before him—had gotten a divorce when he chose a younger wife.

In the early mornings Saulati's father would walk to the mosque, greeting friends who joined him in the lanes. The name of God fresh on their lips, they would stroll home for their first cups of tea.

"What shall we do with you, girl?" her father mused one morning. Behind the wavery steam rising from his teacup, his face looked softer and more mysterious than usual.

"Me, Father?" she blinked.

"You are my eldest. You must go to school."

"A great pity we don't have a Qur'anic school attached to the mosque," said her uncle over his tea.

"A great loss," her father agreed. "Never mind. We must make do with what is at hand." He looked down at Saulati. "You must go to the Catholic school, daughter."

So she was whisked off to the tailor to have a fresh school uniform sewed, her stepmother in charge. A satchel. A lunch packet. All insignia of a new world. She felt important and scared.

"What are you learning?" her father would ask her in the mornings.

"One plus one . . . Two plus two . . ."

"Yes," her father would nod. "What else?"

"A, B, C, D . . ."

"Yes," he would approve. "And—?"

"Hail Mary, full of grace, blessed art thou among women . . ." she recited one morning.

"Ho! What was that?" he barked.

"The prayer, Father."

"Daughter, you have known the true prayers since you were four years old. You know the ablutions. I myself have taught you."

"Yes, Father."

"So no more of this prayer to Mary, giving to a human being worship that belongs to God."

"Yes, Father."

Saulati started skipping religion class. As a result, her grade average dropped. "Daughter, come here at once!" her father growled when he saw her grades." How do you account for these marks?"

She explained fearfully.

He shrugged. "Well, we must compromise. A good academic record is essential for future success. Go ahead. Attend the religion class. You don't have to believe anything in it."

So Saulati grew, wending her way under blinding sunlight or dripping palm fronds to school, to market or to her mother's home. As her father had taught her, she said her Muslim prayers regularly. More than any of her friends, she was faithful. She feared her father, and she feared God.

Yet if a prayer wasn't perfect, God wouldn't hear it. Even wrong pronunciation could ruin it. Saulati wasn't a native speaker of Arabic. How could she ever be sure her pronunciation was absolutely right? How could she tell whether God truly heard her prayers?

With no answers, her prayers dragged. After menstruation, she was slow to resume them. After missing part of a fast because of menstruation, she never made up the fast. There was a decided lack of joyful motivation in all her praying.

Externally she was a success. High school graduation was followed by a university degree. Then she was tapped for a position as an assistant professor. Nor did her father leave her to languish as a lonely spinster. He activated his network, found a promising possible husband in Ibrahim, introduced Ibrahim and Saulati and, when they agreed, arranged their marriage.

The first year of marriage was special. But then people began to ask, "Are you pregnant yet?"

Africans take seriously God's words to Adam, "It is not good for man to be alone." People are created for community. Westerners may explain some of the meaning of human life by quoting the philosopher Rene Descartes, *Cogito, ergo sum:* "I think, therefore I am." To Africans it makes more sense to say *Cognatus, ergo sum:* "I am related to people, therefore I am." That is what gives human life significance.

Community stretches back in time. Some Africans can list ancestors spanning five hundred years. Community also stretches forward in time to the generations yet unborn. In this context, Saulati's childbearing was not a private affair. It would enrich the whole community. It would also glue her marriage together.

Where was the baby? When she stopped by the vegetable market on her way home from the university, louder than the strings and reeds of Arabic-style music on the vendor's radio, louder than the clang of the plantain vendor's metal utensils, Saulati would hear the gurgle of the seller's beautiful baby. Bumping into a woman veiled from head to foot in a black *buibui*—the Swahili word for "black spider"—she would feel a baby being carried. Sweeping her bright red cement floor after supper, she would hear neighborhood mothers calling back and forth to their children. Bringing a gift of bananas and beer to a friend's house, she would be swept into a bevy of children. Where was *her* baby?

During the years of infertility, Saulati nearly lost her mind. Ultimately, she got so depressed that she took an overdose of pills to commit suicide. This landed her in a psychiatric hospital for several weeks. She had to take a year's leave of absence from her university teaching. As she remembers it, she lost 45 kilograms of weight.

Trying to help, her father phoned a man who wrote Qur'anic verses with charcoal inside a cup, poured water into the cup and gave her the liquid solution to drink. Saulati also sought out a pagan curer who performed an exorcism ritual to try to remove demons from her. Once a Christian group prayed for her too. Through it all, Saulati remembers, she longed for God.

Eventually surgery for fibroids cured the problem, though Saulati's pregnancy came so soon afterward that the doctor worried. Thank God, her daughter was born normally, and she was at once absorbed into the big lap of her extended family.

Meanwhile, in spite of depression, psychosis, infertility, surgery, pregnancy and childbirth, Saulati taught well. The government scholarship to study for the master's degree in America was a reward.

Minnesota. Saulati tapped her pen against the book spread on the library table. She stared out the massive glass window at bare trees. Feet shuffled. A whisper floated. Otherwise silence smothered everything, just like the snow outside. The room smelled of cleaning solvents.

What a country, she said to herself. *So little color, so little smell, so little noise. Everybody staring at a computer or a book. Everybody smiling like robots—and showing just about as much passion in friendship. Even the trees look dead, skeletons stretched out against the sky.*

Absently she traced a figure in the moisture on the window. "Thank God for the African students here. If not for them, I'd go crazy." The figure began to take shape as a palm tree. "Probably I'm crazy anyway. Coming here hasn't helped. Just like that Roman poet Horace said in that quote I read yesterday:"

> Those who cross the seas
> may change the skies above,
> but not their own souls.

"That's me. Depressed as ever. Only more so. My little girl half a world away. And everybody else that I care for."

One student from Kenya encouraged her regularly. "Try. You can make it," he urged. He took her to a university counselor. While the counselor didn't help, the Kenyan's friendship did. Still, it wasn't enough.

Wearily she closed the book. "I can't concentrate. Who am I kidding? All I want to do is sleep. If I had a ticket, I'd fly home tomorrow."

Out of her desperation, Saulati hatched a plan. "OK, I'm going to fail. And when I do—when I fail my semester exams—they'll send me home."

She quit studying. She quit handing in her homework. She slept a lot.

Exam week arrived. Of the two graduate courses in which Saulati was enrolled, one repeated material she had studied at the undergraduate level. She expected she might pass that exam even without study.

Sure enough, she did. But she was surprised at how highly she placed.

Then, to her amazement, she passed the second exam too. "I can't even succeed in failing!" she groaned.

This unexpected turn motivated her to try again. "If I can pass courses in spite of all these problems, maybe I can complete this program after all. Let me try."

With that goal, she spent the two weeks between semesters reading and studying. By the time the second semester began, she had caught up with the material and was well prepared for the new term.

Academic success is only a small part of life, however. Saulati desperately needed more. In particular, she longed for God. "I knew there was no way out except with God's help," she recounts. "But since I hadn't performed the five prayers since leaving home, how was I going to be closer to God?"

When another African friend heard that, he said, "Saulati, the way out of your problem is to receive Jesus Christ as your Lord."

"How would I do that?" she wondered.

"I can't explain, but I can direct you to someone who can," he answered, and he gave her the telephone number of a student from her own country named Simon.

Saulati phoned Simon.

He came to her apartment. She poured out the story of her life to him, then asked: "Is it possible to be close to God here in America? Even though I haven't kept the prayers? Can Jesus help? Is there any way that I can tap into God's power?"

Simon listened patiently. Then, speaking in Swahili, their shared language, he explained that we are unable to go directly to God to tell him our problems. There's a barrier, because we're sinners. For example, back home people often went to spirit doctors when they were in trouble. Saulati had done that once, sinning against the one true God. Sins like those build a barrier between us and God.

Yet there is a way over the barrier, and that is to pass through Jesus. Jesus, who was perfect, asked God's forgiveness for us. If we go through Jesus, God will forgive us.

These words and Simon's spirit moved Saulati. "In fact," she says, "The same day I saw Simon, I gave my life to Jesus."

What was the result? "First of all, I could pray to God anytime," Saulati says firmly. "No matter what time of day it was, my prayer would be accepted. And I knew I wasn't guilty before God."

Simon gave Saulati a Bible and a study guide, *Our Daily Bread*. Immediately he recruited his friend Titus to pray and study with her. Titus came from West Africa, far across the continent from Simon and Saulati's homeland. Still, in spite of a heavy schedule, Titus met with Saulati willingly. Meanwhile, Simon looked for an educated Christian woman knowledgeable in Islam who could mentor Saulati for an extended period. Networking through friends, he found Janet.

Over several months, Janet and Saulati met weekly. They studied the Bible, as well as a book on basic Christian life challenges, *The Fight* by John White.

"She gobbles up the Scripture like she was starving," Janet said during this period. "Whenever we meet, she has a list of probing questions. What a joy to share with somebody who takes such active responsibility for her own growth."

By the time Janet and Saulati stopped meeting regularly, Saulati had internalized the habit of daily prayer and Bible reading, using *Our Daily Bread* as a guide. She started with the Gospel of John, reading in English. Then she wanted to begin at the beginning, so she went back to Genesis and read up to the major prophets. The "big prophets" were difficult. She didn't finish them. She read most of the New Testament, along with the *Our Daily Bread* guide.

"There's no way you *can't* believe that Jesus is God," she said after reading about his miracles. "Making the dead become alive again! It is only God who makes people die and rise."

The Psalms also became especially precious to Saulati.

The more she matured in Christ, the more she wondered, *Should I get baptized?*

Five weeks after Saulati invited Jesus to be Lord of her life, her husband, Ibrahim, arrived. She had come to Minnesota as a student. He came as her spouse. Because of her long course of study, the government had made arrangements for him to join her.

What would Ibrahim say when he discovered Saulati had welcomed Jesus Christ as Lord of her life?

He disapproved. However, he remembered that Saulati had had ups and downs before. And back home people consulted a great array of saints and spirits to meet their spiritual needs. Maybe this wasn't all that different. Anyway, he was new to the country. He needed to listen and learn before he could take over. But Saulati had to quit going to Christian meetings if those occurred on days when Ibrahim was home. She had to fit in

Bible studies between classes on those days when she was on campus.

Simon, Titus and David, three African students, welcomed Ibrahim and Saulati into their homes and families. They greeted Ibrahim joyfully as a fellow pilgrim in a strange land. They gathered exuberantly around peanut-and-tomato stew and fried bananas. They relaxed together, free for a few hours from trying to make sense of Americans.

When Ibrahim wanted to discuss religion, they dived robustly into long, lively discussions. When he was fed up with talking about religion, they switched happily to talking about news from home, bargains, politics and sports. After all, who was in charge of their witness? Themselves? Or God? And if God was in control, wouldn't he accomplish his purposes in his own time?

But often they would remark on Ibrahim's name. "How blessed you are to carry the name of a prophet!" they would comment. Ibrahim, the friend of God. Ibrahim, who trusted God to provide a substitutionary sacrifice. Ibrahim, who experienced God's righteousness as a gift. What a high calling to bear such a name.

These three African student families literally opened their homes to Ibrahim and Saulati. The couple moved in with David's family and stayed for months until David's family had to relocate. Later they spent several months with Titus's family. And on Sunday afternoons they visited Simon's family so regularly that Simon confided, "We've decided to cancel all other activities on Sunday afternoons. We just stay at home and welcome them." This, in spite of the fact that Simon was in demand as a Christian speaker.

"When you see how Christians live, you can see they are guided by some special power," Saulati said later. "Especially in marriage. The way Christian couples present their dissatisfactions to each other. The way they solve their problems."

By God's grace, Saulati finished her course work, embarked on her thesis, wrote first drafts of chapters and finally began to staple together final drafts. In a few months, she would graduate and return to East Africa.

Meanwhile, the more Ibrahim had learned of Jesus Christ, the more he saw that Jesus either was Lord of all or not Lord at all. Predictably, Ibrahim argued that the prophet Muhammad stood higher. So they had a stalemate. Toward the end of their stay in Minnesota, Ibrahim told Saulati,

"Well, you won't listen to your husband. But when you go back, you'll have to listen to your father."

All this was in Saulati's mind as she proofread the next-to-last chapter of her thesis. Beyond the pages of typescript, the question shimmered: *Should I get baptized?*

When she asked this question, Saulati may have been thinking of her own mother. Her grandmother had been married to a Muslim. She had borne him several children, including Saulati's mother. Then she had been divorced. A few years later, she had married a Christian. They too had several children.

Saulati's mother was from the first set of children, the Muslim batch. After the divorce, they stayed with their father. But they visited their mother and spent time with their Christian half-siblings. There Saulati's mother learned the story of Jesus.

On his death bed, Saulati's Muslim grandfather made her mother promise to marry a Muslim and have Muslim grandchildren for him. She obeyed, and Saulati was raised Muslim.

In spite of that, she remembers her mother sitting and reading the Bible.

Later Saulati's father divorced her mother, and Saulati's mother moved back to her own mother's Christian home.

When Saulati's mother died a few years ago, her children helped prepare her body for burial. As they were washing her, one sister said, "We should have a Christian burial, because our mother was a Christian."

"Was she?" the brothers and sisters asked each other.

"Maybe. Remember . . ." And they told stories of her life and what she had said to them.

"But was she ultimately a Christian? That determines what burial ritual we will follow."

For Africans, a funeral sums up a life. It validates what it means to be human. Funerals also border on the supernatural, the life beyond this one. People spend a lot of money on funerals. Some last several days. It is important to follow the right burial ritual.

Suddenly a brother asked, "Was our mother baptized?"

The brothers and sisters stood silent, thinking.

"No," said the eldest. "If she was, I never heard about it. Did you?"

Nobody had certain knowledge that their mother had been baptized, so they buried her that afternoon as a Muslim.

But Saulati remembered her mother sitting and reading the Bible.

Now, as she sat proofreading her thesis, all that unfinished business flooded back into her mind. Preparing to leave the land of her new birth in Christ, she felt the need to achieve a certain closure, not only for herself but also for her mother and her grandmother, quiet witnesses in the Muslim world.

On a Tuesday morning in March, a circle of Midwestern deacons shuffled into the choir loft of the large downtown First Baptist Church. Saulati had phoned Sandra, the Christian woman in whose house she had roomed when she first arrived in Minnesota.

"I'm going home in six weeks, Sandra—"

"So soon? Oh, we'll miss you! I wanted to take you to the lake, but it's still frozen—"

"—and before I go back, I want to be baptized. Can you help me?" Saulati blurted it all out in a rush.

Sandra introduced her to her pastor, and Saulati counseled with him. "I want to be baptized, but I don't want my husband to know yet. There will be a time for that later," she explained.

"I see," he mused. "Not a totally public occasion, then. Still, a testimony before others. Hmm. How about a baptism during a regular deacon board meeting?"

So that Tuesday morning Saulati stepped off a city bus, changed into a white gown and slipped into the water of the baptistry. The deacons crowded into the choir loft to be as near as possible. Titus's wife took a day off from work to come. Janet helped perform the baptism.

As Saulati told her story, she began to cry. She feared losing her relationship with her parents. The deacons each wrote a verse on a piece of paper, and one by one gave her those promises to keep. Some of them cried too.

Yet she had a ringing testimony. "Whatever I do, God is in front of me and will help me," she said. "Before, I always said, 'I can't. There's no way out.' But now I know there's always a way out if I let God guide. Like now—I've finished my thesis!"

When it was over, Saulati looked as if she was walking on air.

God's way out was not what we would have planned. Six months after Saulati returned home, she was dead. The details are not clear. Poisoning and sorcery may have been involved.

Yet if Saulati had a chance to do it over again, I think she would make the same choice. The love of Jesus transformed her life. She wanted to mark that through baptism. Her mother had died unbaptized. Saulati did not want that. When she was baptized, Saulati was preparing for her death. She hoped it would be many decades later. But whenever it came, she wanted to die a baptized Christian.

And she did.

10

Money Matters: Who Pays?

A young girl lies on the ground. One old woman pins down her shoulders. Another grabs her feet. The girl's legs are spread apart. With a knife, a third woman slices into the girl's genitals. First she cuts off part of the clitoris. Then she razors away the lips of tissue surrounding the genital area. Finally, she stitches the bloody area together, leaving only a narrow opening through which urine can pass.

This is radical clitoridectomy, or female genital mutilation (FGM). It produces scar tissue which must be broken on the girl's wedding night, and broken even more at childbirth. After delivering a baby, the mother must be resewn. Sometimes infections occur, leading to pain, incontinence, sterility and death.

An alternative, minimal clitoridectomy, involves simply chopping off part of the clitoris. This reduces sexual pleasure. The rationale is that a girl or woman will be less likely to seek sex outside marriage.

While the prophet Muhammad did not require it, this procedure has become Muslim tradition in some places, especially in East Africa. Most governments have issued statements against it, but common loyalty to the custom remains strong. In some places it is increasing as people struggle to reconnect with their roots.[1]

Clitoridectomy complicates childbirth, already the second biggest health issue for Muslim women. The biggest issue is malnutrition. Yes, there are many Muslim women who are wealthy. Many more are comfortable, even when they are not rich. But in the vast land masses of Asia and Africa are millions of poor women, and many of these are Muslims. Some come from generations of poverty. Others have lost everything suddenly through a war or natural disaster such as an earthquake or flood. Now they eke out their lives, some in refugee camps.

To bless these women includes serving their physical needs. We follow the Lord Jesus who "went about doing good and serving all who were oppressed." How have Christians helped Muslim physically or economically?

Shahida. Shahida lives in a slum in Bangladesh with her husband and five children. She longed for her children to go to school. Classes were free, but parents had to pay for books and school uniforms. Shahida had no money for those extras. It looked as if her dream would die. Her family would produce another generation of illiterates.

Then she heard about World Concern, a Christian agency that gives loans to poor people who put forward simple business proposals. Shahida applied for a loan to buy two cows. The milk she would sell to her neighbors in the slum. She got the loan. The milk business prospered. Later she took out a second loan.

Today Shahida owns ten cows and ten calves, and she employs two fellow slum-dwellers to help sell the milk door to door. All her children are in school. They eat well. They have money set aside for emergencies. And Shahida's subsistence-income husband treats her with greater respect.

Zeinebou. Zeinebou is a single mother with seven children. She lives in central Mauritania, in the heart of the Sahara Desert. Droughts have wiped out the herds that used to sustain the economy. People are desperately poor. While the average monthly income for a family of five is $40, it takes $107 to live at the poverty level. Eight of every ten women are illiterate.

No matter how poor, people still need clothes. And in the drab desert, women love bright fabrics. Their main garment is a gauzy cotton wraparound cloth which protects them from sun and blowing sand. Intricate patterns make each cloth unique. These patterns are created by skillful tie-dying.

Zeinebou decided to start a cloth dying business. She asked World Vision's local development bank for a loan amounting to $231. With a stock of fabric and dye bought at wholesale prices, Zeinebou began to labor for hours over a boiling vat of dye balanced on a small coal-burning stove. Sometimes the daily temperatures reach 122 degrees Fahrenheit. But she is thankful for this work. She is netting a profit of $35 weekly, far above the average local family income. She is able to include her children in the business, passing on skills. As a capstone benefit Zeinebou is learning to read, because when the local World Vision bank makes a loan, one condition is enrolling in a literacy class.

Faridah. Faridah is not starving, but she would like to develop some job skills so she could supplement her husband's wages. He is a taxi driver. Yet as an immigrant from Pakistan to the city of Chicago, Faridah feels she is on the outside looking in. If only she could learn English!

Faridah and her husband have found help through the South Asian Friendship Center, located in the heart of a Muslim business district in Chicago. The core of the Center is a bookstore, stocking titles in Urdu (Faridah's language), Arabic and English. There are many Christian books. Couches and chairs, free cookies and Indian tea make for a delightful browsing and reading environment. Cassettes, CDs and videos are available too.

Here Faridah has enrolled in an English class right on the premises. As well, although she hasn't needed to access these services yet, Faridah has discovered that the Center provides help with immigration issues, legal counsel, medical assistance, home visits and even classes in the Hindi and Urdu languages!

Best of all, the people pray. When Faridah signed up for the English class, the woman staff member asked her softly, "May I pray with you that this class will be a good experience for you, and that you will learn well?" Faridah wasn't sure what to expect, but the simple prayer touched her heart. *In such a materialistic, godless country, it is a blessing to meet people who pray,* she thought.

This Center is the multidenominational effort of many area churches.[2]

First Do No Harm

"Would you like to know what it's like to work with Americans?" I was in Mali, West Africa. Daniel Coulibaly asked me that question. He continued, "Let me tell you a story." This is the story he told.

Elephant and Mouse were best friends. One day Elephant said, "Mouse, let's have a party!" So they did. Animals gathered from far and near. They ate, and drank, and sang, and danced. And nobody celebrated more exuberantly than the Elephant.

After it was over, Elephant exclaimed, "Mouse, did you ever go to a better party? Wasn't that an incredible celebration?"

But Mouse didn't answer.

"Where are you, Mouse?" Elephant called. Suddenly he shrank back in horror. There at his feet lay the Mouse, his body ground into the dirt, smashed by the exuberance of his friend the Elephant.

"Sometimes that's what it is like to do mission with you Americans," my friend commented. "It's like dancing with an Elephant."

Charging in to help—that's what we Westerners do. Yet with our hastily conceived short-term solutions we can trample fragile local patterns that have stood the test of time. Steve Saint tells about that. His father, Nate Saint, was one of the five gifted missionary pioneers massacred in 1956 by Aucas, people who live in the jungle of Ecuador. The tragedy flashed round the world. Featured on the cover of *Life* magazine, it caught the imagination of Christians everywhere.

In the years since, other missionaries have gone to the Aucas, now known as the Huaorani. Many Huaorani have believed. Steve himself grew up in the United States and went into business. But his family visited the Huaorani. He was baptized there. He kept in touch with the jungle people. A few years ago they asked him to come back for awhile to serve as a broad-ranging consultant.

What Steve found when he settled back into the jungle was a disturbing pattern of dependency. The Huaorani had been stronger Christian leaders in the 1960s than they were in the 1990s. Short-term missions charging in like elephants had trampled their initiative.

For example, although the Huaorani had built simple churches twenty years before, they were not building them anymore. Why? Foreigners came from time to time and constructed buildings. When they did, they attached aluminum roofing that they had flown in. Huaorani had no aluminum. They could only construct thatched roofs. That wasn't really good enough for God, they decided. So they had fallen into the habit of waiting for foreigners to come and build.

"We can only build like the ancient ones did," they told Steve.

"God would be happy with thatch," he protested. "He lived in a tent with the Children of Israel."

Steve comments, "That was a new thought to them. They assumed the outsiders didn't think what they were doing was adequate, so the outsiders came in and showed them what to do. So they thought, 'We can't build like that, so we should leave that for the outsiders to do.' "[3]

Similarly, the Huaorani no longer ran their own Christian training sessions but waited for short-term mission teams who turned up periodically. Today this is changing, in both economic and spiritual areas, as the Huaorani rediscover their own resources.

A world away, urban mission specialist Ray Bakke began his ministry in an inner-city Chicago church. Here he learned how important it was to help people discover their own resources. "The fact that the church building was falling down was the best thing we could offer, in my opinion. People learned to paint, wire, fix windows, build and repair things. We ran classes in the various building trades in the community, and people came for ten-week courses. This was a way of empowering people. Our builder did not do the work on the church himself: he always taught others who worked with him."[4]

Even more radically, Bakke suggests, "When [short-term teams come], let it be in the spirit of 'mission in reverse.' . . . There it is clearly understood that the indigenous local lay folk are the teachers and the visiting students who assist temporarily are in fact the learners, being taught by the poor how to pastor the poor. There is great integrity in that kind of learning contract."

If we apply this to ministry with women like Shahida, Zeinebou and Faridah, we will take time to learn what they have. We will begin with what they know. On that we can build together for a healthier, richer life. *Umm Ahmad.* Umm Ahmad is a widow in Egypt who manages the family's housework and field work, rotating it among her daughters and daughters-in-law. All her grown sons give her their income. She buys their food and clothes and the family seed and fertilizer. For a time she ran a small store.

To outsiders Umm Ahmad may look needy. There's no question that her family survives on a limited budget. But it would be wrong to say they are without resources.

One day Umm Ahmad's daughter Habiba approached her. "Mother, Ahmad and Faruq want me to sell my gold earrings."

"Why?" Umm Ahmad asked.

"So they can buy a cow, as a shared investment between them."

"Hmph!" Umm Ahmad snorted.

"Well, what do you think?" Habiba persisted. "After all, they're my husband and my brother. Shouldn't I give them the earrings?"

"I wouldn't advise it, my girl," answered the wise peasant mama. "You'd be a fool to let that capital slip through your fingers."

Habiba took heed, and her brother and husband couldn't make her part with the jewelry.

A few months later, Umm Ahmad took Habiba aside. "I have an idea. Why don't you sell your gold earrings and with *part* of the money buy a small calf in a three-way partnership with Ahmad and Faruq?"

"Well . . ."

"Just make sure—" Umm Ahmad warned, "just make sure you get a signed receipt from Faruq. And buy yourself a small pair of earrings with whatever you have left."[5]

This woman is not without resources, physical, mental or social. It would be wrong to approach her as though she had nothing. Rather, our economic help should build on her strengths. There are biblical grounds for this. To be sure, there is a lot that is negative in Umm Ahmad's way of life, just as there is in ours. On the other hand, there are also strengths in her heritage. These positive patterns are gifts from God, who endowed Umm Ahmad's ancestors with creativity in his image.

When we work with women like Umm Ahmad, Shahida, Zeinebou or Faridah, we should look for their God-blessed natural endowments and build on them. Assuming that many of their traditional patterns fit with the local environment, we should enter into economic projects humbly, knowing that we have a lot to learn. We should seek counsel from wise local women and men. As soon as possible, we want to work with and under local leaders.

Plan Systematically, Not Piecemeal

Where should we begin? How should we prioritize?

Health Care. Dr. Ida Scudder built the Vellore Medical Hospital and Training School, one of the outstanding health centers of South Asia. When she was a young adult, however, that was the last thing she expected to do. For two generations her family had been missionary doctors. She did not intend be the third. After college in America she expected to settle down on U.S. soil.

But a visit back to her parents in India changed her plans. One evening a man knocked on the door. "Excuse me. My wife is having a baby and something has gone wrong. Is there a doctor who can come?"

Ida's father picked up his medical bag, but the husband objected, "No, not a male doctor. Isn't there a woman doctor?"

There was not, so the young husband went away. Twice more that night husbands came seeking help for wives in childbirth. Twice more they turned away when they discovered there was no woman doctor. In the morning Ida heard that all three women had died. She went back to the United States, enrolled in medical school, raised funds and returned with enough finances to start her renowned medical center, which has focused on serving and training women. Ida is one of thousands who have reached out to sick, blind and leprous people, moved by the compassion of Jesus.[6]

Dr. Mary Eddy was born in Syria of missionary parents. Educated in the United States, she went back to the Turkish empire to practice medicine. For five months in Constantinople she persevered night and day, studying for a diploma which would allow her to practice under the Turkish flag.

Once she was certified, she traveled widely, camping out, in order to serve the needy. Cataract removal was her specialty. Her first operation was on a slave woman who had been blind for five years. She lived on crumbs from servants she had supervised. As a result of the operation, this woman's sight and her former position were restored. Every year she visited Mary with a gift.

After she had straightened the vision of a number of cross-eyed girls, a local Muslim said, "You have provided these destitute ones with homes by your skill. You have laid up more merit in heaven than if you had been to Mecca."[7]

The heritage of healing continues. John is a foreign Christian doctor in the Northwest Frontier Province of Pakistan. Many of his patients are pregnant women. Multiple babies, dietary deficiencies and lack of sunlight from staying indoors can cause severe bone disease. The disease may contort the pelvis and make normal vaginal delivery impossible. Yet these women desperately desire sons.

"No man wants to be without sons, and many men want several. One gentleman was advised that his wife should be sterilized because further pregnancies would likely kill her. He would not agree because his brother had one more son than he did," the doctor reports.

Mothers-in-law want grandsons, and they can make life miserable until they get them. A few months after the wedding, a couple will begin being asked repeatedly, "Aren't you pregnant yet?"

Iqbal and Aisha's situation was awful. Although they had been married for six months, they had not managed to have sex. In his role as physician, John helped them solve the problem. Talking with Iqbal, John learned that Iqbal had not chosen his bride. Arranged marriages were customary. But Iqbal's father had forced him against his will to marry his cousin.

The older man was eager for this union because he had adopted Aisha many years ago and was responsible to find her a husband. Marrying his son to his niece solved both problems.

Unfortunately, because Iqbal had lived in the same house with Aisha since he was a boy, he looked at her as a sister. Now he had an unconscious fear that he was committing incest. He also had not fully forgotten about a girl he loved who had been married to another man.

John helped Iqbal and Aisha through this excruciating situation. Such medical treatment and counsel not only keeps people alive but also transforms the quality of their lives.

Today national governments provide medical care in many countries. Hospitals that once were Christian are now staffed by local Muslim doctors and nurses. In some countries the comprehensive health services are remarkable. In Iran, for example, contraceptive supplies are free for life, and family planning counseling is required for both the bride and the groom before they can get a marriage license.

Yet in poor countries the need for health services outstrips the supply. In some regions, medical schools train specialists rather than primary care physicians. Nursing may be seen as demeaning work, leading to a shortage of caring, high-quality nurses. In Saudi Arabia, "nurse training programs have been funded at least since 1979, but until recently most of the students came from foreign countries because for women nursing carries a social stigma," says Eleanor Doumato. "In interviews I conducted at the National Guard Hospital in Riyadh in May of 1996, I was told that there were no Saudi nurses employed at that hospital."[8]

Where there is need, foreign Christian volunteers can make a contribution. For example, where radical clitoridectomy is practiced, some Christian doctors do reconstructive surgery on women who suffer disastrous damage following childbirth. In so doing, they give these women back their lives.

Where populations are huge, public health education is a never-ending challenge. Yet teaching women in a community about clean water, fluid therapy for infant diarrhea, waste disposal and immunizations can reap enormous benefits.

The capital of Mauritania has seen a great influx of former nomads fleeing drought in the desert oases. These newcomers' hygiene practices are unsuited to crowded city living. Sickness and child death rates are high. World Vision in Mauritania embarked on a national public health education campaign using a range of media: radio spots, a radio storyteller and radio talk shows; TV music minivideos; traveling drama troupes; newspaper opinion pieces; school textbook inserts; a telephone campaign; billboard murals; posters, stickers; T-shirts with slogans.

Mauritanian imams supported this campaign. Some even have appeared in World Vision TV ads advocating family planning. This media package has won an award in an Africa-wide competition.

Christians also have been invaluable in AIDS education, from chastity campaigns to networking AIDS orphans into families.

Agriculture. Health care is not enough, however. Economists point out that modern medicine keeps more people alive than poor countries can support. In the West, because industry developed before modern medicine, national economies grew to support the increased populations, the weak, the old and the babies who formerly would have died. In the missions movement, however, we have sent more doctors and nurses than business people.

Have we been saving people to starve?

Increasing food production is essential. In the long run people need not just charity but the skills, land and capital to produce their own food and goods. This means seeds, tools, animal stock, a dependable water supply, fertilizer, pest control, agricultural consultants, veterinary care, and market channels and information.

Twenty years ago Martin Price was a professor of biology at Geneva College. He and his wife left that secure position to sink all their savings into a few acres in Florida. They began to experiment with food plants that flourished under difficult conditions—heat, cold, dryness, pests. When people requested them, Martin and Bonnie shared seeds, but they asked for feedback on where the seeds were planted and how they grew.

This data went into information banks, books, booklets, videos, a newsletter and a web page. Missionaries began to drop in to study at Martin and Bonnie's place, which is named the Educational Concerns for Hunger Organization (ECHO). Container gardening, growing vegetables without soil and rooftop gardening are some of Martin's more recent enthusiasms. These creative alternatives make it possible for a lot more people to grow their own food.[9]

Animal husbandry has been the Christian Veterinary Mission's avenue for service in many parts of the world over the last two decades. Women veterinarians are serving in some vital locations.[10] Although Bob Blencoe is not a veterinarian, he too found himself in a "ministry of meat." Right after the Gulf War, Bob went to Kurdistan in northern Iraq. He lived there for the next six years. One day, while he was enjoying the food at a community feast, the man next to him remarked, "Do you realize that the meat in that stew was not vaccinated?"

Bob lost his appetite.

The man next to him turned out to be a veterinarian, unemployed because of the political upheaval. Bob learned that the sheep and goats all throughout Iraqi Kurdistan were unvaccinated. Using USAID connections, he got vaccines and refrigerators spread across the country at fourteen-hour intervals. Then he put together a team of veterinarians that included local Kurds as well as foreign Christians. They vaccinated well over a million animals. Kurds who had never owned a sheep or goat began investing in them as portable bank accounts.[11]

Business. Like health care, food production alone is not enough. When people don't own land, whether they are urban or rural, they will need something more—either a job or the means to create one. Muslim women are in the workplace. "Incomplete statistics from Tunisia, Morocco, and the Gulf suggest that nearly a third of Middle East women from these countries work full-time outside the home, and that most of the rest work part-time in or out of their homes."[12] Shahida, for example, struggles for a financial foothold in Bangladesh. Zeinebou does the same in Mauritania.

Christians can offer women like Shahida and Zeinebou a hand up. Skills training is a key part. A woman may need to learn about accounting, quality control, marketing, government regulations. She also may need capital and equipment. This is so important that we will devote the next major section to it.

Politics. Production is not always the problem. The distribution system may be corrupt. We want to help people own their own land and businesses. We want to encourage them to gain increasing control of their own political processes. We want to stand with them when they confront oppression. Sometimes this will require us to be advocates at the international level. We will have to join or form a group to write or speak to multinational corporations, the United Nations, or our own government about unfair policies.

On the other hand, sometimes what's required is advocacy at the local level. The Bangladesh Rural Advancement Committee, a group supported by Oxfam-America, worked in a village where 40 percent of the people owned no land. Two percent of the population were rich landowners. Yet fallow vacant land lay all around. It had been abandoned by people who fled to India during the 1971 war of liberation. Now government land, it was used illegally by the rich for grazing and cultivation.[13]

BRAC taught the illiterate landless villagers to read, using curricula that focused on real problems facing village Bengalis. The laborers learned to name their problems and identify resources at their disposal. As a result, once they had the learned to read, they formed the Rajasan Landless Cooperative Society and started petitioning the government to grant them title to some of the abandoned land.

Two years later, after unrelenting corporate pressure from the landless cooperative, the government ceded them sixty acres. This amounted to one-and-one-half acres per family.

Then the local hassles started. The rich landowners were alarmed because they were losing their illegal use of the abandoned land. Also they were losing their stranglehold on the poor laborers. They incited other villagers to break the irrigation canal on which the cooperative's land depended. They tried to keep the cooperative from using the river. But they didn't try too hard, because they suspected that starting from scratch would prove too difficult for farmers with little land and no tools or capital.

"They'll be mortgaging their farms right back to us. Give them one season," they laughed to each other.

Instead, the new farmers got a loan for equipment from BRAC at twelve percent interest. (The alternative would have been a loan at fifty to two hundred percent interest from the local moneylenders.)

In spite of bad harvest weather, the new farmers paid back the loan plus interest at the end of the first season. After that, they began to discuss extending their joint activities to fishing. They started seeking better health care services. They even asked for information on family planning.

Whether at the local, national or international level, sometimes serving the poor means political advocacy to help them gain control of the fruits of their labor. There is an old saying:

Give a man a fish, and you feed him for one day.
Teach him to fish, and you feed him for many days.

The politically sensitive Christian adds: Who owns the pond?

All in all, this means tackling women's money problems systemically rather than piecemeal.

Microloans and Small Businesses

What helped Shahida was a loan, so she could buy cows and start a milk business. With a similar loan, Zeinebou started a cloth dyeing enterprise. This strategy holds so much promise that consultants from 110 countries who met at a Microcredit Summit in 1997 set a goal to help 100 million people escape poverty through small loans by the year 2005.

Muhammad Yunus was one of the early promoters of "microloans." He was a professor of economics in Bangladesh when a famine developed. Suddenly it seemed that the theories he was teaching in the classroom didn't apply to the thousands of people dying outside. "Economics seemed hollow. I was totally disenchanted with what I was doing. I left the classroom and stepped out into the villages of Bangladesh," he says.[14] Here Yunus observed a woman who earned two pennies a day making bamboo stools. For her supplies she had to borrow from a moneylender. The moneylender took most of her income.

Yunus explains, "I realized if this money was available at normal interest rates the woman would earn a decent living and get out of poverty.

"I went around this village to look for other people who also were stuck in poverty for being dependent on loans from traders and money lenders. I came up with a list of 42 such people. Their total credit requirement was only $30. I gave out the money from my own pocket as a loan. I thought if normal banking institutions could take on such functions these people could have an easy way out of poverty. I was wrong. Conventional banking institutions do not provide to the poor or to rural women.

"The bankers I met laughed at me. They didn't think it was possible to give out money without collateral. I ran from one bank to another. They all said the same. I offered myself as guarantor for the loans. This was good for a few hundred dollars. . . .

"I went back to the banks showing proof that poor people do pay back. They said it works in your one village but it wouldn't work over many villages. I tried it over many villages."

Finally Yunus said to himself, *Why am I knocking myself out chasing after banks? I'll create a bank.* So he did. The Grameen Bank was born in 1983 as a bank for the poor. It has loaned over two billion dollars in small amounts, with dazzling success.

Today many missions and nongovernment agencies have set up microloan programs. Women entrepreneurs are the focus of one mission loan program in a very poor Asian Muslim country. In a recent six-month period this agency made business loans to 591 women. The women started businesses in these areas: garments, services, manufacturing, livestock, embroidery, handicraft, food processing. In spite of terrorism, political unrest, the government's slum eviction program, which disrupted many of these women's businesses, and a devastating fire, repayment rate has been 86 percent.

In this program, field visits provide continuing education in bookkeeping, marketing, product quality control, cooperative buying and selling and so on. They can spell the difference between success or failure. Field staff have been motivated by performance bonuses to give more quality time to field travel. A friendly competition has developed.

Interestingly, lower- and middle-class women have repaid their loans better than upper-class women with larger loans, according to a staff report. However, since the agency has started sending out "uncommon faces like the program coordinator, auditors, and accountants to solve the problems of problematic clients," repayment overall has improved. "It showed our strength that we could speak to them boldly," the staff report observes, adding, "It is good to recruit married and taller persons as field staff. . . . But a smaller and unmarried person with quality can do well also."

Some of the loan staff are believers and others are not. The believers often tell their clients that they are Christians. To meet a native Christian is a new experience for many of the borrowers. It expands their categories. They welcome the staff into their homes. The warm relationships that develop constitute "a quiet influence on society, which we hope is a foundation for the salvation of many in the future," the agency says.

All Christian and non-Christian staff meet for morning devotions every workday. Testimonies, Bible stories and Bible verses sow the seed. "On loan disbursement days, the project manager and other Christian staff share with all the businesswomen who are present about God's plan for human beings: that he loves and cares for all people, that he created all of us in his own image but due to our sin we were separated from him. He wants to reconcile us with himself, and we should come back to him in repentance. However, we haven't shared with them in this public setting that they must accept Christ as their Lord and Savior." That must be done on a person-to-person basis, the agency believes.

Even where there is no such agency, focused investment in an individual woman can pay off. This should be done in the context of an overall plan. Take Aziza, for example. She is an African, born in an ethnic group that is among the most resistant to the gospel on that continent. But Aziza married a nominal Christian. Because of this she began to attend a Bible study. Just as she started, her Christian husband divorced her! She was left with a two-year-old child and no means of support.

Aziza's response was striking. "I don't want this bad experience to stand in the way of my learning about the gospel," she said.

Her family pressured her to give the child to his father's relatives. "You have to get rid of this child, because he's the child of a Christian," they urged. But Aziza loved her child, and she loved hearing about Jesus.

"How can we help her during this difficult time?" a missionary wondered. "How can we empower her without fostering dependency?"

They found her a scholarship for a one-year course in tailoring. A small group of local believers who were not of Muslim background helped her with rent and food. An international agency that assists persecuted Christians paid for her tuition and childcare.

Among the local believers Aziza discovered a loving community. Here she spent her spare time, and here she came to faith in the Lord. Today she is employed in a women's tailoring and handicraft cooperative which serves refugee women. She is the assistant in charge of accounts, and it is her joy to serve other women in need. The church still supplements her food supply a little. She maintains active contact with her extended family, phoning home once a month. Her credibility with them is growing. Their original fear was that she would be immoral as a Christian. Now they see her responsible adult life, her godly behavior, and her love and care for them. Judicious investment in Aziza helped to make this possible.

Encourage Accountability, Community and Simplicity

Accountability. To succeed, an economic project must produce *something*

people will buy. It must maintain *quality*. It must manage *inventory* so that
waste and backups do not drain profits. A great strength of microcredit
programs is that they offer not only loans but also business advice. As a
result, these small business lending efforts show a startlingly high repayment rate, often over 90 percent. Monitoring by compassionate consultants makes the difference.

Making a *profit* is one measure of success. Another is *fair wages* paid by
middlemen to entrepreneurs, and by entrepreneurs to their employees.
Shahida, for example, borrows money to buy two cows. Her dairy business
prospers. She now employs two people to deliver the milk. What does she
pay these employees? Her original loan should have stipulated fair and
increasing wages for employees. This should be monitored. It will not happen automatically unless it is required from the outset.

A loan recipient may even consider *profit-sharing* with her experienced
employees. Or she may eventually help them secure their own
microloans. One way or another, she must be committed to passing on the
benefits. She must have social as well as economic goals.

Some projects go even further. A study of microborrowers in fourteen
African countries found that 95 percent had trouble paying medical bills,
77 percent had trouble paying for funerals, and 50 percent had trouble
supporting orphans in their kin group. As a result, some microlenders now
include preventive health education as part of their business training. Topics may range from handwashing to condoms to health insurance.

A third measure is whether the products *serve the poor* or are luxuries
for the rich. Crafts export businesses do the latter. These are not evil businesses. They enrich both the sellers and the buyers. It is better, however,
when we can help a woman serve her neighbors, providing for some of
their basic needs. Shahida sells milk, for example. Zeinebou sells ordinary,
pretty cloth. We must resist the temptation to focus on products that will
sell to global islands of the elite simply because that is where the greatest
profit lies. When we do that, we play into the hands of Marxists who argue
that capitalism creates luxuries for the rich before it turns to necessities for
the poor.

A fourth measure concerns *management skills*. When a woman applies
for a loan, does she have the experience or skills to succeed in her pro-

posed business? Who will monitor her? What accountability structures are in place? Will a regional consultant visit regularly, or will monitoring be handled locally?

Here is a checklist of criteria for success:

☐ The business makes a profit (quality product, steady inventory, sound bookkeeping)

☐ The business pays fair wages, increasing as it prospers (wage increases, employee profit-sharing, microloans)

☐ Products are essentials, serving the economically needy or the spiritually underreached

☐ The seller has adequate skills and receives regular visits from a consultant

☐ The business conserves the local ecology and the local cultural heritage

☐ The seller has been praying to God for economic help

Community. Just as we encourage accountability, so we must encourage community. Many programs operate through peer accountability groups. In the Grameen Bank structure, for example, five women in a given neighborhood will hold each other accountable to repay their loans. If one defaults, all of them will have problems when it comes to future loans and benefits. With this motivation, sharp-eyed friends note each other's small excesses and nip them in the bud.

Long before the modern era, women in some countries were forming credit cooperatives. West African women's traders' associations have operated on a big scale for generations. Such a group capitalizes women; connects the new trader with a network of customers; shows her how to reinvest profitably; buys in bulk; regulates trading to prevent anyone underselling the rest; and limits the number of traders to what the market will bear. Personal benefits may include generous gifts on the birth of a child, sick benefits and substantial sums of money to the bereaved on the death of a member. The Nigerian Egba Women's Union of Abeokuta has had a dues-paying membership of 80,000 and has run a maternity and child welfare clinic. They also have sponsored English literacy classes for traders who need a common language to register goods and deal with wholesalers and customers from various tribes. A microcredit program should look for local networks like these and build on them.

In urban centers women may not know or trust their neighbors. Here some microlenders use "stepped lending" instead of "peer accountability." A borrower puts up half the capital, and the lender matches it. This may constitute a very small loan. When the borrower repays, she gets a larger loan. She borrows successively, step by step. This strategy has been successful.

An added benefit is that the loan agency acts like a bank. The borrower does not have to hold onto large sums, but she can return to the agency for more. Really poor people can't afford to have large sums of money in their possession. They can't secure it safely. Stepped lending protects them.

Community doesn't come naturally when local cooperative structures are lacking. It is easy to fall into habits of private capitalism focused on improving life for *my* family. The venerable founder of the Christian Community Development Association, John Perkins, discusses this in his book *Restoring At-Risk Communities: Doing It Together and Doing It Right.*[15] Development must bless a *community*, he argues. From the beginning, those who benefit must look outward. They are blessed to be a blessing.

Simplicity. How much is enough? When we help women economically, we should be careful not to stimulate an acquisitive spirit. People deserve to have basic economic needs met. Starvation is not God's will. Watching your babies die is not good for any woman. And beyond basic needs, people deserve beauty and festivity. But how much is enough?

The Davos World Economic Forum meets in Switzerland annually. This year a panel on the twenty-first-century corporation described this "age of digital Darwinism" in scary terms. "The key to winning in business today is adapt or die, get wired or get killed, work 24 hours a day from everywhere or be left behind," according to Thomas Friedman, columnist for the *New York Times.*[16]

Listening to this panel, Howard Stringer, chairman of Sony America, finally could take no more. He stood up. "Doesn't anyone here think this sounds like a vision of hell?" he asked. "While we are all competing or dying, when will there be time for sex or music or books? Stop the world, I want to get off." Long ago a poet said,

> Give me neither poverty nor riches; Feed me with food convenient for me:
> Lest I be full, and deny thee, and say, Who is the LORD? or lest I be poor,
> and steal, And take the name of my God in vain. (Proverbs 30:8-9 KJV)

Centuries later the apostle Paul observed, "I know what it is to be in need, and I know what it is to have plenty. I have learned the secret of being content in any and every situation" (Philippians 4:12) and "Godliness with contentment is great gain" (1 Timothy 6:6).

Even in America today there are groups of women who are voluntarily learning how to live more cheaply. Some garden, can or dry food, and sew. Others exchange babysitting and haircuts. They clip coupons, cruise garage sales and buy together in bulk. They drive older cars. They enjoy inexpensive recreation. Little by little, they're finding they can live happily with less. As we help to empower Muslim-background women economically, we must cultivate joy in simplicity ourselves.

Think of the women in the Bible. Did Hannah have indoor plumbing? Did Esther own a washer and dryer? Did Mary use a laptop? Yet their lives were as valid as ours. They dominated nature less. Fewer alternative products, customs and ideas were available to them. But they experienced friendship, love, parenthood, creativity, learning, responsibility, choice, dignity, adventure and relationship to God. They had as many significant experiences as any modern woman.

We Can Do Something

On Christmas Eve, my niece and nephew tumbled through the door. "Where are Joel and Michael?" they clamored, looking for my sons.

"Upstairs—ordering Christmas presents on the computer," I admitted.

You can't get much more last-minute than that. Still, on Christmas day, because of a World Concern gift catalog, nineteen- year-old Joel and seventeen-year-old Michael could announce, "Marilyn, Don, Melanie, Wil—there's a family in Haiti that is receiving a dairy goat in your name. Heather and Steve—a family in Rwanda will be getting a pair of breeding rabbits in your name. Grandma and Grandpa—there are five families in Somalia who are going to receive fishing kits in your name."

We can't do everything, but we can do something. So we should. Money matters.

11

When You Seek Me
with All Your Heart

Born in northern Iran, Simin was the oldest of three girls. Because her father had no sons, he tutored his daughters with great attention. All were top students. When national leaders came to northern Iran, Simin often was chosen to welcome them. Twice she met the Shah and his family.

"The Lord was preparing me to go first before an earthly king and then before a heavenly King," Simin says now. "My father gave us good qualities that now are working for the kingdom of God."

From an early age, Simin had a hunger for God. And God seems to have responded in some unusual ways. One day when Simin was four, she heard screaming. Up the stairs she clambered, across her roof and onto the adjoining roof, and the next, and the next, and the next. Finally she looked down to discover what was causing the noise. In the courtyard below, she saw a dead baby. A woman was washing it. As she poured the water, she howled. Eventually a group of people carried the baby out of the yard. Simin followed, creeping along behind. Their destination was a cemetery. Because Iranians don't use coffins, Simin saw them put the baby in a hole in the ground.

Running home, she begged her grandmother, "Why do they take human beings and put them in a hole in the ground?"

"Because people die. Where have you—?

"Why do they die?"

"Fate. When it's their fate, when it's their time, they have to go. We all have to—"

"When they die, where do they go?"

"Ah, there's the mystery. They say there is a bridge ten thousand times finer than human hair. If you are good enough, you will be able to cross it when you die. Then you'll be in paradise. Food, music, pets, friends, luxury—ah, but you, with all your naughtiness, you're more likely to end up in hell—fire, pain, screams of agony. You'd better watch out, pay attention, obey, be a better girl, shape up—"

Hell. Simin began to have nightmares.

A few months later, soldiers came to the village to conscript young men. Knock! Knock!

"Salaam Aleikum, Madam," they greeted Simin's grandmother. "Peace be with you. It is our duty to inform you that we have a notice of conscription for two young men in your family, Ali Razak and Hussein—"

Simin fled out the back door. Regardless of what they said, she knew who they were: demons, sent to drag her to hell! All day Simin hid out behind a wall. All day she prayed, "God, I'll do whatever you want, just don't take me to hell. Don't turn me into a demon."

Toward evening she went down to the river to wash her hands and face. There she saw a man on the water.

"What are you doing here?" he asked her.

"Washing my hands," she answered.

"Why don't you do that at home?"

Simin explained why she was afraid.

"What are you worried about?" the man smiled. "I am the one who decides who goes to heaven and who goes to hell. And you are going to be with me."

Peace flowed over little Simin. She wanted to hug the man. But she couldn't walk on the water to him. Instead, thoughtfully, she went home. For years Simin treasured that memory. How different this glimpse of the supernatural seemed from her grandmother's. Years later she would continue to hunger for God, sometimes impetuously and almost blasphemously. Not for religion. Not for a set of standards to keep. But for the God who made her. The God who knew her. The God who kept pursuing her, even as she pursued him. Fourteen years after her conversion to the Lord Jesus Christ, when asked her favorite verse, Simin would say quietly and firmly, "The promise of God in Jeremiah 29:13: 'You will seek me and find me when you seek me with all your heart.' "

Her story witnesses eloquently to the truth of that verse.

At age twenty-two Simin got a brief glimpse of heaven. One day when she was working as a student nurse, a seven-year-old-girl was brought in. As Simin prepared her, she saw fluids flowing out of the little girl's body in the wrong places. "This child is sicker than the doctor realized," she gasped.

"Nurse," a small voice interrupted, "Do you hear the music? Do you see the angels?"

In a few minutes the little girl closed her eyes and was gone. But Simin treasured that brush with heaven.

As a top student, Simin felt superior to other Iranian women. Then British-educated nurses arrived. "Iranian nurses' training? Very second-rate," they mocked.

"Look, we Iranian nurses perform many of the functions that doctors do in other countries," Simin and her friends protested.

"All the more fools you. You perform the functions, but you lack the background theory. You diagnose by symptom rather than understanding the comprehensive etiology."

This bothered Simin. One night, while eating a piece of watermelon all by herself outside the nursing students' quarters, she prayed impulsively, "Lord, I want to get out of this country." She felt that God affirmed her resolve. She walked back in and announced to the other nurses, "I'm going to the U.S."

"Impossible!" they hooted. The year was 1971. How would she get a visa?

Making the rounds of embassy offices, Simin began the battle of the red tape. A few days later, during lunch break at the American embassy, Simin stopped in a restaurant. She was ushered to an almost empty upstairs room. She took the opportunity to pray. Then "the joy of the Holy Spirit filled the whole upstairs of the restaurant, as if God himself was happy I was getting out," she remembers.

In one week, Simin got her impossible visa.

When she put her foot on the gangway at John F. Kennedy Airport, Simin experienced once more what seemed to be the happiness of God himself, as though God was glad for her and with her. Where would he take her? What did he intend for her? Would she ever know God more personally? Simin thanked God. She worshiped him. And she wondered.

After a few days in the United States, though, she was thoroughly homesick. At loose ends one afternoon, she took a dictionary and strolled aimlessly down the streets. In front of an attractive big building, she stopped. "Church," she read on the sign in front.

Church? she wondered, and riffled through the pages of her dictionary. "A place of Christian worship," she read.

The soaring stone arches drew her with their hints of spaciousness and serenity.

Well, now I'm in this country, and I need all the help I can get, she thought to herself. So she pushed open the thick oak door of the church and slipped inside. She tiptoed to the aisle. The quiet, the stained glass windows, dust motes dancing in shafts of sunlight, the warm wood of carved pews—Simin was touched. She walked softly to the front and knelt down. Peace washed over her. Suddenly, as she began to unwind, as she began to relax from the stresses of culture shock that had piled up inside her, she started to cry.

In time an old man came and knelt beside her. He talked comfortingly. He prayed.

Simin hardly could understand a word. Just enough to give him her address when he asked. After that, he invited her to his home for dinner. He took her to church. And he dropped in for a visit at her apartment almost every day. While there he would read from the Bible, King James Version.

Again Simin couldn't understand. "What's he saying?" she would ask her roommate, who had been in the United States longer.

"He's trying to convert us," her roommate would sneer.

"Well, let him come," Simin answered, "No fear. We won't get converted."

So, day after day, the doorbell would ring. "Oh no, here he is again!" her roommate would groan, squinting through the peephole in the door. But Simin recognized the old man's warmth and love.

What *did* Simin believe about God at this point? She knew that God was the Creator and Sustainer of the world. He spoke to people through prophets and through scriptures like the Qur'an. But he would never go through the humiliation of taking on human form, as Christians believed he did in Jesus. Like other Muslims, Simin believed that Jesus had existed as a great prophet. But he hadn't died on the cross to conquer sin, death and the devil, or risen from the dead to generate new life for us. There was no redemption from sin. We rise out of our misdeeds by our own human determination to obey God's laws. This was Simin's background. Its legalism repulsed her. On the other hand, its high view of God called forth reverence from her. Besides these orthodox teachings, she had picked up some folk beliefs about demons, charms, mantras and magic.

After a few months on the East Coast, Simin moved to the Midwest, where she took a job as a nurse's aide in a convalescent home. One of her charges was an old lady. Simin washed and brushed her hair with care and dressed her attractively. The woman's daughter, a Catholic, appreciated Simin's thoughtfulness.

"Do you know Jesus, Simin?" the daughter asked one day.

"No. Only as a prophet," Simin answered.

No more was said on the subject. But Simin remained aware that the old woman's daughter always looked at her with eyes full of love and concern.

Again Simin moved. Neither the Catholic woman nor the old man who had read her the King James Bible ever would know what abundant fruit their seeds of love produced. Yet because they were faithful in small things, God continued showing himself to Simin through them.

Simin enrolled in college in California. But life in America was becoming disillusioning. While her Iranian friends didn't seem to have much meaning in their lives, neither did her American friends. She began to withdraw, spending more time alone. She would go out into the hills around Ventura and talk to God, asking him to show himself to her. "I see people turning into animals. No one is searching for you," she told God.

A brief visit home provided little help. Her family didn't know what to make of this Americanized Simin. She walked differently, and she talked differently. She smoked two packs of cigarettes a day. As for Simin, she recounts, "After two days Iran was the same as America"—social patterns without significance.

Her mother called her to pray with the family at one of the regular daily prayers. But tradition was no longer enough for Simin. She wanted an authentic personal encounter with God.

"I'm not going to kneel down unless God confronts me personally," Simin lashed out. "I've been kneeling down too long without knowing why." She wanted God, not religion.

Drawing her into the next room, her mother protested, "You don't have to raise your voice in front of your brothers and sisters. Don't rattle *their* faith, at least."

"Why not?" Simin retorted. "They need help too. Where is God? What has our faith really done for us? How has it helped us to understand life better?"

If orthodox Islam seemed vague, the neighbors' ouija board parties didn't offer anything better. Although these well-meaning friends urged her to join them for some sociability, Simin refused. "There has to be a Creator in charge, not just dead souls giving messages helter-skelter," she insisted.

Her vacation over, she returned to California. Back in school, her hunger for God continued. She began asking people, even people she had just met, people coming out of a supermarket or a bank, "Can I ask you a question? Do you believe in God?" She started making a religious survey of her fellow students. She didn't find one "born again" person.

"All of me was a question mark," she recounts. But she saw that the people around her were empty.

No doubt cultural displacement and the challenges of being an unattached young adult in California exacerbated her stress. In any case, she became depressed. Looking back now, she says her search in the flesh came to an end. Thoughts of suicide began to flit through her mind.

"God, I've been looking for you everywhere and I can't find you. Why are you hiding? You're cruel. Can't you hear somebody calling for you?" Simin would cry.

One day in anatomy class she was dissecting a cat. Her partner was an Iranian man. Both were excellent students. In this exercise, one was supposed to read the instructions while the other performed the operation. But today all she could think of was the cat's Creator. "Who made you?" she kept asking the cat.

She and her partner got sidetracked, discussing life.

When the professor came around to observe their work, he scratched his head and said, "I can't give you a good grade, because everybody else is in the abdominal cavity and you're still on the superficial muscles."

Simin's partner was upset. He went to the professor. "May I talk to you privately, sir? I think Simin is suicidal. That's why we didn't get much dissection done."

When the professor called her in for a consultation, Simin unloaded. Why didn't anybody else demand significance from life? "The whole world is full of animals that don't know where they've come from and where they're going!" she exclaimed.

"You're wasting your time," the professor soothed her. "There is no God. Evolution has produced us. So enjoy. You're a young girl. Life is before you—"

"Even a blind person knows there's a God," Simin retorted. "But I want to communicate with him. I've been talking. He hasn't been answering. I want to meet him face to face. There are some things I want to discuss with him."

When she left the professor's office she thought in despair, "Tonight I'm going to kill myself."

Wisely, though, the professor asked her to undertake a further dissection as his partner. They were to open a human cadaver. Therapy for a suicidal person? Strangely, it was.

"How old do you think this man was?" the professor asked her as they began.

"Oh, quite old," she said, noting the many signs of aging.

"He was ninety-three."

"Ninety-three years old!" Simin exclaimed. She said to herself, "What gave him the power to go on that long? Did he know God?"

When the cadaver was opened, Simin saw the glory of God. "Lord," she breathed, "I see your signature over the liver, over the stomach. The wrist section is like guitar strings. You're beautiful, Creator. But can a human being know you?"

In a still small voice, it seemed that God answered, "Did you know I can come and live in you?"

Simin was thrilled. As soon as she could, she told her friends, "Would you believe, God spoke to me!"

They didn't believe. They thought she was a little crazy. A day or so later she began to think so too. At this point, she still didn't know anything about Jesus Christ as Lord. She started to think she was mentally ill since she had heard a voice. The pressure during this period was tremendous. She felt squeezed, as if she was going through a birth canal.

During this period, Simin wrote God a letter.

> Do you remember when I was talking to You in my anatomy class? I'm from Iran. I'm a young girl. Everybody thinks I have so much. But I don't have anything because I don't have You.
>
> God, I'm tired of running my life. Would You make friends with fools? If You would, here is one. I'm very lonely. All the things that other people on earth enjoy don't do anything for me. But I confess I'm nothing but trouble for You. . . .
>
> I don't know what mailman to give this letter to. Yet if You're powerful enough to create the cadaver, You're powerful enough to see me writing this letter.
>
> I don't know what to call You. Some call You energy. Some Allah. Some Buddha. You tell me who You are. I know You must have a personality."

And three times in the letter, Simin thanked God for himself.

When she put down the pen, the Spirit of God seemed to come around her and hug her, and she received confidence that her letter would be answered.

But the squeeze was on. The next day, October 28, once again depressed, thinking she had been deluded, Simin picked up a crochet hook to plug it into an electric socket. Forgetting for the moment that the

United States had 110-volt current, she thought she would give herself a 220-volt jolt and end it all.

But the crochet hook flew out of her hand and across the room.

Dejectedly, Simin took a bath, crying into the tub. "God, either You take my life and do something with it, or let me take it."

A big wind rushed into her bathroom. It filled her being. Simin bowed over with sudden consciousness of her sin, of her unworthiness to negotiate with the Creator of the universe. "Oh yes, You're beautiful, You're majestic," she breathed, "but You're also a person before whom we have to fall flat on our faces."

"Congratulations!" God seemed to say to her. "You have been born again!"

Very much like the French philosopher-mathematician Blaise Pascal, when he recorded his climactic experience of God in 1654, Simin was flooded with joy. From 2:30 in the afternoon throughout the whole night, bliss and confidence washed over her. She didn't dare sleep. She didn't want to miss a minute of the enjoyment of God's presence.

Sometime during that afternoon, God seemed to say, "Now that I've revealed myself to you, what are you going to do for me?"

Simin walked over to her picture window and looked down on the people thronging the sidewalk below. "Those crazy idiots walking around down there, they're going to know about you," she vowed.

Then the Spirit said to her, "Pray for truth, and I will show it to you."

What more truth do I need, now that I have this experience of You? she wondered. But she prayed as the Spirit directed.

In the morning her doorbell rang.

"Hello. The Lord Jesus loves you," smiled the woman at Simin's door. She handed Simin a leaflet. Startled, glancing through it, Simin read, "Here I am! I stand at the door and knock. If anyone hears my voice and opens the door, I will go in and eat with him, and he with me" (Revelation 3:20).

"Who said this?" Simin asked.

"Jesus Christ," the woman answered.

No! No! No! Simin shouted inside. *I'm never going to give up the Muslim religion. If this is what You wanted to show me, God, I shouldn't have started looking for You. This is like asking me to take off my clothes and run across the grass naked.*

Surely the God who had met Simin so sweetly couldn't intend this. Surely her visitor was misguided. Out of pity for the woman, wanting to help even Christians come to a true experience of God such as she now had, Simin agreed to go to church with her visitor.

After she had shared her experience with some of the people at church, the pastor quietly invited her, "Simin, would you like to be born again?"

"I *am* born again!" she exploded. "Didn't you hear what I said?"

"But do you follow Jesus? There is no other way to be born again except through Jesus. He is the way, the truth and the life—"

"No, Jesus is only a prophet as far as I know. And as for you, you people ought to fall down in awe and reverence and worship God, not a man."

Although this exchange was stalemated, the worship continued. Soon they reached the point in the service when most of the congregation went forward and knelt down for prayer. Simin did too. Falling on her knees, she prayed that these church people would have the joy of being born again like she was.

Some people's prayers were audible to Simin. They were speaking languages that weren't English. One lady said, "*Tavakol beh Masih,*" which in the Persian language means "Trust in the Messiah."

When Simin raised her head, she was enraged to see that all around her Christians were praying for *her,* stretching out their hands toward her, though at a distance.

As soon as the service was over, Simin went to the woman who had said, "*Tavakol beh Masih.*"

"Do you speak Persian? Have you lived in Iran?" Simin asked her.

The woman seemed dumbstruck. Her husband nudged her. "Honey, you speak Persian!"

"Oh, I do?" the woman wondered.

"No, we've never been to Iran," the man explained to Simin. These are heavenly languages we're speaking. The Holy Spirit gives them to us. We don't always understand what they mean."

What kind of crazy people are these, Simin thought, *that they don't even know what languages they speak!* She made her exit as quickly as she could.

But a woman ran after her down the sidewalk, calling, "Lady! Lady!"

Simin turned. "Yes?"

"Take this," panted the woman, holding out a Bible. While Simin hesitated, the woman began to explain the basic divisions, the Old Testament and New Testament. Seeing other people streaming out of the church toward her, and not wanting to get further entangled, Simin took the Bible quickly, muttered thanks and got out of there.

All night long, until eight o'clock the next morning, Simin read the New Testament, not even changing position in her chair.

A still, small voice spoke to her about the Trinity—God the Father, God the Son and God the Holy Spirit.

Simin got mad. "I don't want Jesus and I don't want the Holy Spirit. I just want *You!*" she begged.

She kept on reading the Bible, but she didn't go back to church. About ten days later, a general bulletin from the church landed in her mailbox. It included a questionnaire for new visitors and a brochure. On the brochure an artist had drawn a loaf of bread and a stalk of wheat. Underneath were the words, "I am the bread of life."

"Truly, God, You *are* the bread of life, our necessity, our nourishment. But why is Jesus claiming this?" Simin murmured.

Scanning the questionnaire, she decided, *I'd better let these church people know that there's no way I'm going to become a Christian.* So she filled in the blanks with negatives.

"Are you interested in learning more about the Christian life?"

"No!"

"Are you interested in praying to receive Christ into your life?"

"No!"

And so on.

Finished with that, she wrote a letter telling her father how stupid American Christians are, worshiping a man instead of God. Then she scooted across the bed in order to get up, go out and mail the two letters. As she reached the edge of the bed, suddenly she envisioned a pair of bare feet coming toward her. Then she saw the lower part of a garment above the feet. The cloth had a Jewish patterned figure, such as she had seen when she had done public health nursing in a Jewish community in Iran. The vision put its hand on her face and said, "Go to sleep. The Lord is with you."

Drowsiness overcame her. She fell back on the bed and slept sweetly until morning.

Then, as she woke, bits of the vision came back.

"God, who was that Jewish man in my room last night?" she asked sleepily.

"The Lord Jesus Christ. The Lord Jesus Christ. The Lord Jesus Christ." Voices murmured it over and over. Unearthly music swelled.

Simin fell flat on her face. "Oh Lord Jesus, forgive me," she cried. "I don't know if you know my background. I'm from Iran. I'm a Muslim. It's so hard for us to think of You as God . . ."

Going back to the church, Simin asked for the microphone and told her story. That was twenty years ago. Since then God has brought many beautiful Christian friends into her life. Still, it hasn't been easy. The first four years of her Christian life were constant fighting, Simin recalls. "God loved me, but he didn't like much about me." Nor was she quick to yield to him.

When she told her family, her father said, "No Americans can change my daughter. The children that I brought up are rooted in truth." He asked the American embassy to deport her. Imagine his surprise when they told him they couldn't do that, since people have freedom of religion in America.

"Now when I see Iranians, I cry for them," Simin admits. Quite a few Iranians in the United States have come to know the Lord Jesus through her witness. People trust her, she says, because although she is blunt she is kind and will not gossip. She has served as an elder in the two-thousand-member New Jerusalem Church in southern California. In addition to demonstrating a gift in evangelism, she also is known for a special gift in healing.

One night, for example, Simin was the nurse in charge of her ward at the hospital. The shift was quiet. She sat at the nurses' station, reviewing charts. Suddenly she sniffed. What was it? An odor, musty, fetid and foul.

"Death," Simin thought. "I smell death."

Pushing up out of her swivel chair, she craned her neck. Down the dim corridor, a black shape drifted. A shape like the demons she had seen as a child in Iran. The shape floated into a side room.

"Lord Jesus, be with me," Simin breathed. She stalked down the antiseptic-smelling hall and followed "death" into the room.

Here lay a man. The needle of his monitor was drawing a straight line. No vital functions were operating. According to his monitor, he was dead.

"In the name of Jesus, I command you to come back," Simin called out. "I bind death."

"Nurse!" An aide rushed into the room. "Oh, are you here already? This patient's reading is completely flat at the central station monitor. Oh, but I see by this monitor his heart's beating again. And he's breathing—"

So he was.

"Were his leads disconnected? That's what I rushed in to check," the aide burbled on. "Did you reconnect them?"

"I believe they're all connected," Simin smiled. When she checked, they were.

The next day, the patient's wife told Simin, "Last night I heard a hideous laugh. A voice said, 'I'm going to take your husband's life tonight.' So I prayed with all my strength, 'God, send a Christian nurse or doctor to my husband's room.' "

Days later, when the man could talk, he told his wife, "Honey, I died. I met Jesus. And he said, 'Go back. There's a nurse praying for you.' When I came back to consciousness, sure enough, there was a nurse praying. I don't know who. All I know is that she had a foreign accent."

Who was Simin, with the foreign accent? A woman who hungered for God, who searched for God—and who learned the truth of God's promise, "You will seek me and find me when you seek me with all your heart" (Jeremiah 29:13).

Yet who was seeking whom? Not only did Simin pursue God. Even more, God pursued her. Like Hagar in the desert so long ago, Simin discovered that God knew her name. God knew her location. And he came to meet her.

In the end, all evangelism is really the attempt to introduce people to the One who has been pursuing us our whole lives. How different from the demanding deity of Islam is this divine love, which refuses to be denied or derailed in winning our hearts. This is why Muslim women deserve our energy and our care.

Notes

Preface
[1]Those wondering about the source for a case are advised to contact the author. Confidentiality will be maintained, but the level of documentation will be disclosed.

Chapter 1: Why Muslim Women Come to Christ
[1]Ismail R. al Faruqi and Lois Lamya'al Faruqi, *The Cultural Atlas of Islam* (New York: Macmillan, 1986), pp. 62-63.
[2]Edward Said, *Orientalism: Western Conceptions of the Orient* (London: Penguin, 1995).
[3]Judith MacLeod, *Woman's Union Missionary Society: The Story of a Continuing Mission* (Upper Darby, Penn.: Interserve, 1999), p. 12.
[4]See Erik Freas, "Muslim Women in the Missionary World," *The Muslim World*, April 1998, pp. 141-64; and Guli Francis-Dehqani, "CMS Women Missionaries in Persia: Perceptions of Muslim Women and Islam, 1884-1934," in *The Church Mission Society and World Christianity, 1799-1999*, ed. Kevin Ward and Brian Stanley (Grand Rapids, Mich.: Eerdmans, 1999), pp. 91-119.
[5]Francis-Dehqani, "CMS Women Missionaries," p. 118.

Chapter 2: Every Woman Is an Exception
[1]Dawn Chatty, "Changing Sex Roles in Bedouin Society in Syria and Lebanon," in *Women in the Muslim World*, ed. Lois Beck and Nikki Keddie (Cambridge, Mass.: Harvard University Press, 1978), pp. 399-415.
[2]Jay Rasooli and Cady Allen, *Dr. Sa'eed of Iran* (Pasadena, Calif.: William Carey Library, 1957), p. 117.
[3]Chatty, "Changing Sex Roles," p. 408. See also Lois Beck, "Women Among Qashqa'i Nomadic Pastoralists in Iran," in *Women in the Muslim World*, ed. Lois Beck and Nikki Keddie (Cambridge, Mass.: Harvard University Press, 1978), p. 368.
[4]Laila Abu-Lughod, *Writing Women's Worlds* (Berkeley: University of California

Press, 1993).

[5]Susan Shaefer Davis, "Working Women in a Moroccan Village," in *Women in the Muslim World*, ed. Lois Beck and Nikki Keddie (Cambridge, Mass.: Harvard University Press, 1978), pp. 416-33.

[6]Nancy Tapper, "The Women's Subsociety Among the Shahsevan Nomads of Iran," in *Women in the Muslim World*, ed. Lois Beck and Nikki Keddie (Cambridge, Mass.: Harvard University Press, 1978), pp. 374-98.

[7]Sawsan el-Messiri, "Self-Images of Traditional Urban Women in Cairo," in *Women in the Muslim World*, ed. Lois Beck and Nikki Keddie (Cambridge, Mass.: Harvard University Press, 1978), pp. 522-40. See also, in the same volume, Suad Joseph, "Women and the Neighborhood Street in Borj, Hammoud, Lebanon," pp. 541-58.

[8]El-Messiri, "Self-Images of Traditional Urban Women," p. 535.

[9]Tahire Erman, "The Importance of Migration on Turkish Rural Women: Four Emerging Patterns," *Gender and Society*, April 1998, pp. 148-65.

[10]Ibid.

[11]Compare this with the first teacher-training school that opened in Turkey in 1911. Since no aristocratic women professors could be found, the government hunted out the ugliest and oldest men professors. These men lectured from behind a partition, chaperoned by older women from their own families.

[12]Naila Minai, *Women in Islam* (New York: Seaview, 1981), p. 38.

[13]Ibid., pp. 29-34.

[14]Ahmed Rashid, "Sister Courage: Hazara Women Take to the Battlefield," *Far Eastern Economic Review*, Nov. 27, 1997, p. 30.

[15]Yasmin Alibhai-Brown, "Unveiled: The New Adventurers," *Telegraph*, May 13, 1996, pp. 32-36.

[16]Soraya Altorki and Camillia Fawzi El-Solh, eds., *Arab Women in the Field: Studying Your Own Society* (Syracuse, N.Y.: Syracuse University Press, 1988).

[17]Minai, *Women in Islam*, p. 229.

[18]Elizabeth Fernea, "The Challenges for Middle Eastern Women in the 21st Century," *Middle East Journal*, Spring 2000, p. 187.

[19]Elizabeth Fernea and Basima Qattan Bezirgan, *Middle Eastern Muslim Women Speak* (Austin: University of Texas Press, 1977), pp. 251-62.

[20]Ibid., pp. 193-200.

[21]Minai, *Women in Islam*, p. 75.

[22]Valerie Hoffman, "An Islamic Activist: Zaynab al-Ghazali," in *Women and Family in the Middle East*, ed. Elizabeth Fernea (Austin: University of Texas Press, 1985), pp. 233-54.

[23]Ibid.

[24]Ibid.

[25]Minai, *Women in Islam*, p. 76.

Chapter 4: What Is Liberation for Muslim Women?

[1]A. A. Stockdale, "God Left the Challenge in the Earth," *His*, December 1964, p. 20.

[2]Badru Katerrega and David Shenk, *Islam and Christianity: A Muslim and a Christian in Dialogue* (Nairobi: Uzima, 1980), p. 15.

[3]Kenneth Cragg, *The House of Islam* (Encino, Calif.: Dickenson, 1975), p. 68.

[4]Kenneth Cragg, *The Call of the Minaret* (1956; reprint, Maryknoll, N.Y.: Orbis, 1985), p. 41.

[5]Ruth Tucker and Walter Liefeld, *Daughters of the Church: Women in Ministry from New Testament Times to the Present* (Grand Rapids, Mich.: Zondervan, 1987), p. 47.

[6]Geoffrey Parrinder, *Jesus in the Quran* (London: Faber, 1965).

[7]J. I. Packer, *Systematic Theology Overview: Theology Course Lecture Notes* (Vancouver, B.C.: Regent College Publishing, 2001).

[8]Edwin E. Calverley, "Christian Theology and the Qur'an," *The Muslim World* 47 (1957), p. 289.

[9]Cragg, *Call of the Minaret*, p. 227.

[10]Khalid Gauba, *Prophet of the Desert*, cited in Cragg, *Call of the Minaret*, p. 227.

[11]Cragg, *Call of the Minaret*, p. 227.

[12]Seamands, *Tell It Well*, p. 161.

[13]Ibid.

[14]Cragg, *Call of the Minaret*, p. 235.

[15]Vivienne Stacey, *Christ Supreme over Satan* (Lahore, Pakistan: Masihi Isha'at Khana, 1986). Available from Interserve, P.O. Box 418, Upper Darby, PA 19082.

[16]Paul Hiebert, "Biblical Perspectives on Spiritual Warfare," in *Anthropological Reflections on Missiological Issues* (Grand Rapids, Mich.: Baker, 1994), pp. 203-15.

[17]Dana Robert, *American Women in Mission: A Social History of Their Thought and Practice* (Machine, Ga.: Mercer University Press, 1996), pp. 140, 144-45, 148.

[18]Elizabeth Fernea, "The Challenges for Middle Eastern Women in the 21st Century," *Middle East Journal* (spring 2000): 190.

[19]Eleanor Abdella Doumato, "Women and Work in Saudi Arabia: How Flexible Are Islamic Margins?" *Middle East Journal* 53, no. 4 (1999): 576.

[20]Mary Elaine Hegland, "The Power Paradox in Muslim Women's *Majales*: North-West Pakistani Mourning Rituals as Sites of Contestation over Religious Politics, Ethnicity, and Gender," *Signs: Journal of Women in Culture and Society*, 23, no. 2, pp. 391-423.

[21]Alaine Hutson, "The Development of Women's Authority in the Kano Tijaniyya, 1894-1963," *Africa Today*, summer-fall 1999, pp. 43-64.

Chapter 6: Family: Sex, Singles, Husbands, Children

[1]Lawrence Rosen, "The Negotiation of Reality: Male-Female Relations in Sefrou, Morocco," in *Women in the Muslim World*, ed. Lois Beck and Nikki Keddie (Cambridge, Mass.: Harvard University Press, 1978), pp. 566-68.

[2]Fatima Mernissi, *Beyond the Veil: Male-Female Dynamics in a Modern Muslim Society* (Cambridge: Shenkman, 1978), p. 63.

[3]Ibid.

[4]Ismail Faruqi and Lois Lamaya'al Faruqi, *The Cultural Atlas of Islam* (New York: Macmillan, 1986), pp. 149-51.

[5]Michael Fischer, "On the Changing Concept and Position of Persian Women," in *Women in the Muslim World*, ed. Lois Beck and Nikki Keddie (Cambridge, Mass.: Harvard University Press, 1978), p. 194.

[6]Naila Minai, *Women in Islam: Tradition and Transition in the Middle East* (New York: Seaview, 1981), p. 18.

[7]Geraldine Brooks, *Nine Parts of Desire: The Hidden World of Islamic Women* (New York: Doubleday, 1995), p. 61.

[8]Betty Mahmoody and William Hoffer, *Not Without My Daughter* (New York: St. Martin's Press, 1993); Jean Sasson, *Princess* (New York: Avon, 1993).

[9]Nesta Ramazani, "Arab Women in the Gulf," *Middle East Journal*, spring 1985, p. 268.

[10]Carol Mukhopadhyay and Patricia Higgins, "Anthropological Studies of Women's Status Revisited" in *Annual Review of Anthropology* (Palo Alto, Calif.: Annual Reviews, 1988); and Naomi Quinn, "Anthropological Studies on Women's Status" in *Annual Review of Anthropology* (Palo Alto, Calif.: Annual Reviews, 1977).

[11]Nadia Hijab, *Womanpower: The Arab Debate on Women at Work* (London: Cambridge University Press, 1988), cited in Elizabeth Fernea, "The Challenges for Middle Eastern Women in the 21st Century," *Middle East Journal*, spring 2000, p. 189.

[12]Alaine Hutson, "The Development of Women's Authority in the Kano Tijaniyya, 1894-1963," *Africa Today*, summer-fall 1999, pp. 43-64.

[13]Will Durant, *Age of Faith* (New York: Simon & Schuster, 1950), p. 973 (on Aquinas); Augustine *On the Sermon on the Mount* 1.15.41; Tertullian *On the Apparel of Women* 1.1. For calling my attention to these comments by the church fathers I am indebted to Ruth Tucker and Walter Liefeld, *Daughters of the Church* (Grand Rapids, Mich.: Zondervan, 1987), pp. 103, 124, 164-65.

[14]Mufti Jafar Husain Sahib Qibla, *Nahjul Balagha* (Karachi, 1972), p. 177, quoted in Fischer, "Changing Concept," p. 195.

[15]Hutson, "Development of Women's Authority," p. 56.

[16]Emrys L. Peters, "Women in Four Middle East Communities," in *Women in the*

Muslim World, ed. Lois Beck and Nikki Keddie (Cambridge, Mass.: Harvard University Press, 1978), p. 341.

[17]Camillia Fawzi El-Solh, "Gender, Class, and Origin: Aspects of Role During Fieldwork in Arab Society," in *Arab Women in the Field: Studying Your Own Society*, ed. Soraya Altorki and Camillia Fawzi El-Solh (Syracuse, N.Y.: Syracuse University Press, 1988), p. 105.

[18]Seteny Shami, "Studying Your Own: The Complexities of a Shared Culture," in *Arab Women in the Field: Studying Your Own Society*, ed. Soraya Altorki and Camillia Fawzi El-Solh (Syracuse, N.Y.: Syracuse University Press, 1988), p. 125.

[19]Harriet Papanek, "The Woman Field Worker in a Purdah Society," *Human Organization* 23, no. 3 (1964): 160-63.

[20]Fawzi El-Solh, "Gender, Class, and Origin," p. 106.

[21]Patricia St. John, *Until the Day Breaks: The Life and Work of Lilias Trotter* (Carlisle, U.K.: OM Publishing, 1990).

[22]Mildred Cable, *The Gobi Desert* (London: Hodder & Stoughton, 1942).

[23]Ruth Tucker, *From Jerusalem to Irian Jaya: A Biographical History of Christian Mission* (Grand Rapids, Mich.: Zondervan, 1983), pp. 242-46.

[24]Dana Robert, *American Women in Mission: A Social History of Their Thought and Practice* (Machine, Ga.: Mercer University Press, 1996).

[25]Mary Lou Cummings, *Surviving Without Romance: African Women Tell Their Stories* (Scottsdale Ariz.: Herald, 1991).

[26]Julia Duin, *Purity Makes the Heart Grow Stronger* (Ann Arbor, Mich.: Vine, 1988).

[27]Anne Morrow Lindbergh, *Gift from the Sea* (New York: Pantheon, 1955).

[28]Salwa Abdel Hameed Al-Khateeb, "Women, Family and the Discovery of Oil in Saudi Arabia," *Marriage and Family Review* 27, no. 1 (1988): 174.

[29]Hutson, "Development of Women's Authority," p. 57.

Chapter 7: Southeast Asian Sisters

[1]Clifford Geertz, *The Religion of Java* (New York: Free Press, 1960), p. 59.

[2]Avery Willis, *Indonesian Revival: Why Two Million Came to Christ* (Pasadena, Calif.: William Carey Library, 1977), p. 139.

Chapter 8: Singing Our Theology

[1]Vivienne Stacey, unpublished manuscript.

[2]See Fran Love and Jeleta Eckheart, eds. *Ministry to Muslim Women: Longing to Call Them Sisters* (Pasadena Calif.: William Carey Library, 2000).

[3]Contact Keith@idmail.com to order or for information about the *Jesus* video.

[4]See note 2.

[5]Tim Matheny, *Reaching the Arabs: A Felt Need Approach* (Pasadena, Calif.: Wil-

liam Carey Library, 1981), pp. 146-52.

[6]William Conley, *The Kalimantan Kenyah: A Study of Tribal Conversion in Terms of Dynamic Cultural Themes* (Nutley, N.J.: Presbyterian & Reformed, 1975), pp. 45-279.

[7]John Webster et al., *From Role to Identity: Dalit Christian Women in Transition* (Delhi: ISPCK, 1997), pp. 129-31.

[8]Kenneth Cragg, *The House of Islam* (Encino, Calif.: Dickenson, 1975), p. 41.

[9]Lila Abu-Lughod, *Veiled Sentiments: Honor and Poetry in a Bedouin Society* (Berkeley: University of California Press, 1988).

[10]Viggo Søgaard, *Everything You Need to Know for a Cassette Ministry* (Minneapolis: Bethany House, 1975), p. 102.

[11]When researching women's singing in a Muslim culture, consider this model article: Irina Naroditskaia, "Azerbaijanian Female Musicians: Women's Voices Defying and Defining the Culture," *Ethnomusicology* 44, no. 2 (2000): 234-56.

[12]Eli Shouby, "The Influence of the Arabic Language on Arab Psychology," *Middle East Journal*, Summer 1951, p. 300.

[13]Elizabeth Fernea, *Guests of the Sheikh* (New York: Doubleday, 1965), p. 135.

[14]Abu-Lughod, *Veiled Sentiments*, p. 173.

[15]John Seamands, *Tell It Well: Communicating the Gospel Across Cultures* (Kansas City: Beacon Hill, 1981), pp. 139-41.

[16]Ibid.

Chapter 9: African Sisters

[1]Ron Nelson, "Some Crucial Dimensions of Ministry to Fulbe," *Missiology* (April 1983): 201-18.

The Hausa evangelist's use of Fulani concepts, including this dialogue, is adapted from Nelson (see note 1).

Chapter 10: Money Matters: Who Pays?

See Lindy Williams and Teresa Sobieszczyk, "Attitudes Surrounding the Continuation of Female Circumcision in the Sudan: Passing the Tradition to the Next Generation," *Journal of Marriage and the Family*, November 1997, pp. 966-81. Note also this observation by Elizabeth Fernea: "In 1995, women and men in Egypt challenged the Rector of Al-Azhar University who had issued a new fatwa stating that female circumcision, like male circumcision, was part of one's adherence to Islam. They argued the contrary, took the Rector to court, and to some surprise won their case; female genital mutilation is illegal in Egypt once more, as it had been since 1979" ("The Challenges for Middle Eastern Women in the 21st Century," *Middle East Journal*, spring 2000, p. 191).

[2]Wendy Zoba, "Islam, U.S.A.," *Christianity Today*, April 3, 2000, p. 48.

[3]Rick Wood, "Fighting Dependency Among the 'Aucas': An Interview with Steve Saint," and Steve Saint, "Looking at Missions From Their Side, Not Ours," *Mission Frontiers*, May-June 1998, pp. 8-19.

[4]Ray Bakke, *The Urban Christian* (Downers Grove, Ill.: InterVarsity Press, 1987), pp. 93-94.

[5]Lucie Wood Saunders, "Umm Ahmad: A Village Mother of Egypt," *Middle Eastern Muslim Women Speak*, ed. Elizabeth Fernea and Basima Qattan Bezirgan (Austin: University of Texas Press, 1977), pp. 219-30.

[6]Ruth Tucker, *Guardians of the Great Commission: The Story of Women in Modern Missions* (Grand Rapids, Mich.: Zondervan, 1988), p. 155.

[7]A. Z. Zwemer and Samuel Zwemer, *Moslem Women* (West Medford, Mass.: Central Committee on the United Study of Foreign Missions, 1926), pp. 202-4.

[8]Eleanor Abdella Doumato, "Women and Work in Saudi Arabia: How Flexible Are the Margins?" *Middle East Journal* 53, no. 4 (1999): 570.

[9]See the home page of the Educational Concerns for Hunger Organization: <www.echonet.org>.

[10]See the home page of the Christian Veterinary Mission: <www.vetmission.org>.

[11]Other dimensions of Bob Blencoe's work in Iraqi Kurdistan are described in his award-winning book *Ethnic Realities and the Church: Lessons from Kurdistan* (Pasadena, Calif.: Presbyterian Center for Mission Studies, 1998).

[12]Fernea, "Challenges for Middle Eastern Women," p. 186.

[13]Frances Moore Lappe, Joseph Collins and David Kinley, *Aid as Obstacle: Twenty Questions About Our Foreign Aid and the Hungry* (San Francisco: Institute for Food and Development Policy, 1980), pp. 143-46.

[14]Muhammad Yunus, "The MicroLoan," *Seattle Post-Intelligencer*, September 29 1996, pp. E1-3.

[15]John Perkins, *Restoring At-Risk Communities: Doing It Together and Doing Right* (Grand Rapids, Mich.: Baker, 1995).

[16]Thomas Friedman, "Back from Davos: Backlash Brewing Against Technolog," *New York Times* News Service, January 30, 2001.